City Life from Jakarta to Dakar

City Life from Jakarta to Dakar is an important new book examining the potentials of urban life from unexpected places that has been consciously written for undergraduate urban courses, while not oversimplifying its subject.

Through powerful stories as well as an incisive theoretical point of view, the book puts cities in Africa and Southeast Asia as a cutting edge in thinking about the urban world of today. It shows how much of what is considered peripheral to urban life is actually critical to it and thereby opens up new ways for understanding what it is possible to do in cities from now on.

AbdouMaliq Simone is an urbanist and Professor of Sociology at Goldsmiths College, University of London. Since 1977 he has had many jobs in different cities across Africa and Southeast Asia, in the fields of education, housing, social welfare, urban development, and local government. His best known publications are *In Whose Image: Political Islam and Urban Practices in the Sudan*, and *For the City Yet to Come: Urban Change in Four African Cities*.

Global Realities
A Routledge Series
Edited by **Charles C. Lemert**, *Wesleyan University*

The Series **Global Realities** offers concise accounts of how the nations and regions of the world are experiencing the effects of globalization. Richly descriptive yet theoretically informed, each volume shows how individual places are navigating the tension between age-old traditions and the new forces generated by globalization.

City Life from Jakarta to Dakar

Movements at the Crossroads

ABDOUMALIQ SIMONE

Goldsmiths College,
University of London

Routledge
Taylor & Francis Group

NEW YORK AND LONDON

First published 2010
by Routledge
270 Madison Avenue,
New York, NY 10016

Simultaneously published in the UK
by Routledge
2 Park Square, Milton Park, Abingdon,
Oxon OX14 4RN

Routledge is an imprint of the Taylor & Francis Group, an informa business

© 2010 Taylor & Francis

Typeset in 11/14pt Joanna by RefineCatch Limited, Bungay, Suffolk
Printed and bound in the United States of America on acid-free paper by Edwards Brothers, Inc.

Library of Congress Cataloging-in-Publication Data
Simone, A. M. (Abdou Maliqalim)
    City life from Jakarta to Dakar : movements at the crossroads / AbdouMaliq Simone.
        p. cm.—(Global realities)
    Includes bibliographical references and index.
    1. City and town life—Africa.   2. City and town life—Southeast Asia.   3. Urbanization—Africa.
    4. Urbanization—Southeast Asia.   I. Title.
    HT384.A35S56 2009
    307.760959—dc22   2009019701

ISBN10: 0–415–99321–0 (hbk)
ISBN10: 0–415–99322–9 (pbk)
ISBN10: 0–203–89249–6 (ebk)

ISBN13: 978–0–415–99321–0 (hbk)
ISBN13: 978–0–415–99322–7 (pbk)
ISBN13: 978–0–203–89249–7 (ebk)

Contents

List of Illustrations

.

Series Editor's Foreword: From the City to Cityness

For a good bit of human history, people spoke of *the* City. They often meant a specific city or large town, like Rome, Mecca, Jerusalem, Constantinople, or Paris. But when they did, the city thus held in mind was imbued with a cosmic meaning— Rome, the eternal city; Paris, the city of lights. The practice of taking a local place of a certain demographic proportion as the center of a global reality continued down into the late modern era. Thus, in the social sciences in the century or more from the 1890s on there was a field called urban studies, the subject of which more often than not was *the* City—as in the city as megalopolis or, more recently, the global city. Even the general idea of urbanization was for the longest while understood as an unrelenting kind of uniform, global process that ate up the rural past and its allegedly less modern locales. The early twentieth century tradition of urban studies as an ecology of urban populations is a notable but by no means singular example.

In our time, still early in the 2000s, the practice of thinking of cities as more than their geographically local limits has begun to fall away. To be sure, there are still urbanists who specialize in *the* city and poverty or *the* urban neighborhood or *the* gated enclave—as if these particulars of late modern city life were vectors of growth and decay that spread across the earth wherever populations gathered in very large numbers to live or struggle. Yet, as happens from time to time, the received scientific and practical wisdom of professional urbanists is challenged in ways so empirically commanding that one by one people who care about city life begin to see and feel and think anew.

AbdouMaliq Simone, perhaps more than any I know, has been just that kind of urbanist—one, that is, who breaks the mold of traditional thought by the utterly straightforward method of visiting real cities and visiting with a particular vigilance for cities of the global South that are least convenient to the thinking of a city as an instance of *the* City. I can remember the first time I read Simone's work. It was an earlier essay on invisibility in four African cities that I would never have come across had a brilliant student of mine not found it somewhere in a remote corner of the internet. That relatively short text changed everything I had been thinking about globalization and the so-called global city. There and in *City Life from Jakarta to Dakar*, as in other writings that have established him as one of the world's most original observers of city life, Simone brilliantly captures the contradictions and absurdities of city life that we who live in cities recognize without realizing what they mean.

Thus it is that the subject of *City Life from Jakarta to Dakar* is not *the* City, but *cityness*, which is to say a much more global phenomenon and one intractably local and irregular. For Simone, cityness captures those elements of city life that cannot be captured, least of all by the organizing categories of modern social science. Cityness is about surprises—contradictions that are the source of human enterprise, absurdly illegal activities about which the most ordinary people possess the finest detailed knowledge, the visibility below surface appearances of, yes, terrible human misery but also of people working together in order to live. What Simone sees is the startling possibility that in the most peripheral regions of city life, where there is neither clean water nor sewage, it is the people themselves who are the infrastructure. This one insistence, among the many that sneak up on the reader in this book, turns the table on urban studies—infrastructure is human not material, people not pipes matter most, and city life—the lived reality—replaces the City. Cityness is about local living, not abstract planned cities.

Simone does not, however, write as jet ethnographer, a phrase Pierre Bourdieu once used. Over many years he has lived in and studied the cities of the world, most poignantly those of the impoverished Southern tier. The experiences of a trained observer when put to the page pull the reader, often against her will, into the worlds of cityness that play out in far corners most would never visit. Yet, without a lot of arm waving, Simone is also deploying the most current of theoretical ideas—none more compellingly than that of the global realities as a series of rhizomatically joined assemblages. From Gilles Deleuze to Manuel Delanda and others influenced by them many have tried to reckon with this puzzling notion that in our time life moves constantly, unpredictably without organizing tap roots. Worlds are assembled by inscrutable forces. People live in them on the move against all odds; and the poor who must live in the margins are, as Simone seems to say, those who are the better, not less, able to make them work.

As so many have helped us see—Giorgio Agamben chief among them—it is life itself that is at stake in the new global assemblages. And what Simone does is to move the more philosophical ideas of assemblage and naked life into the language and experience of city life and toward the cityness in which all of us are sooner or later caught. There is to my mind no better guide book to cityness and its consequences than *City Life from Jakarta to Dakar*.

Charles Lemert
New Haven, CT
June 20, 2009

This is a time of cities. More precisely, cities have preoccupied people from many walks of life for a long time. But particularly now, there is a sense that cities have attained new capacities and challenges that require multiple ways of talking about and engaging them that do not always seem to easily fit together. After all, to live in one city today means living in many, as any individual city folds in and stretches itself across urban experiences, information, and economies throughout the world.

So the realities of Lagos, Jakarta, São Paolo, or Cairo—to name just a few of the largest cities of the so-called Global South—are not distant from the critical events and processes that affect the lives of urban residents in other parts of the world. The histories of settlement and administration, as well as the mechanisms and practices at work in shaping the everyday experiences of residents, may be different from those in New York, Omaha, or Leipzig—as individual cities everywhere have their singular dynamics, and cities of the South their own problematic and long-term connections with Europe and North America, as well as with each other. But these differences are not simply matters of various development stages or technological progress. They don't simply tell us about essential ingredients that cities either possess or lack.

Rather, these differences broaden our understandings about

what cities are and could be. They point to cities—not as outgrowths of specific histories, nor as organic or technical systems available to new levels of adaptation or change—but as places and occasions for experimentation, for seeing what happens when bodies, materials, and affect intersect, and the various ways of living that can proceed from that intersection.

So this is not a book that simply wants to include cities from Jakarta to Dakar—across Southeast Asia, the Middle East, and Africa—to the normal curriculum on urban studies. Rather, by focusing on these cities, and particularly on the ways in which residents themselves try and make urban lives, the intention of the book is to help change what we think it is possible to do in whatever city we may find ourselves.

At times the book emphasizes the experiences of cities that on the surface would seem very far removed from conventional understandings about what works and is the norm. At other times, it concentrates on the very particular everyday tactics through which residents decide where to locate themselves, how to spend limited resources, who to talk to or affiliate with. These specificities are not intended to convey an otherwise invisible dimension to cities or to point out that our usual sense of what a city needs may not always be the case. Rather, delving into the economies, social relationships, and everyday practices of large and often messy cities of the South is meant to emphasize what all urban residents everywhere must often do or at least consider in order to put together their lives in the city. Sometimes, only by looking elsewhere can a person recognize important aspects of their own life. Thus, the "destination" of this book is not for specialist studies of specific regions or development problems. Rather, it hopes to be a tool-box of ideas, stories, and points of view applicable to making urban conditions everywhere a little more creative and just.

Acknowledgments

I wish to acknowledge the following persons for their ideas and support with various facets of this project, and without whom it would have been impossible to present this work: Wardah Hafiz, Marco Kusumuwijaya, Dian Tril, Rachmat Rhamdahni Fauzi, Rizqi Muhammed Ghribran, Dominique Malaquais, Jean-Christophe Lanquetin, Eléonore Hellio, Androa Minde Kolo, Achille Mbembe, Chhun Oeurn Heng, Prem Chap, Penny Edwards, Kirsten Harrison, Graeme Gotz, Edgar Pieterse, Martina Rieker, Kamran Ali, Mohamadou Diop, Irene Leung, Ellen Boccuzzi, Ananya Roy, Marilyn Douala-Bell, Jennifer Robinson, Matthew Gandy, Scott Lash, Filip de Boeck, Michael Keith, Vyjayanthi Rao, Satya Pemmaraju, Michael Goldman, Ghalya Saadawi, and Karin Santi.

Map 1
Regions from Jakarta to Dakar

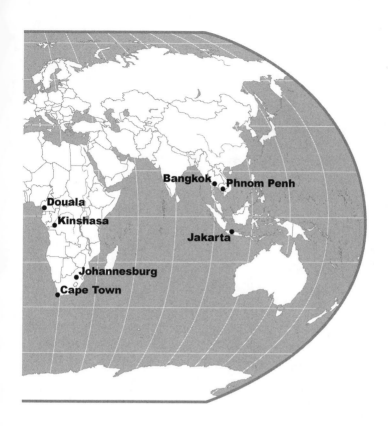

If you think of your life in the city, how many streets have you never gone down, how many elevators have you never taken up, how many beds have you never slept in, bars never pulled up to, fashion trends not gotten behind? If you think of your life in the city, how many times have you wanted to follow someone into a new life, how many arms have you imagined grabbing you from behind and pushing you into new versions of yourself? How many times have you just missed a bus where there was an empty seat next to a friend or partner you wouldn't be finding ways to get rid of? How much do you know about where the water that you use to wash off a bad dream comes from, or how the light at the end of the tunnel will be replaced when it burns out?

Why do I ask these questions? We all know that cities can often be overwhelming places, and that we need a determined attitude and clear focus in order to navigate their complexity. We know that maintaining even the semblance of a functional life in cities requires efforts to make them familiar and manageable. This requires particular ways of paying attention to what is going on and decisions as to what it is important to take seriously, as well as what things and events have something to do with our lives. Routines and structures exist to facilitate familiarity and predictability. The coding of cities with their various designations of names, districts, functions, and zones; transport infrastructures which shape predominant ways of circulating through urban space; and the distribution of services and facilities that link together the provision of specific consumption needs—all are a means of structuring our urban experience.

But this is going to be a book about movement—the movement in cities and between cities. It is about people taking sudden turns into new realities even when they are accustomed to often mundane and repetitive details of making ends meet. It is a book about things darting back and forth, of events moving in and out the shadows. It is the motion of work, of how urban works gets done. In this regard it doesn't so much emphasize structures and policies as it does the processes where urban residents try to actively figure things out, take chances, hedge bets, and make small experimentations. It is about all of the calculations, intuitions, and speculations that go into trying to keep heads above water. The cities dealt with in this book are particularly salient contexts for these kinds of explorations since urban life in them largely relies upon wits, psychological maneuvers, small escapades, and impulse. Importantly, the very process of making things stable doesn't entail following a set of rules, formulas or best practices. Rather, it entails shaking things up, playing in larger arenas, and paying attention to new territories and people.

The book tries to embody these dimensions by moving within and between districts and cities. The book is not about a city or a set of cities in particular, but rather uses different cities to emphasize the various intricacies of everyday urban life, the challenges that residents face on a daily level, the scope of their accomplishments, and the usually ambivalent results they produce for themselves by being able to use the city in many different ways. Often the very ways they get out of trouble put them into trouble of a different kind. And they have to start figuring things out once again—sometimes alone and sometimes with various combinations of known and unknown people. The book is also about anticipation, about how residents try to stay one step ahead of the game. Residents have to operate in often ambiguous spaces and times; it is not always clear what outcomes their actions will produce and they have to live with this ambiguity. The book attempts to talk about what this experience is like and what kinds of individual and collective behaviors ensue.

Above all, the book attempts to talk about various aspects of cityness. The demands of putting together livelihoods, managing domestic spaces, and demonstrating accountability to key institutions and personal networks all limit the ways in which we engage cities. Yet these opening questions point to what is the simultaneous promise, threat, and resource of cityness—i.e. the city's capacity to provoke relations of all kinds. Cityness refers to the city as a thing in the making. No matter how hard analysts and policymakers might try, practices of inhabiting the city are so diverse and change so quickly that they cannot easily be channeled into clearly defined uses of space and resources or patterns of social interchange.[1] In other words, at the heart of city life is the capacity for its different people, spaces, activities, and things to interact in ways that exceed any attempt to regulate them. While the absence of regulation is commonly seen as a bad thing, one must first start with the understanding that no form of regulation can keep the city "in line."

In a neighborhood such as Oju-Elegba in Lagos, the day's commerce gives way to the night and a different kind of operation, even if what is bought and sold during the night is largely what is bought and sold in the day. But a new "regime" of authority seems to kick in. For while the local government, trade associations, police, security companies, and sanitation crews are still officially in charge of their domains of activity, still in charge of maintaining order, much of what really takes place is ceded to a new format where the rules may still be the rules but are now, for these hours, slightly qualified. Exceptions are made as to what activities will now be interdicted, or how certain spaces are to be used. Not that any of such rules are really operative to the letter during the day. But for the night, things are allowed to happen with an enhanced visibility. Residents that otherwise would not been seen dealing with each other during the day are busy having much to do with each other in the night.

Deep into the night at 3 a.m., the assemblage of discrepant activities seems to pile up on each other given their proximity. Small stalls sell huge marijuana cigarettes next to those that sell votive candles, and then there are sales of rice, cigarettes, laundry soap, and batteries throughout the night, as well as cooked meals, many stalls specializing in various regional cuisines. Pharmaceuticals, charms, and local medicines are hawked both by ambulatory sellers and various forms of makeshift stalls. Set back further along the streets are stores whose histories have known hundreds of functions and whose identities even now fluctuate according to the time of day. At this hour, hardware stores become outcall services for sex workers delivered to almost any location in the surrounding vicinity; a small business center takes calls and sends out a fleet of young repairmen on motorcycles for various domestic emergencies such as broken water pipes or shorts in overtaxed electricity distributors that often occur when too many households try to connect to a branch line. Schools that teach computer classes during the day host all night prayer meetings next to bars and small discos, next to a small law office which at this hour serves as a kind of floating "design workshop," where a local politician holds court soliciting ideas, plans, drawings, and models for new housing developments, roadways, drainage systems, and a host of small improvements on every aspect of life in the area.

Local patrons take turns holding all night dispute resolution meetings for various neighborhood and domestic conflicts; a small storefront church rents out its facilities for local bands to rehearse; and there are the constant operations of local bakeries, furniture fabrication, and car repair. While theft and the illicit always work their way into the scene, a strong sense of security is maintained. Eyes are always trained on what is happening; local youth are tightly organized into both mobile and stationary patrols. Anything out of the ordinary or any prospective threat is immediately cut off, and there are tight chains of command. In part, this is both to keep thieves and conmen at bay, but also to make sure that the hundreds of different kinds of activities taking place all have their space, and to ensure a fluid transition between the night and the day—as spaces have to be turned over to their respective owners and functions. Yet, all these different things happen side by side. Even when each turns a kind of blind eye to the contradictions or discrepancies that are produced, these activities still find themselves "happening upon" the other, and they are aware of the larger "neighborhood" in which they are able to exist. Every activity has to know something about the other and to find ways of acknowledging their mutual existence in order for them to take their space, to find a consistent means of operating night after night.

In a fundamental way, this cityness has become and always has been largely peripheral to city life. That is, the very dimension that characterizes the city—its capacities to continuously reshape the ways in which people, places, materials, ideas, and affect are intersected—is often the very thing that is left out of the larger analytical picture. Rather, cityness is something that we are to know implicitly and take for granted. It is to be the common sense of our urban experience, and as such, we can easily move on to consider the wide range of issues concerning what kinds of relationships are most important and what conditions sustain or break them. We can move on to the vast problems of segregation, inequality, security, escalating, or declining land values and jobs, changes in the quality of life, the costs and quality of essential services. We can then pay attention to how best to calibrate relations among people, places, institutions, responsibilities, economic activities, and social functions through more proficient forms and practices of urban governance. These calibrations are structured according to law, policy, and specific ideas about norms, efficiency, and justice. But they are also subject to relations of power. Here, specific individuals and institutions use the uncertainties incumbent in urban life and the need of most residents to have a sense of order as occasions to accumulate the material and symbolic resources that are used to exercise authority over how relations get made.

As cities historically have been rough and tumble places, where some people can acquire a great deal of money and live in increasingly spectacular conditions while others barely scrape by, the diversity of the city can easily foster highly competitive relationships. There is competition over how land is to be used, competition over who can do what kinds of activities in a particular place, competition to make one's voice heard, competition over a set number of jobs and opportunities. While competition has rules, the city—with its plurality of relational possibilities, deal-making, loyalties, and affiliations—enables competition to be often vociferous and cutthroat. As such, the city has been seen as something that needs to be tamed and kept in line.

HOW DOES CITYNESS RELATE TO EFFORTS MADE
TO KEEP THE CITY IN LINE?

Urban development attempts to resolutely settle the question of how things within the city get articulated once and for all. This has been an effort to sum up the ways in which built, social, political, and ecological environments will be connected—a process now often reflected in the emphasis on public–private partnership, and urban governance as a blending of various sectors, actors, positions, and institutions. This attempt at summing up, of synthesizing and maximizing the synergies that can be attained through holding resources, people, and places in continuously re-stabilized relationships—concretely framed through infrastructure—is itself the result of many small gestures, maneuvers, and innovations. Yet, because this objective and its subsequent results do not often effectively engage local histories in recognizable ways, such trajectories of urban development face a particular conundrum.

The conundrum is this: Buildings, layouts, provisioning systems, and organizations try to hold together and stabilize relationships between materials, environments, bodies, and institutions. Urban infrastructure attempts to bring these elements into circuits of association that constitute both bodies and territories in ways that must be continuously calibrated and readjusted. But any collective is a collection. As a collection, each component has to deal with the others, but they also have a life outside the collection, something that came before and that is ongoing. So when technology, people, things, and space operate as a collection, this process has various implications for the different networks in which each of these elements is individually situated. Water, power, people, effort, and materials that are collected in order to attain a kind of optimal functioning are drawn from many other places. Any collection of these things in one place inevitably has an impact on the places from which they were drawn. And they act back.

As a result things and people come and go, intensify and withdraw their engagements, and, in the end, every arrangement is temporary. Connections break down, and collections generate unanticipated outcomes, penetrate across territories and situations for which they are unprepared. Because certain collections aim to build more monumental, inclusive, efficient, all-encompassing, and far-reaching operations, they also bring together larger numbers of heterogeneous elements, processes, and histories into their ambit. Instead of proficiently coordinating these different compositional elements into a regular and thus predictable pattern of interaction, the very power of these operations destabilizes the relationships the collected elements have with other environments and networks. Rather than conveying stability, these major urban developments impart a sense of their own temporariness and insufficiency.

For all the efforts made to ensure order, accountability, and the transparency of how things work and decisions get made, cityness continues to haunt the city. This is because in the same place and time, another set of conditions, another way of doing things, and another reality have always already been possible—and in an important way, were always already in place. It is precisely this virtual presence of cityness in each and every major and mundane action undertaken to structure urban life that is made peripheral—even if the viability of urban economies, governance, and innovation needs that cityness as an essential resource.

Thus, in cities there are two senses of time in operation. In other words a city is full of memories about what has taken place in the past, and those memories also include a certain amount of imagination—of hopes and dreams that the city could have been a certain kind of place, but one that never seemed to reach fruition. These imaginations have never fully gone away, as the city remains a place of dreams, present and past, of bits and pieces of ways of doing things that never really had enough time or support to fully implant themselves. Cities were and are places full of experiments, of different ways of being with people, spaces, and things. While many of these practices never really "take off" or become institutionalized, they remain in people's memories and sensibilities. So, cityness also includes a sense that behind the present moment there is another time operating, other things taking place, unfolding, waiting, getting ready or slipping away, and that we know only a fragment of what is taking place.

We can extend this notion to other forms of "double time." For example, in some cities that were strongly marked by a colonial history, the time of the "postcolonial" finds many of their inhabitants believing that it is impossible to make a life in the city in which they live. Conditions are too uncertain and fluid, or they are certain that they have no prospects to make a life within them. As a result, these inhabitants demonstrate a capacity, however tentative, to live anywhere, regardless of the extent to which this willingness is voluntary or involuntary. Lives are risked, everything is sacrificed in order to move; territory is claimed and has no other function but to be sacrificed in pursuit of some other place that holds out the promise of a better life. At the same, but in a different time, there is the persistence of colonialism, but now as something which comes to characterize the conditions in most any city. For example, the spatial segmentation and highly particularized interests and ways of doing things that seemingly cannot be integrated, and which once characterized life in the colonial city, are true of cities everywhere.

In Europe particularly, urban space is hollowed out and

dislocated in such a way as to take apart the physical environments through which different kinds of people might come to know each other. Still, there remain prolific in-between spaces. More precisely, seemingly marginal, wasted, or carceral spaces become something more in-between, always pushing, always under threat. But they still act as a platform for a non-territorially fixed sense of being in place that short-circuits the efforts of governments to make certain urban residents always feel "out of place." In the suburbs, inner cities, *banlieues*, peripheries, and estates, people's lives are clearly constrained and their movements and life possibilities circumscribed. Yet, people pour in and pour out of these places, mix it up in fights, cooperation, generosity, and toughness. Money is moved, things fall off the truck, and conference calls are made between Lagos, Bangkok, Shenzhen, and São Paolo on battered folding chairs in the back room of some instant coffee café. Even as the interweaving of diasporas and localities takes place with complex forms of calculation and anticipation, neighborhoods are flooded with people who try to make sure that they are taken for something they are not, as well as by a desire for anonymity.

Of course neighborhoods are also full of traumas experienced elsewhere. People are trying to get away from wars, family dramas, persecution, and hopelessness. These traumas make places volatile. Thus, it becomes difficult for residents to really locate themselves, particularly in face of all the different policing, social work, educational, and welfare agencies that are either omnipresent or nowhere to be found. As a result, many residents remain silent, and their anonymity is often enforced. As the French urban activist Gustave Massiah put it, the poor and the strange must never stop proving their innocence. Still, more residents and more spaces of the city are staying out of representation, are demonstrating a flexibility to be linked to any scheme, any agenda, anywhere else. After all, the colonial world was full of various diasporic, cosmopolitan subalterns pursuing various tricks of the trade to go from here to there—and the world's cities are generating new versions of these mobile subalterns all the time.

As Rose and Osborne point out, while the city was always an unstable domain requiring constant intervention, it needed, at the same time, a spontaneous, undetermined, and unfixed character. In fact, the ability to govern the city would emerge out of its fluidity. To govern was not to immobilize the city's energies but to harness them in the interest of each and all. For an ongoing process of generating and then re-connecting various forms of life, relations of space and time, and different actors was both the motivation for government and the source of its power.[2] So no matter how proficient urban management systems may be, this desire to "fix" things, to make precise identifications of space, problems, or populations, becomes increasingly difficult. Events can be positioned in so many ways at such great speeds as to make any consensus on what events mean impossible.[3] Bodies, as message-bearing systems, must rush to accelerate their "circulatory migration" through proliferating networks of communication and exchange, always displaced in order to maintain place.

Urban spaces are also lived in ways that disrupt hegemonic mappings. For the seemingly coherent landscape of the city is only possible when unruly eruptions, interference, and murkiness are negated or erased. With this erasure, whatever appears coherent about the city is fundamentally tenuous and uneasy. For the extent to which "urban development" is able to conceal the sheer fact that something is being erased is never certain. The extent to which those who govern cities can cover up the specific hopes embedded in the ways of doing things that end up being erased or pushed aside is never certain.

Concerted efforts have been made to govern the city through zoning, cadastre, property, and administration. Yet, these efforts do not completely erase the unruly yet dynamic intersections among differences of all kinds to which the city offers both a setting and a cause. The choreographed coherence of the city wanes at the very point at which the attempted control of space and bodies weakens this dynamism. It wanes as the capacity of residents to navigate the unruly spaces and realities of the city are diminished and then inevitably remain weakly implicated in every system of governance. Ash Amin talks about the frontiers that proliferate across the city and whose effective use and navigation require the suspension of familiar cultural assumptions and social strategies. The real articulations among different facets of urban life then take place in the very crossing of these frontiers in what he calls "banal transgression."[4]

Even efforts to use every aspect of the urban environment in order to observe, calculate, and order the behavior of urban residents—through smart buildings, CCTV cameras, traffic systems, 3G cellular technologies, GPS, and other locational systems—are limited in terms of how comprehensive they can be. As Steve Graham and Mike Crang indicate:

> Urban ubicomp clearly has a fetishistic power in appearing to finally offer solutions by rendering place and space utterly transparent in some simple, deterministic way. Indeed, we would argue that there is a danger that locative media are equally seen as a technical fix for oppositional voices and alternative histories in art projects. In this sense the myths matter and have effects. But they are only mythologies of a perfect, uniform informational landscape. In reality, the seamless and ubiquitous process of pure urban transparency that many accounts suggest will always be little but a fantasy. In practice, the linking of many layers of

> computerized technology is generally a "kludge" . . . Far from the
> pure vision of what de Certeau calls the "concept city," we may
> find the production of myriads of little stories—a messy infinity of
> "Little Brothers" rather than one omniscient "Big" Brother.[5]

In Andrea Arnold's recent film *Red Road*, the main character, Jackie, spends her days monitoring CCTV cameras for the Glasgow City Council. She diligently uses her gaze as part of an apparatus that attempts to keep urban life in line. One day, however, she spots a man in an abandoned field near a huge housing estate with a prostitute. Zeroing the camera in she recognizes him as the man behind the wheel in a hit and run that killed her husband and small child, and who was supposed to be serving a long prison term. While the cameras have been able to place the man in a given area of the city, Jackie must go where the cameras cannot in order to get close enough to him in order to carry out her intention of revenge. Even as she is watched on other shifts by the cameras she routinely sits behind, she hurtles to some abyss trying to track the guy down in the real world of the city's streets and housing projects. Jackie takes an unexpected path into a life and version of herself that she would never have imagined, one opened up by the very act of surveillance itself.

No matter how we pay attention, no matter how street wise and calculating we might be, the city is the world where everyone can be simultaneously swindled and dazzled, and where everyone can be a trickster playing to a crowd he or she otherwise would never deserve. As such, to then affirm that we now know the "real deal" and precisely what to do risks wiping out those confident portrayals of a city capable of taking on the unexpected, of dealing with almost anything that anyone brings to it. For it is this sense of surprise, of not knowing exactly what will happen, that enables us to be "taken in" to all that we believe the city offers. After all, we are city dwellers full of visions that are colliding with and eating off the other, always electric, wired for sound, and always looking for a connection.

DESPITE THE CONTROLS, WHY THE PERIPHERY IS STILL IMPORTANT TO URBAN LIFE

Still, cityness remains at the periphery of our attentions. What I want to do in this book is to talk about different forms of periphery as they relate to cities, and ways in which the periphery can be productively "brought back in" to our considerations of urban life. While this project aims to be applicable to cities across the world, the reflections here are based primarily on cities either that have been at the periphery of urban analysis or which embody urban processes and realities that have largely been left out when these cities are taken into consideration. Thus, reference is made to a swathe of urban life running roughly from Dakar to Jakarta.

Cities that can be located across this invented latitude vary immensely in terms of their characteristics, histories, and positions in an increasingly globalized network of relations among cities. Dakar, Abidjan, Lome, Lagos, Kinshasa, Johannesburg, Nairobi, Dubai, Karachi, Dehli, Mumbai, Bangkok, Phnom Penh, and Jakarta are not brought together here as objects of comparison or to consolidate them as indications of new urban trends or theories. The working assumption is that these cities have something to do with each other, both directly and indirectly—some through various combinations of shared colonial histories, development strategies, trade circuits, regional integration, common challenges, investment flows, and geopolitical articulation. There is no overarching framework that makes these cities instances of a particular type or of economic trends that cement particular connections amongst them that are more powerful than, say, their connections to cities elsewhere in Europe and the Americas. Yet, the rather artificial lines that can be drawn west to east and vice-versa, skirting the usually obligatory reference to cities of "the North," do have a real materialization. This materialization is found in the ways key policy and commercial actors in these cities make reference to each other's urban realities and the migratory and trade flows that leave long-term historical marks and possibilities.

In an important way, these cities "move toward" each other. They do so in gestures and inclinations shaped by the search for economic and political strategies that enhance their "normalization" as viable cities according to standards still largely shaped by occidental notions of modernity. But there is also the search for strategies that address particular practices of inhabitation, livelihood formation, spatial diversification, and social contestation which, while certainly not unknown in cities of the North, assume a different kind of importance for these particular cities—no matter how different from each other they may be. There is a growing recognition that cities can effectively operate in the world without having to adhere to a uniform set of prescriptions—either of economic development, governance, or the shape of the built environment. Instead, cities must find their own particular way to consolidate their histories, locations, and populations and make themselves something more than eligible sites of inward investment from multinational companies. Instead, the question is how they can be active players in making new kinds of economic relationships across different scales and spaces.

Rather than simply being capital or port cities, regional hubs, entrepôts, or major tourist destinations, cities in the South could engineer new kinds of spatial relationships. These relationships would permit new kinds of synergies, cross-investments, commodity chains, distribution networks, production complementarities, and alliances in the multilateral forums where key policies and deals are made. For the cities identified above, the opportunities for producing new spaces—new connections, new opportunities, new exchanges, and so forth—are then largely with each other. Here the financial, political, and technical predominance of New York, London, Frankfurt, Tokyo, Los Angeles, and Paris need not exert an overarching force.

These efforts may be identifiable only in the hundreds upon hundreds of small initiatives that affect, even unwittingly, some kind of articulation—and not in some grand, self-conscious design these cities might collectively launch. As such, these initiatives remain peripheral to the predominant considerations of global urban change. These cities both occasion and embody the often unruly intersection of very different ways of life—intersections that have purportedly been "well regulated" in cities of the North. By trying to work out effective ways of regulation that make sense to their histories, capacities, and inclinations, these cities experiment with different ways of operating in the larger world. Taken together, then, these two forms of the peripheral—the intersection of spaces, peoples, and ways of life "inside" the city and what these cities are trying to do on the "outside"—combine to generate important new ideas about what cities are and can be.

THE HISTORICAL CONDITIONS WHICH MAKE URBAN SPACES AND PRACTICES PERIPHERAL

In my explorations here I will not deal specifically with each of the cities itemized above. For the most part, I will stick to those I know well—which mostly include the major cities of Africa, as well as Phnom Penh, Jakarta, and Dubai—while making occasional reference to others. This partiality does not obviate the overall points I want to make regarding new forms of urban regionalization underway in the bands across Africa and Asia. Certainly there is sufficient secondary material out there that can be woven into the discussion; but the direct ethnographic materials and policy experiences are primarily garnered from those cities in which I have some substantial experience.

Most of the observations here have been developed through many years of work in the slums of Africa and Southeast Asia. The designation "slums," while important to the work of political advocacy and policy development, tends to group particular kinds of urban spaces across the world into generalizations that end up obscuring important features about how the poor actually live and use cities. This is not to deny that perhaps the majority of residents in cities of the Global South live without adequate income and access to some form of stable assets, shelter, and safety nets. They live without access to clean water, sanitation, and power, and enjoy highly limited protection of rights, law, and political voice. In 2003, United Nations Habitat estimated a global slum population of 900 million.

The growth and persistence of slums clearly have a deleterious impact on cities as a whole. Without access to sufficient space, healthy living conditions, basic services such as water and sanitation, and security, people's efforts are primarily devoted to providing for basic needs, and this takes up a great deal of their time. States at both national and municipal levels simply do not provide a comprehensive distribution of market-supporting goods—such as water, clear legal frameworks, power, and sanitation. Therefore, people have to spend a lot of time trying to find things like water, pay high prices because they can only afford to buy a little bit at a time since there are no economies of scale, and spend time trying to get over water-borne illnesses because they have no access to clean water.

In part, this failure to integrate the city through the distribution of goods that would support economic activity and increase incomes stems from the colonial history of many of these cities. Colonial authorities rarely invested in the planning and governance of cities under their jurisdiction as coherent, integrated entities, because they were primarily interested in the extraction of resources and the affordable control and mobilization of urban labor.[6] Rather, these authorities usually identified specific local brokers, customary rulers, and imported military officials—in other words, fragments of previously interlinked ethnicities, societies, and regions—to carry out the day-to-day operations of rule.

Extensions of trade, religion, and domination have originated in many parts of the world, spreading their influences, control, and ways of doing things in various trajectories. Cities have long histories of being at the confluence of different trade routes, as well as contestations over political and religious influence. All of these push and pull existing populations in various directions, and prompt the additions of new peoples and economies. Therefore, it is impossible to ever assume that cities existed at some point as integrated entities, their residents and activities all effectively coordinated under an overarching set of values, rules, or institutions. Yet, European colonialism, as well as many of the postcolonial investments and affiliations with the urban South, has operated through partial institutions and powers. The continued reproduction of customary chiefs, military cliques, dominant ethnic entrepreneurial groupings, ruling families, and political associations makes it difficult for effective state structures to emerge—ones that have the interest of a general urban citizenry in mind.

Thus, city life in many parts of Asia and Africa simply becomes the purview of the few. As a result, the viability of the city—its economic output, accumulated revenues, and development resources—is generated by only a small proportion of its territory and population. Even when slums do demonstrate economic capacity, in terms of all the goods and services that its residents do and can produce, governments tend to treat them in highly punitive ways. Residents are forcefully evicted from areas where, no matter how bad the living conditions, they have established an entire fabric of relations critical to their livelihoods. Governments crack down on so-called illegal, unlicensed businesses and trades. In many cases, where small entrepreneurs attempt to legitimize their status through securing property, capital, and licenses, they are shut out from such prospects by municipal agencies and banks.

In most ways the picture of contemporary urban life for residents of much of the urban South is bleak. Too often political regimes enforce their power by making life as precarious as possible for a significant part of urban populations. Despite disadvantageous colonial histories, many national governments once cultivated an elite from competing regions and/or ethnic groups within a nation through a balanced investment in education opportunities, human services, and accumulation opportunities, and then tied them to the state. But marked changes in the position of nations within global economies have substantially diminished the public resources available to do this.[7] At one time, these governments ensured educational opportunities. Thus access to the most lucrative wage labor— usually located within the public sector—was made available to elites across various ethnic and regional communities. Urbanization and state employment produced at least the semblance of solidarity across these communities. At the same time, the mechanisms that have been employed for distorting agricultural markets, and thus extracting implicit forms of taxation from the non-urban areas in favor of the urban elite, are legendary. Prices paid to local producers for important commodities were kept artificially low; state marketing boards would dispose of large quantities of important products on black markets and pocket the profits for important elites rather than for state coffers.

Still, many of these distortions were aimed at maximizing resources for the state. These resources were to be distributed throughout the country. Increasingly, with massive budget reductions for education forced upon states, they no longer have the resources to engineer such solidarity across different regional and ethnic divides—although the extent to which states that have been granted substantial debt relief will manage the retention of funds that otherwise would go to service high levels of indebtedness remains to be seen.

As states over the past two decades shed many of their former responsibilities and oversaw a substantial retrenchment of public employees, resulting in the subsequent decline of urban incomes and the privatization of major economic interests, governance became more informalized.[8] Specific dominant groups use this process of dismantling to transfer significant resources to private spheres, and the state then uses its authority to mask these transfers.[9] Widespread privatization of state assets has frequently been used as a vehicle to maintain control of these assets in the hands of those occupying state power but now acting in a private capacity. The procedures through which these assets are sold and subsequently organized are often organized with the complicity of the state and are often irregular.

WHEN PERIPHERALIZATION, POVERTY, AND NEW
POSSIBILITIES BECOME ENTANGLED

Those who are disadvantaged in this process increasingly resort to plunder and looting.[10] Employment of any kind—formal and informal—is increasingly difficult to access.[11] As a result, extended family and residential support systems find themselves overburdened.[12] It is estimated that roughly 75 percent of basic needs are provided informally in the majority of African cities, and that most sectors and domains of urban life are largely informalized, even as formal institutions continue to multiply and grow.[13] Whereas unemployment has long been a persistent reality for African cities, available compensations now require more drastic action.[14] At the same time, various components of economic rationalization have opened up possibilities for the appropriation of formerly public assets—land, enterprises, services—by private interests, particularly for the emerging elite, well positioned in the apparatuses managing the restructuring of national economies. Structural adjustment policies have been more than simply instruments of institutional realignment or fiscal calibration in their impact on the public sphere.

While a semblance of social cohesion and collaboration continues to be reproduced or reworked, how people are connected to each other is something that has given rise to great anxiety, conflict, and experimentation, particularly in urban Africa. Increased mobility of urban populations among places marked by ever-increasing disparities in economic capacity means that city residents witness more people suddenly accumulating and losing material wealth. As a result, the pressures on maintaining a sense of cohesion within extended family systems, and on the practices of resource distribution that go with it, are enormous.[15]

Even efforts at consolidating a sense of place can make the

city seem less cohesive. For example, Dakar, Accra, and Lagos have witnessed the explosive growth of housing starts in the past two decades, as repatriated earnings are invested in land acquisition and home construction. While at one level, this investment represents an ongoing commitment to consolidating a place in the city, the widespread corruption and shabby work of contractors, the inflated costs of building materials, and the volatility of financial transactions have acted against the long-term security sought by investors. In addition, since the bulk of such investment is placed in construction, rather than in explicit production-centered activities,[16] the notion of what place is becomes increasingly narrow. In other words, property is often divorced from the prospective viability of the larger economic context in which it is situated. As a result, more transactions with other places, most usually Europe, are required in order to sustain these investments in property.

For the youth particularly, there is greater uncertainty as to what it takes to get ahead or to stay out of trouble. Clearly old-fashioned networking, school connections, and political loyalty are important. But there are marked ebbs and flows characterizing incomes and opportunities. On one day a neighbor suddenly has a lot of money; two months later they have nothing. As a result, few individuals can put together a viable perspective on how to secure a consistent livelihood over the long run.

In the city, households must rely upon many different renditions of so-called customary ties—through which households are able to extend kin-like relations, and thus support and obligation. At the same time, they must increasingly find ways to operate outside these frequently claustrophobic sets of relations. The efforts to forge networks across different ethnic groups and geographic territories are fraught with uncertainties given either the absence or wearing away of strong organizational cultures through which such relations could be socialized. Outside of school, church, and work there are few contexts through which people can collaborate in situations not focused on entrepreneurial activities. At the same time, the more provisional networking efforts happening outside of institutions are actually less vulnerable to manipulation by the state.

During the past two decades, international institutions such as the United Nations and the World Bank have focused on decentralizing the governance of cities to very local levels. States, however, have often used this process as a way of maximizing their control of urban neighborhoods without necessarily delivering better services or tolerating real democratic decision-making.

Additionally, civic associations that do exist in neighborhoods and districts tend to be organized along highly hierarchical lines. Individuals seek to disrupt these hierarchies, but at the same time, try to maintain their ostensible purpose, which is to offer clearly defined positions and responsibilities for their members. Still, many popular civic associations are prone to political manipulation—both in order to lessen their potential political force as formal associations and to disrupt their ability to coordinate local actions. The majority of residents are either unable or unwilling to negotiate their way through these political games in a context with few real job or financial opportunities, especially in places where state power consistently transgresses the established rules of the game. Accordingly, alternative means of accumulation must be secured.

The content of deprivations are numerous and interlocking, and have ramifications that extend across generations and territory. They impact on global climatic conditions and political stability. Yet, the long lists of deprivations do not in themselves summarize what actually does take place in slums.

In other words, the absence of certain material conditions assumed to support a viable life does not rule out life altogether. Residents find particular ways of dealing with those absences in particular combinations of generosity, ruthlessness, collaboration, competition, stillness, movement, flexibility, and defensiveness. Some residents will hold their limited ground to the end; others will live lives all over the place, willing to become anything for anyone almost anywhere. What these combinations will look like depends on the particular histories of cities and their relationship to other combinations—i.e. the combinations of economic policy, spatial organization, political culture and contestation, and how particular localities are situated in relationship to others, as well as other cities, regions, and economic poles.

The combinations of sentiment, action, inclination, and effort are also the stuff of available local economies. Although their economic activities are mostly focused on sheer survival without hope of making large earnings, street sellers, hawkers, repairers, and hustlers all pay attention to these combinations and try to anticipate what might happen as a result. Take a busy transport center, with buses and cars of all kinds taking passengers from a given city to somewhere else. Take the assemblage of drivers, loaders, sellers, touts, mechanics, and hangers-on. There are no systematic market surveys, passenger and customer profiles to inform these economic actors about what to do. There are usually few institutional authorities available to mediate their relations with each other, assign specific places of operation, or calibrate their dealings with one another. Still, they pay attention to who is dealing with whom, what kinds of passengers gravitate toward different cars or buses serving the same destination. They pay attention to what kinds of items they purchase before or following their journeys. They pay attention to the kinds of words exchanged between taxis looking to pick up arriving passengers, and the kinds of arrangements made between supposedly competing transport companies—how services and money are shared; how passengers are passed along to other cars or drivers because they seem to be part of a fortuitous fit with the other people who have now been "committed" to a specific car or bus. Here, the possible interactions amongst people sharing a particular journey might produce some unexpected information or possibilities which baggage handlers, drivers, ticket collectors, and attendants might make future use of.

By paying attention to all of these circuitries of exchange, of words, money, favors, obligations, and information going back and forth, each actor here tries to anticipate what various combinations might bring about. There is no clear way of reading or determining what is going on. Yet, these observations and engagements become tools for shaping the moment, for being in it in ways that not only maximize what an individual might get out of it—in terms of tips, information, favors, and opportunities—but that bring other scenarios into being. Scenarios that actively shape this market place of transactions in ways that set up more opportunities in the future. With so many bodies in circulation—some on their way somewhere, some coming from somewhere, others just finding ways to intersect with these movements—the transport center becomes a staging area of anticipation.

There is not enough time, resources, or authority available for the actors gathered here to experiment in a free-wheeling way. Efforts have to be based on some kind of calculation, some kind of reading of what could be the most advantageous set of words and styles with which to approach a potential customer, collaborator, patron, or client. The key is also not just how to turn individuals into one of these fixed identities but to keep open the possibility that any particular individual that is engaged could act as several at various times. An economy of anticipation then actively gears individual and group actions toward shaping a wide range of possible outcomes from the combinations of the many different actions, feelings, styles, and functions that operate in a given market place. As this economy of anticipation is generalized across the city, it clearly shapes what the city then becomes.

The challenge in dealing with slums is that global economic trends and policies do have an effect on where people live and what they are able to do. The problems of accumulation—of generating sufficient profit—have been displaced onto the poor. This happens by cheapening labor and disinvesting in public services. The past three decades of economic orientations focused on shrinking the role of the state and public sectors in providing jobs and services for people and eliminating barriers to the circulation of capital and commodities have had a global effect, producing remarkable similarities in the conditions faced by urban residents across the Global South. Mike Davis' book *The Planet of the Slums* has been particularly useful in demonstrating these trends and how they have come about.[17]

Work is seemingly more precarious everywhere, and for those at the bottom the horizons of possibility are narrowed to a series of provisional relationships through which they might approximate some sense of being part of something and anchored somewhere. More of the world's population is forced to eke out survival in an economy of part-time service jobs, hustles, and schemes where nothing and no one can really be counted on, and where a premium is placed on "getting over," deceit, and trickery. At times, everyone seems to trick each other, play each other for some kind of fool. And once you've tricked someone, you have to move on; just as it is easy for one to overstay in a part-time dead-end job, even as people fight to hold on to them as some kind of sign of normalcy. When a person has to move from one improvised economic arrangement to another, fantasies about staying put grow strong. As Lauren Berlant points out, in times of great uncertainty and temporariness, possessing the fantasy of some un-conflicted, normative life-world can provide at least the emotional sense of a place of rest, even if it is concretely experienced as just a mirage of solidity and stability.[18]

This is why people operating within precarious econo-mic circumstances, where even family ties are tenuous and disappointing, attempt to force some sense of obligation in someone which can come to stand in for their desire for recognition and for a normal way of life. No matter the form or what it takes, there is often a desperate fight for some kind of intimacy. This is because intimacy is still seen as a way of attaining a kind of commensurateness with a general set of prevailing values. These put emphasis on the importance of belonging, of making a good life—a life which, Berlant says, doesn't always have to be reinvented.

But the challenge also rests in trying to understand how these global trends toward the deepening and extension of urban impoverishment, the shedding of national and metro-politan responsibility for taking care of urban residents onto urban residents themselves, and the increasing dependence on work outside formal, waged jobs (and thus work of all kinds) are themselves urbanized. In other words, let us assume that cities remain places where relations of all kinds unfold. Residents, forced to operate outside of stable regulatory frame-works governing how they put food on the table and how they will deal with each other, must come up with all kinds of tac-tics, practices, emotions, risks, and commitments in order to survive. If this is the case, then how do the combinations of all these aspects produce particular kinds of urban residents in a given place and time? How are particular kinds of conflicts, possibilities, skills, and vulnerabilities produced? The sheer enumeration of how bad slums are—a practice certainly not new in urban history—does not tell us what specific cities are capable of. It does not tell us where attention should be placed in terms of trying to begin to change things within a specific city.

USING PERIPHERAL STATUS AS AN ADVANTAGE, OR GETTING THE MOST OUT OF INVISIBILITY

Mayo, a district of 300,000 inhabitants, 20 kilometers outside of central Khartoum, is probably one of the most difficult slums in Africa. Over the past three decades, its four sub-districts have contained political refugees escaping war in Southern Sudan and the Nuba Mountains, and economic and political refugees from the west, including Darfur. Many residents of Southern Sudan are considered displaced persons with no formal rights to the city, even though many have lived nowhere else but in Khartoum. Living far from any available work, most residents are unemployed. Those that do find work as domestic servants, construction workers, or tea sellers exhaust a large proportion of their earnings simply in transport costs. The illegal brewing and sale of alcohol, as well as sex work, constitute a major part of the local economy, as do raids on trucks and other petty criminality. The district retains a mostly strict territorial order according to ethnic and regional identification—with different groups of Dinka, Shilluk, Nuer, Nubu, Azande, Equitorian, Baggara, Borgho, Fellata, Fur, and Zaghawa peoples living in their own zones.

Years of deprivation and constant harassment by national authorities and the police have greatly undermined the coherence of each group's cultural practices. Rampant demoralization has produced new generations operating largely outside the ambit of either household or local cultural authority. Despite being grouped into their sub-territories, different ethnicities have been forced by their circumstances to thicken and broaden all kinds of interchange, giving rise to a hybrid form of Arabic for their communications with each other. Implicit in this "urbanization" of interchange has been the growing adoption of either Islam or Christianity, with their emphasis on individual responsibility, moral culpability, and salvation. This has taken individuals away from indigenous belief systems that emphasized the interpenetration of the visible and invisible in all aspects of social life, in that social life was the embodiment and integration of forces of all kinds. Here harmony, custom, and reciprocity were to be valued over individual efficacy and success.[19]

The organization of relationships according to shared monotheistic affiliation and secular concerns provides a platform in which to think about local development and governance, as well as a way for a younger generation of Mayo residents to try to link themselves with the larger city. But this means that much of the framework that ties individuals into a particular cultural group is lost. Yet, as these links with the larger city become increasingly problematic and communities experience greater levels of disintegration within the household and neighborhood, people turn to accounts of invisible forces. These forces are no longer domesticated and familiarized within a prevailing cultural practice which once enabled individuals to explain what was going on in their lives. In other words, the invisible world becomes an antagonistic one. It is a world where forces are no longer known, no longer rooted in the day-to-day experiences of people joined together by common understandings of who they are for each other, and what they are expected to do with each other.[20]

Yet, if these forces then have nothing to do with how Dinka, Shilluk, or Nuer, for example, try to maintain a sense of coherent practice constantly in touch with a past that remains vibrant, then they can possibly be put to use in other ways. For example, while the alcohol and prostitution business has severely disrupted local moral orders, it has meant that these slums do have some vehicle through which the city "comes" to them in order to buy these services. In recent years, residents in these businesses have tried to take note of where their regular "customers" come from, and have sometimes gone to elaborate efforts to track the cars, using lookouts stationed at various key road junctions with cell phones. Sometimes taxis are hired at key points once cars are tracked back to Khartoum in order to pinpoint the person's office or home. On future visits, then, calls are made on cell phones for "operatives" in the town to leave mystifying amulets or signs. Sometimes attempts are made to rob the house. Even if there are absolutely no connections made, even when these efforts produce no discernible result, which they almost never do, residents still talk about the fact that they make some impact on the city, that they are steering it in a particular direction that will ultimately have some kind of pay-off.

The effect of cell phones has been substantial. Even for households who can barely feed themselves, it is not unusual for the household to have at least one phone. In Mayo most of them are stolen; SIM cards and air time are shared, but even here some residents have found ingenious ways to manipulate using cell phones for almost no cost. So when women spread out across Khartoum, going to their different domestic jobs, or scouring the city looking for them, they pay attention to the surroundings, perhaps now in new ways. Groups gather at night talking about the city, in terms of not only developments that directly affect the security of their camps and districts, but also the facets related to the city's explosive development, the construction of new districts, buildings, and shopping malls. In their excursions to and from work, or searching for work, calls will be placed regarding the offloading of building materials on a particular lot, or a house that has been left weakly guarded, or car seemingly abandoned in a spot for several days, or the arrival of new stores of food or other supplies where the workers have smuggled off part of the proceeds to some nearby bushes, vans, or crevices to be disposed of later. These calls will be relayed to friends and relatives, who will contact others more capable of taking direct advantage. Sometimes groups of women will themselves rendezvous to intervene in an opportunity where just a few hands are needed. They will carry off some pipes or tin sheets into the desert, or stuff their dresses with calculators that a hole in a warehouse fence has left exposed.

Most often it will never be clear to them just what was done with the observations they reported on their cell phones, or by whom. But they are convinced that, somewhere down the line, a Baggara merchant selling bits of cloth in the main commercial area of Mayo offers a discount as a returned favor for something that transpired a few weeks before, or that their sons have a few extra Sudanese pounds in their pockets because some Fellata[21] with a truck picked up on a load of cement blocks that had been delivered to the wrong address. Significant here is that many of these residents explicitly see themselves turning into the invisible forces that have haunted them—that have brought illness and misfortune. These invisible forces no longer are the familiar vehicles of consolidation existing within a set of coherent cultural references. Rather they are signs of estrangement of Mayo residents from both a past and a viable future. As such, they are to be inhabited instrumentally as a way of trying to act on the city as a whole. Residents act as if they are some kind of invisible force moving across the city, finding the loopholes, or, at least, acting as if there are many different ways in which the city is unable to defend itself, unable to keep the residents of Mayo out, to keep them from living a city life.

These invisibilities are combined with the equally opaque trajectories through which money pours into Khartoum from all over the world. Here, the built environment serves as a platform that concretely links repatriated earnings from Sudanese working in the Gulf, various earnings and pay-offs related to the Chinese domination of national oil production, inflows of finance and investment from the Arab world, and the proceeds of the city's distribution activities that link Asian imports to markets across the lower Sahel through Cameroon to Douala—just to take a few examples of such elements. It seems that rather than paying attention to the conditions that presently exist, both rich and poor are looking at the city in terms of what can be destroyed and remade.

In July 2006, John Garang, the former leader of the Sudan People's Liberation Movement, arrived in Khartoum following the signing of a peace deal with the Sudanese government. Two million Dinka, Nuer, Azande, and Shilluk gathered in the center of the town to welcome him. The gathering sent Khartoum into shock, since most residents did not, and probably had refused to, acknowledge the number of so-called "foreigners" in their midst. Largely condemned to live at the periphery as they were, visual images of their consolidation were not readily available. Yet, since it was impossible to stay put in the periphery, they had continuously dispersed across the city for decades, spreading out through its crevices, its layout among deserts and rivers—a quotidian invasion of the city practiced under the radar.

These invisibilities constitute the city as a place of play, as something always in play, immune to any overarching image or plan of what it is to be. Too many discrepancies are produced within the dense relationship between the poor's conversion of themselves into invisible spirits and the invisible deals that circumvent municipal development frameworks. Money is put to work in hasty constructions not really built to last—as if they were high-class shanty towns. There are too many lingering questions about who people really think they are and about what forces are at work making things happen. Together, these two kinds of invisibility make it difficult to grasp what would constitute a clearly recognizable and stable citizenry or set of locations that could be brought together under the auspices of municipal justice or equanimity.

GIVEN THE ENTANGLEMENTS OF PERIPHERY AND POSSIBILITY, WHAT MAKES ANY ACTION EFFECTIVE?

It is true that the ability to change urban conditions requires a groundswell of actions—actions undertaken in a coordinated fashion by multilateral institutions, corporations, states, municipalities, research centers, associations of mayors, local authorities, builders, and providers of infrastructure. Such coordinated action does rely upon sweeping discourses that sum up a wide range of specificities across the world. But without a better understanding of what residents themselves are actually doing in specific sites and how those actions are reworked or abandoned for new ones, new policies may shape the actions of politicians, technicians, bureaucrats, and service providers without them having any foothold in the worlds of the urban poor. Even the many nongovernmental organizations (NGOs), community-based organizations, and urban social movements that attempt to represent these lives and to consolidate new ways of improving them often reduce them to a bare minimum or overestimate their capacities.

Many of the so-called lacks—of amenities, infrastructure, livelihood, markets, and governance—become occasions for residents to assemble ways of working together that otherwise would not be possible given existing cultural norms, political practices, and urban experiences. These are collective efforts that cannot be characterized as associations or community organizations. On the one hand, the efforts to secure urban resources or opportunities may seldom look efficient or viable in their own terms—for these efforts require individuals to "stretch" their performance beyond the prevailing terms of what is acceptable, normal, or worthwhile.

Take, for example, "the Building"—a large dilapidated housing development in Phnom Penh, Cambodia, that runs uninterrupted the equivalent length of several football fields. The structure—with its stairwells, balconies, apartments, and sheds—is continuously being remade by various groups of residents, in part to accommodate and facilitate new social realities. The development has been segmented into three sections corresponding to the three major stairwells—the "police section" at the southern stairwell that originally had housed police officers (most of whom had sold off their apartments and moved elsewhere in the city); the "artists' section" at the middle stairwell, inhabited by musicians, dancers, and actors who once worked at the former nearby national theater; and a "sex workers' section" at the northern stairwell. Out of the 160 units that we were able to establish contact with, 37 indicated some affiliation to the performing arts and 25 indicated their involvement in sex work. Given the social stigma associated with sex work, such overt self-identification suggested a large degree of consolidation of this sector within the neighborhood. While artists and sex workers may not have constituted the majority living in the sections attributed to them, those parts of the building were seen as being predominantly defined by their presence.

In part, the participation of an important subset of residents in the same livelihoods—respectively, sex work and the performing arts—provides them grounds for a ready commonality that did not exist for other residents. This did not mean that the sex workers or performing artists constituted homogeneous groupings or that residents involved in other livelihoods did not have ways of associating together. Rather, it points to the process whereby specific residential territories get to be known as the sphere of a particular identity. So in addition to the wide diversity of livelihood practices relied upon by residents (and typical of low-income and poor urban communities), certain symbolic economies come to the fore that have particular constraints, values, and possibilities in terms of the relationship of a specific locality to the larger city.

In the early 1990s, an influx of residents from the refugee camps along the Thai–Cambodian border became another important anchor of the Building. But, despite its very mixed population, the Building carried negative connotations in other quarters of the city. It simultaneously embodied a failed project of "modernist living" and the dangerous contiguities of sex, art, crime, popular culture, and informal commerce—in short, as the place where one can acquire nearly anything.

On the surface, the Building, with its buzzing small markets, stalls, cafés, gaming parlors, computer rooms, improvised classrooms, and storage places, seemed unlinked to any part of the city, and certainly to the buildings and functions in the surrounding areas. Within the warren of staircases, narrow halls, cramped apartments, and densely packed commercial spaces, all rubbing up against each other, the management of everyday transactions and security in the Building is labor intensive. There are barely any formal agencies or associations that might lend some predictability or order, yet disparate agendas and inclinations do manage to interlock through residents' need and ability to observe what each other does and to render this a matter of conversation, both serious and playful.

The scores of small cafés, inserted in the ground-floor openings that had been initially built for flood control and ventilation, are one example of the many local spaces "carved out" of the original construction in order to manage and circulate everyday information. In those mostly frequented by youth, the social scene is usually heterogeneous in terms of who is sitting and talking together. Even though youth identify particular group affiliations through the use of tattoos, clothing, and hairstyles, or ways of speaking, these cafés are not the hang-outs of any particular group but remain as places for a kind of mutual witnessing and exchange. Thus, youth who are able to attend university or the scores of tertiary-level training programs across the city will routinely mask the fact that they live in the Building in order not to be shunned. At the same time, they have access to information and points of view that youth who consider themselves *chukan* (gangsters) and who strongly assert their residential location do not have.

In the cafés there is great emphasis on an exchange of different interpretations of the rest of the city made possible by these divergent trajectories of engagement. For the *chukan* do not sit still within the Building but attempt to figure out ways to move across the city, through a field of antagonisms and alliances with other gangs, or by doing the dirty work for syndicates (most often Vietnamese). This exposure generates stories and information that the university students then use to communicate a street wisdom that not many of their fellow students possess. At a more concrete level, the cafés and youth become contexts for the advertisement and acquisition of goods and services obtained through theft, bartering, or as the by-product of favors rendered to *okhna* ("big men"). For both poor and middle-class residents, who struggle to maintain specific levels of consumption, access to such low-cost goods is critical. Across the area, this profusion of talk, information exchange, rumors, and transactions also takes place in the billiard and snooker sheds and over card games. Even as the different residential segments—art, sex, police—provide distinct zones of anchorage, the proximity of these different sections enables them to provide opportunities and support to each other.

This example from Phnom Penh shows that once lines of conventional identities are crossed, the efforts to, for example, retrieve water, share tools and space, or put various materials or services together often force a reworking of power relations and privilege—of what can be kept apart and put together. If and when such residents "hit the road" and migrate elsewhere, these ways of creating collaboration where none seemed possible constitute a "tool-box" that can be re-tried in other settings.[22]

Despite disparate distribution patterns and impoverishment, as well as the fact that many urban residents in a given city would rather be somewhere else, city dwellers do make concerted efforts to invest in an urban existence. Even when their consumption levels decline significantly, they continue to secure access to at least the bare minimum.[23] Thus, the collective orientation of the poor—i.e. to engage the city as an embodiment of specific long-term aspirations—does contrast markedly with the almost parasitical inclinations of the ruling elite. The elite are not averse to running cities into the ground as they pursue sometimes perverse levels of consumption.[24]

Attaining even the minimum often requires complex ways

of staying attuned to the shifting intersections of gestures, excitements, languages, anxieties, determinations, and comportments enacted across markets, streets, and other venues. Acknowledging this is not to romanticize the slum or the poor. But this is the way the issue is too often framed. For example, the renowned architect Lebbeus Woods states:

> Living in the slums, which means living without many beneficial, even necessary, things, but also with so many threatening, even dangerous, things, is a great test of human ingenuity, and of the human spirit, which means nothing less than finding, or creating, a degree of satisfaction in being human . . . but admiration must be tempered by the realization that they do not struggle because they choose to, out of principle, or in the service of high social or political ideals, but because of their desperation at the brutal limits of survival. It is a mistake—and a grave disservice to them—to imagine that their ingenuity, resourcefulness, and capacities for self-organization can in any way serve as models for our present global society.

But this is not the point here. The point is not to suggest models or admire resilience. Rather, the point is to pursue the dogged work of trying to understand the implications of what people do, particularly as it is clear that residents, even in the desperate ways they may talk about their lives, usually think about them as more than survival alone. Yes, survival is the overwhelming preoccupation for many. But the pursuit of survival involves actions, relations, sentiments, and opportunities that are more than survival alone. It is these thousands of small excesses which also act on the city, remaking it ever so slightly into something different than it was before.

These changes are not measured by any easily discernible standard that would allow one to say that the city is becoming more just, equal, cutthroat, revolutionary, messianic, or hellish. And thus the important work is perhaps simply to document these efforts on the part of the poor to give rise to a new moral universe, a sense of value, of potential, and of the unexpected to which people's attention, no matter how poor, is also paid. If there are policies that could possibly bring about a more judicious distribution of resources, income, and opportunities, the grassroots will also have to mobilize themselves to meet them. And they will have to do something from a history of trying to make ends meet anyway they can, but with a sense of keeping open certain possibilities—of livelihood, feeling, and relations with others.

THE PERIPHERY IS MANY THINGS

Until this point, I have been talking about the periphery as including both a marginalized cityness and the sidelining of the poor from conventional understandings about how the city is put together. As a site for remaking urban life, the notion of "periphery" is used here with several additional connotations. In its common usage, the periphery refers to the outskirts of cities—to an area that may be part of the city's overall administrative domain, but whose character does not yet fully reflect the "stamp" of the city. Here, activities and ways of living persist that are not completely integrated into city life.

Additionally, the realities of cities in Africa and Southeast Asia have largely been peripheral to the processes in which theories about cities and urban policies are made. The efficacy of urban life has usually been measured by benchmarks that seem to inevitably leave African cities in particular lacking a wide range of normative characteristics.

In the conventional parlance of political geography, the periphery is a region that is simultaneously included and excluded in the formation of a nation, municipality, or region. The periphery is included in that it fully falls under the jurisdiction of the local or national state—subject to its laws and policies, while also being seen as counting for little in terms of its overall contribution to the substance of the polity itself. Given this double status, the periphery depends on the largess and guidance of a center—since it is a space of insufficiency and incompletion.

Yet this lack also means that the periphery is never really brought fully under the auspices of the logic and development trajectories that characterize a center, and therefore embodies an instability that is always potentially destabilizing of that center. This negative potentiality then requires supplemental forms of engagement that would never be applied to non-peripheral parts of the nation or metropolis. In other words, these areas are sometimes in need of special development, humanitarian intervention, restructuring, investment, policing, or emergency controls. Thus, the periphery both is ignored and, at the same time, occasions excessive attention. It forces the state to admit to the necessity of exceeding its own "core" values and technologies in order to rein it in, as perhaps the periphery's only concrete indication of its relevance.

The periphery is also a buffer, a space in-between the nation or city and something else that is formally more foreign, more divergent than the city or nation for which it acts as a periphery. In other words, the periphery can exist as a frontier in that it has a border with another city, nation, rural area, or periphery. When this is the case, the practices and values of the center, and thus the state, do not necessarily have to face directly, compete with, or risk modification or dissolution in close contact with other cities or nations. Thus the periphery can become a hybrid space—a space where different ways of doing things, of thinking about and living urban life, can come together. Here, more direct forms of confrontation among cities, regions, and nations are deferred through a space that absorbs the tensions inherent in any intersection of substantially different ways of doing things. Theoretically, the periphery is then a potentially generative space—a source of innovation and adaptation. Yet, it is precisely this generative role which is usually foreclosed or vilified.

Claude Jacquier reminds us that it is not always clear exactly where certain peripheries are located:

> Nowadays this concept corresponds less to an external limit (the topological meaning of periphery) than to a range of fractures, discontinuities or "hinges" disseminated over urban territories. The entrance to a territory occurs less and less while crossing its periphery (access by seaports and custom posts on traditional borders).[25]

Rather, such entrance takes place via its core, through cities, and generally by railway stations and airports.

Many generalizations are made about distressed neighborhoods and the spatial distribution of hardship. But hardship is constituted in many different ways and temporalities—from periods of short-term crisis and vulnerability to longer-term structural deficiencies in the availability of employment and shelter. Additionally, some enclaves of poverty are strategically located in urban systems so that some actors and districts can take advantage of the fluidity of labor purportedly housed by them. At other times, the distribution of poverty, distress, or hardship occurs through narrow bands across urban systems, squeezed in-between well-resourced areas.

Sometimes entire districts are stigmatized. This is reflected in the ways institutions engage and observe particular sectors of their populations—such as education, police, health, and social welfare. Additionally, residents of district are always particular kinds of residents—racially, ethnically, politically, or culturally—and these designations have particular connotations within the urban system as a whole. Sometimes districts are stigmatized because the form of housing in which they live—self-built pavilions or publicly managed tower blocks—are popularly understood as breeding a wide range of social ills.

At other times, districts are stigmatized simply because conventional mechanisms for assessing livelihood and access to money do not apply to the ways in which people earn an income. This is particularly the case for relatively invisible forms of accumulation in black markets, local community economies, domestic exchange among households, and activities which straddle the licit/illicit divide. Additionally, location near particular kinds of commercial facilities, distance from main transportation grids, or the lack of high-tech facilities is often thought to connote a sense of the area "being out of it."

Districts differ in terms of the people who live within them, how they relate to other districts and functions in the urban system, and the kinds of institutions that exist within the district or which are brought to bear on it. Jacquier points out that the combination of these differences gives rise to a wide range of possible futures, priorities, and perspectives. As such, districts that would on the surface appear to look the same and be subject to the same social and economic forces may end up with very different futures. These divergent possibilities have different impacts on the people, places, and institutions themselves. They impact on what residents consider to be the important practices and ways of being in the city, on what they see as possible to do, and how.

As such, districts differ in terms of how residents and outsiders use them and for what purposes, as well as the extent to which available resources are put to work in these activities. Here, there are important considerations as to how many residents spend most of their time inside or outside a given district; about where their loyalties lie, and where their affiliations are located. How much do they pay attention to the activities and needs of those with whom they ostensibly share space? At times, particular districts will pursue projects—of accumulation, management, social engineering—because they seem to be the normal things which everyone is pursuing, or because of the political pressure exerted by particular segments of the district. Sometimes these projects are not well suited to the character of the place in terms of the people who live there and the resources and aspirations they have. Sometimes particular projects are imposed in places regardless of local sentiment, or, alternately, are refused in favor of accommodations that may work to smooth over local differences and contestation, but in the end don't really advance the economic needs of a district.

Also significant is how much a given district "stands out" in terms of the districts that surround it and what the relationships are among them. All of these considerations affect what we could identify as patterns of growth, renewal, or decline. All of them constitute particular criteria in the assessments made by key municipal institutions as to the kinds of attention and investment they will put into specific districts, as well as what they will consider as possible and viable courses of action. Thus, districts can become increasingly peripheral for a wide variety of reasons. The reasons why a district is peripheral or not are not to be found in the specific character of the district's built environment or social composition.

For example, the remarkable growth of Shenzhen during the last quarter-century from a series of rice-growing villages into one of the world's largest port cities reflects the confusion around what is peripheral and what is not. In order to accommodate the massive inflows of migrant labor from the rest of China, the existing villages were allowed to parcel their land and to construct various residential developments on them. As these villages existed administratively outside of the official Shenzhen municipality and, as such, its residents were designated non-urban dwellers, much of the region's development happened outside of any formal regulation. Even though they came to house half of Shenzhen's 13 million people, these villages were officially considered "rural areas" and were not eligible for schools, hospitals, and other public amenities.

As these uncoordinated and unplanned developments started to attain substantial density, various features of public life were inserted into interstitial spaces. Parking garages doubled as classrooms, improvised stores and recreational centers were set up on streets, nightclubs and health centers were set up in makeshift constructions in small alleyways that separated large apartment blocks. The Shenzhen municipality has tried to officially incorporate these villages into its administrative ambit and, as a result, has destroyed many of them. It has, however, reduced the pace of demolition because it finds itself unable to come up with affordable solutions to housing the enormous migrant population. Thus, the so-called peripheral villages take on an increased importance to the metropolitan system as a whole.[26]

FIVE MANIFESTATIONS OF THE PERIPHERY

Given the multiple connotations and sometimes conceptual confusion concerning the definition of the peripheral, especially when it comes to cities, I will deal with five manifestations of the peripheral in my explorations of African and Southeast Asian urbanities here. These concern dimensions of urban life that have either been paid insufficient attention or been understood in highly limited ways.

First, mobility as both practice and aspiration is extensive for many residents in Africa and Southeast Asia. This entails mobility both inside cities and across cities. Most conventional readings of such mobility emphasize its involuntary nature, the fact that people have little choice but to keep in motion as the places that are nominally home are either environmentally precarious, overcrowded, fraught with political or criminal violence, provide little opportunities for livelihood, or provide insecure tenure.

While these are the structural conditions for large numbers of urban residents, they do not obviate a wide range of desires to use the city as a means of acquiring experiences and sensibilities forged from a more expansive exposure to the world. This has been evident in the motivations of migrants over a long period of time. The question becomes how the involuntary and voluntary aspects of mobility both diverge and intersect. What are their degrees of complicity? What are the ways in which certain inclinations and aspirations impact upon the ability of certain kinds of residents to hold their places within given cities? Who fights, when and how? How do poor yet mobile populations make particular urban spaces provisional or make these spaces amenable to gentrification or more restricted use? How do efforts made by various urban social movements and advocacy organizations to attain security of tenure and the stability of particular localities disrupt local economies based on a complementary distribution of mobility and stasis? In such circumstances some people rarely leave a highly circumscribed space, while others are almost constantly on the move through short-term employment, scavenging, or sojourning.

The second form of the peripheral concerns the role of

different cities in Africa and Southeast Asia in a hierarchy of urban functions and capacities. This is not just a matter of the ways in which cities of the Global South may be largely forced to play "catch up" in terms of their respective levels of development or managerial proficiencies. It is not simply a matter of certain cities continuing to be important only as sites for managing the extraction of important primary commodities or resources—in a continuation of basic colonial relationships. Rather, another form of "the colonial present," as Derek Gregory designates it, remains important. What he means is that actions and policies undertaken in various cities across the South become laboratories for experimenting with renovations and adjustments whose real targets are the urban areas of the North. Here, cities in the South are practice areas; places of experimentation that can be disrupted or wasted when the experiments go wrong.[27]

These experiments not only involve the more abstract renovation and transfer of techniques of urban governance based on making distinctions between citizen and subject. In other words, they do not necessarily center on finding new ways to make distinctions between people who have rights to the city, have a right to develop a long-term life in the city, and those by whom the city is not to be considered home, and therefore who have little opportunity to shape it. Rather, this laboratory concerns how relationships between cities of the North and South will be managed and how these relationships are shaped through various financial infrastructure, migration, and economic circulations at all scales.

For example, large numbers of urban Africans are risking their lives trying to get into Europe as a way to make a living. The cities they call home, many of which originated only as colonial entities, remain largely incapable of helping spur national economies. Rather, they are stuck in their role as sources of oil, cocoa, diamonds, metals, cotton, flowers, or cashews, and thus are unable to provide jobs for growing populations. This "black" African demand on European space, and the demand for economic opportunity, education, residence, autonomy, is a by-product of the logic of colonial administration. This logic wavered between Europeans wanting to keep African peoples as something apart, something fundamentally different and, at the same time, Europe's need to prove the efficacy of its values and culture by imparting them to a certain section of the African population.[28]

The demand is shaped by the extension of that logic and its impact on "white" European citizens—something implanted largely before this demand for access to Europe was articulated. For the practices of segregation experimented with in the colonies were then transferred as instruments for regulating the populations of Europe. Not only does the racialized logic of organizing urban space impact on territorial arrangements but it reproduces the limited capacity of whites and blacks to really take each other into consideration. This leaves both white and black vulnerable to occupying and using the city in highly circumscribed and sometimes destructive ways.[29]

The third instance of the peripheral concerns the relative invisibility of what could be called popular working-class or working-poor neighborhoods (*quartier populaire* in French tends to cover the widest ground here) as an important part of urban economies and a mode of residence. Most attention paid to cities in the Global South tends to focus on how fast they are changing in terms of spectacular new projects, the remaking of city centers, the pushing out of large numbers of urban residents of all social classes, and the extent to which cities are becoming more alike through these major development projects. Alternately, focus is placed on the poor, on massive slums, insalubrious environmental and social conditions, and the potential threats posed by impoverished and unsettled urban populations. What lags behind is attention paid to the continued small and medium-level developments of residential and commercial districts that have occupied specific territories within cities for a long time.

While it is true that many of these districts have been taken apart and remade, or remain vulnerable to such, many continue to make significant investments in upgrading local infrastructure, diversifying local economies, and renewing important social institutions that promote cohesion and a sense of belonging. These efforts are sometimes undertaken as a kind of hedge to defer their vulnerability to displacement, but more often reflect a solid confidence in the ability of these districts to remain viable parts of the urban system. Importantly, while residents living on a block or particular sub-section of an administrative district and historical neighborhood may have a lot in common based on similar levels of household income or ethnic identity, these blocks and sections are usually situated in a larger territory of often remarkable heterogeneity.

In a fundamental way, then, in these districts people of many different backgrounds, incomes, residential histories, aspirations, and orientations to the city intersect. This heterogeneity, while sometimes prompting debilitating disputes and polarization, often works as a key resource for the very survival of the district. While it is true that larger numbers of residents are being pushed to the outskirts of cities or actively seek new residential locations outside of overcrowded, noisy, and increasingly dilapidated central city areas, the capacities of residents to hang on, to undertake their own versions of remaking, are undercounted and undervalued.

Warakas Papango is a mostly lower-middle-class district of some 35,000 residents in North Jakarta. Within a roughly 40 square block area, each of the small houses and compounds which line narrow lanes are repainted every two years; every house has planted extensive shrubbery and exhibits potted plants on its property in order to positively affect local climatic conditions; the open drainage systems on each block are continuously attended to by residents; each block sponsors collective childcare facilities and afterschool programs. Even though the service provision of formal local government is nearly non-existent, the district draws upon a long, twenty-seven-year history of collaboration. The residents are almost all long-term civil servants, teachers, nurses, and bureaucrats whose salaries have never kept pace with inflation, and whose households all have to find creative ways to make ends meet. Yet the competition to maintain the semblance of a middle-class lifestyle does not impede collaboration on local affairs and neighborhood conditions. In fact, this cooperation becomes a way for residents to combine skills, networks, and contacts to earn extra money on the side.

The fourth consideration of the peripheral concerns ways in which particular collective urban experiences are forged simply as a way of putting together disparate experiences in relationship to one another for the purpose of seeing what might happen. Here, people operating in different locations may use sociologically and politically vague markers of commonality as an instrument to pay attention to each other and take something from each other when no other condition or platform would exist for such exchange. For example, the appropriation of a common "blackness" can operate as a vehicle through which black residents in Dakar, Brooklyn, Kingston, Bangkok, London, and Recife not only compare their distinctive urban experiences but cultivate a discourse through which they generate particular understandings of the city and their place and possibilities within it. Here, blackness becomes a device of inter-urban connection—a device for approaching one's urban existence in terms larger than the specificities entailed by a particular place of residence. It is a way of seeing oneself as part of a larger world of operations, powers, and potentials.

While Dakar and Brooklyn, for example, may have highly particular histories, the economic and political forces which implanted black populations in these cities and made "blackness" something important to those histories can be connected as an interrelated phenomenon. The extent to which blackness means similar things today in these contexts as an empirical issue is not so much the point. Rather, what is important is the wide range of practices that residents use in these cities as a way of paying attention to and taking things from a larger urban world in order to navigate the local contingencies of their own urban lives. This is the case even if the prevalent notions of "identity" and a common blackness may be highly limited and limiting.

Race becomes increasingly politically and sociologically peripheral in terms of our understanding of contemporary urban processes. The question is: To what extent do the racial histories of different processes of urban formation around the world prepare us analytically to more effectively engage with new forms of segregation and control? What are the ways in which racial determinations are reinvented in new guises that make distinctions between the relative value of particular kinds of people and their practices?

In many ways, blackness has been largely "freed" from being a component of particular kinds of sociological and political judgments. If the social sciences and politics tell us that class, personal initiative, and culture are the "real components" of social division, then blackness would seem to be something increasingly irrelevant. If this is then the case, might blackness be available as a more mobile device through which residents of different cities across the world might experiment with new forms of connection in a process analogous to those undertaken by the policymakers of cities referred to earlier?

The final consideration of the peripheral is the urban practices and dynamics of the so-called urban peripheries themselves—something which I will outline in some detail here and will not concentrate as much on in the rest of the discussion. For, despite the conceptual flexibility pointed to earlier about what these peripheries actually are and where they are located, any discussion of the urban periphery would have to make at least some reference to what has been known as the peri-urban interface—that purportedly interstitial zone between the urban and rural. This interface usually refers to, but need not be restricted to, the Global South. These are territories of transition and connection that function in several ways. First, they are a repository for inward migrants whose initial urban settlement stops short of the city. These areas function as a vantage point from which migrants can implant themselves in the urban system at lower costs and move closer to the city over a protracted period of time if necessary. Second, these are territories of agricultural production that enter into varied circuits of consumption—from supporting subsistence in the peri-urban area itself, to providing low-cost inputs to local urban markets outside the major retailing networks, as well as the production of specialized goods for niche urban markets. Third, these are territories to which certain environmental costs have been exported, such as waste, polluting industries, and crowded transportation hubs. Fourth, these are spaces to hedge bets as a way in which tentative, residual, or nascent links to both city and rural areas are maintained and intersect.[30]

Peri-urban areas are also marked by substantial economic

shifts. A shrinking public sector, and the concomitant phasing out of agricultural subsidies, extension programs, and marketing programs attenuate the links between rural life and larger markets and institutions. Incentives for export-led primary production have intensified the marketing of land and production at big scales, constraining small farmers from expansion, boxing them into overuse of limited land holdings, and often disrupting the various ways in which rural actors can negotiate access to opportunities and resources. At one time, a few family members living in a city could send a substantial amount of money back to their families living in rural areas. As levels of remittances decline, in part due to increases in the cost of urban living, the absolute dependency on them for daily sustenance has increased, forcing larger numbers of people to come to the city.

As the cost of urban living has risen enormously in the past decades of neoliberal structural adjustment, a two-fold character to urban provisioning has emerged. On the one hand, trade liberalization regimes have flooded local markets with cheap imports, undermining what limited manufacturing sectors did exist in urban areas. On the other hand, some national economies have contracted so much that even these cheap imported provisions have become too expensive for local consumption. Dependency grows on an urban hinterland for the most basic consumables. Depending on the geographical positioning of cities, as well as the characteristics of the built environment, transport and communications systems, natural resources and institutional proficiencies, this burgeoning reliance on urban hinterlands can have negative ecological consequences or pose new opportunities for urban sustainability.

In Africa particularly, the enlarging footprint of the city remains a critical issue as the city must draw water and biomass fuel far beyond its boundaries and thus competes more directly with rural uses of land. The interface may not simply be one of physical proximity but more broadly relational as well, where the interface is configured over a large geographical region. Here, urban residents maintain some connection to a rural existence as a socio-cultural disposition. Access to work, shelter, and sociality in urban areas is often contingent upon how urban residents relate to particular rural resources, such as land, rural livelihoods, and local politics. In other words, what urban residents are able to do in the city— e.g. how they can acquire urban shelter, how they can work collaboratively with others to elaborate urban livelihoods— can sometimes be a function of how they position themselves in relationship to their historical rural ties.

Rural and urban areas are often linked in complex moral economies that at one and the same time require clear differentiation between the two domains but also thick interlinkages that make clear distinctions between domains difficult. Residents frequently tolerate poor urban living conditions as a means of maintaining relatively prosperous rural positions, while many rural residents are clearly dependent upon inputs derived from urban social networks.[31]

As the price of food and shelter increases, attachment to rural areas is reiterated in order to access food. Given economic hardship, such complementarities require both the reiteration of reciprocal obligations between rural and urban households as well as a means of modulating the degrees of mutual demand. How can rural and urban households help each other out without either being overwhelmed by the demands of the other? Such a task requires moral economies that both lessen the "distance" between the urban and the rural and amplify it as well. This relationship requires that people imagine themselves living within a translocal topography which incorporates the urban and rural, not as clearly defined and opposed domains, but fractured ones, with different connotations, expectations, practices, and strategic orientations.[32]

Given such an imaginary topography, the peri-urban is also a mélange of temporalities. What this means is that it is often difficult to get a precise handle on just what kinds of developments are on their way out or just coming up—what is ascendant or in decline. Across almost all major cities, architecture, infrastructure, and land development are being used as instruments to compel, some might say extort, new urban institutional and social relations, from how decisions get made, what is viewed as possible or useful to do in cities, how financial responsibilities are to be defined, and risks assessed. The usual case is that most low-income and many middle-income residents are pushed to the peripheries of the city. Once these areas are serviced and then connected to major transportation grids, they become objects of speculation as cheap land is acquired by those with the aspirations to build big in ways that are prohibited in more centralized locations.

The presence of heterogeneous residents within central city areas enabled a kind of mutual witnessing of how they were implanted and operated in the city. It sometimes elaborated various complementarities among them. The push to the periphery, while not necessarily stopping an inflow of low-income residents in their pursuit of work, renders the city an often opaque place.

This opacity is the result of the inability to clearly identify just what is "coming and going." Surrounding the core of the city, the periphery, with its intersection of the scattered remains of old projects and those of the new in various states of completion—from factories, shopping centers, housing developments, persistent rural economies, informal and formal low-income settlements—poses an uncertain future for this core. Old golf courses are contiguous to new lakeside theme parks, which are next to old factories next to mega-family restaurants next to warehouses and chemical dumps. Material sediments are overlaid with discrepant zoning and land use policies.

The periphery remains a literal archive dependent as much upon what is subtracted and destroyed as upon what is added to it. In some peripheries—in between these comings and goings, ups and downs—there exist complex translocal economies. These economies span many different cities and countries. They appropriate deteriorating yet functional infrastructure, forge flexible relationships with lower tiers of municipal bureaucracies, straddle legal and illegal regulatory systems of commerce, piece together hybrid articulations of transport, machinery, storage and finance, and network under-utilized and undervalued spaces of the built environment.

WHAT KIND OF URBAN RESIDENT DO THE PERIPHERIES CREATE?

In all of these considerations of the peripheral there are questions about the kind of urban resident referred to. Cities in Africa and Southeast Asia not only assemble the styles and performances associated with modern urban citizenship—with its emphasis on the self-cultivation of entrepreneurial capacity, self-management, and continuous self-improvement—but also harbor more peripheral dynamics regarding social life and relations. Who are the subjects of these cities? How do they understand their experiences and possibilities, and what are they likely to do on the basis of those understandings?

I want to briefly discuss two ethnographic studies that help elucidate these issues. In 1997 a region-wide Asian financial crisis was set off by the Thai government's decision to float its national currency. The baht was pegged to the dollar since it could no longer afford to continue to support its fixed level of valuation given severe financial overextension and debt largely prompted by excessive real estate investment. With reduced export earnings stemming from the devaluation, Thailand could not cover its debt obligations and inflows of capital began to dry up. What was particularly interesting about this sudden collapse was the relatively strong support Thai economic policy enjoyed from the International Monetary Fund (IMF) and the World Bank. With the collapse of an economy that they largely guided, these institutions had to cover themselves by retrospectively pointing out the excess number of irrational and illegal practices that prevented the economy from really working.

Blame couldn't be placed on the irrationality of the major Thai economic players—even though they used all kinds of references to magic and spirit belief to fund large-scale public and private projects that lacked accountability—and with whom the IMF and World Bank needed to re-cement working relations. Instead those with little access to the state, let alone to international institutions, were accused. Poor rural households, in particular, were blamed for an abundance of moral hazard, where people take risks otherwise seen as irrational because they believe that some structure exists that will bail them out when the going gets tough and compensate them for any substantial loss.

Thus, a wide range of popular practices engaged in by people with tenuous incomes were demonized. Alan Klima describes the funeral casino, where deaths are marked by various games of chance played widely by a local community.[33] This is a practice where risks are undertaken in such a way as to intensify the exchange of money through which households that have experienced the loss may access extra income to smooth over hard times, as a portion of the money gambled is given to these households. As Klima argues, it is precisely in times of death that the occasion for risk is most productively intensified as it generates an aid package for those in need. Thus, a certain moral hazard underlines the very act of being social. For in risky situations, the rational thing to do is to increase the risk. Not because a pre-existent safety net exists. Rather, as Klima points out, only through increasing the risk can one ensure that such a net will be woven for you, simply because extending the risk begins to implicate more people in the details of your particular situation.

While this game is actively pursued through the bailouts of major financial institutions that have engaged in highly risky and speculative investments, for many local communities, practices that adhere to a similar logic are made illegitimate, illegal, and, above all, peripheral to how social life should be conducted. Instead these populations are to be weaned from local exchange and distribution systems and hooked up to discount stores, such as Walmart, and high-interest credit cards. The very practices that enabled the vitality of social relations as a critical means of not only cushioning economic hardship but maintaining strong levels of equanimity among economic actors are made peripheral. As many of them are actively made illegal, some of the sentiments and tactics involved in these practices are reinserted in more distorted and clandestine ways.

The second study is Saba Mahmood's investigation of the women's prayer movement in Cairo.[34] Many academics and policymakers have been bewildered as to why growing numbers of Muslim women become devout in ways that would seem to suggest a willing embrace of female submission. Certainly, on the surface, the focus on covering the body, on modesty, devotion, prayer, and familial duty would seem anachronistic in light of women's struggles to liberate themselves from patriarchal norms. But Mahmood argues that individuals do not simply free themselves from certain constraints in order to express a purpose and sense of self that have been existent all along. Rather, it is necessary to put together a self that makes sense in terms of what it is possible to do within the specific conditions in which that self is to be performed. The body is not simply a container or a physiological support for an essential kernel of being, but rather a tool to shape and convey particular affects and objectives, as well as an instrument to attain a particular consciousness of what one is.

The question is how to use the body, to act on it, its comportment, and its presence to others as a means of attaining a particular state of mind and being within the models that are available. So if Muslim women affirm a belief in the Quran as the direct word of God, as a divine plan, then how do they put together some kind of relationship to it; how do they make a connection between their inner states of belief and feeling and their outer conduct? How is feeling to be coordinated with speech? Here, reference to particular models of comportment is a way of realizing a certain potentiality, a way for these women to measure their ability to live up to the virtues and codes that their religious traditions specify. Far from being a willing subjection to archaic authority, and thus a subsequent loss of agency, the taking on of certain styles of dress, discipline, and devotion becomes a tool for cultivating an ethical self, a way of becoming active in the world, capable of affecting others and demonstrating their value.

What these two studies indicate are the various possibilities of how one can be a person, and what is to be done with that personhood. It is precisely the range of these possibilities that is often made peripheral in the predominant approaches to urban life—particularly its governance and development. Therefore, it is important to rediscover the possibilities of ways of being in the city, learn from the usually difficult conditions through which urban residents attempt to become persons, and place these efforts front and center in our collective considerations of urban life.

In order to further talk about these urban possibilities, I want to throw the reader into some of the details of district life in the northern section of Jakarta. This is a very messy city, but one that contains within it the vast spectrum of challenges and possibilities inherent in urban life. By talking specifically about the politics involved in trying to make do in one of the world's largest urban systems, I want to illustrate the extent to which the viability of urban life depends on its capacities to cause the divergent aspirations and practices to intersect with each other without the availability of a "common language" or a consensually determined approach.

Towards an Anticipatory Urban Politics:
Notes from the North of Jakarta
Two

In Chapter 1 I talked about the notion of cityness as a way of existing that emphasizes the importance of difference and relations between differences. The idea is that bringing differences into some kind of relationship produces unforeseen capacities and experiences that are valuable—valuable because they extend what we think is possible. Increasingly, however, cities become mechanisms that attempt to make these differences serve the interests of narrowly drawn notions of what is valuable and what is possible. This is something that Mezzadra calls "a unitary language of value."[1] In other words, instead of intersecting the histories, ways of doing things, and aspirations of residents into a particular way of dealing with the larger world, cities have become conduits for feeding resources, ideas, and labor to the growth and movement of capital.

Still, it is also important to consider the (re)emergence of ways of life that oscillate between full exposure to the exploitative maneuvers of this kind of urban management and a more shadow-like existence in between the governments, corporations, and institutions that run cities. In other words, it is important to consider spaces that exist between the mega-projects which substantially remake the city and the forms of residence and economy that are under perpetual threat.

The use of the city as a way of extending market power is never a smooth accomplishment. The intersection of different ways of thinking, feeling, calculating, and deciding carries a range of unpredictable trajectories, however fleeting.[2] The remaking of the city into narrowly considered frameworks of global efficacy and appeal does not tell the entire story—as much is taking place that at least generates significant tensions, complicities, and perhaps even openings that retain the city as a space for production of all kinds. These urbanized provocations and openings may not be sufficient to change the critical economic infrastructure of cities, but they do, nevertheless, constitute a platform to explore the elements of what might be called an anticipatory urban politics more capable of mitigating exploitation. Here, anticipation refers to the art of staying one step ahead of what might come, of being prepared to make a move. For, what this move is and what it will entail can't really be known in advance. It is a movement at the crossroads, where decisions have to be made quickly and people have to do all it takes to try and make the most out of them.

This chapter looks at how these dynamics of anticipation and movement play out in several districts across Northern districts of greater Jakarta. The observations are the product of an ongoing project with a popularly based urban organization known as the Urban Poor Consortium, which has brought poor communities, advocates, and technicians together for over two decades. From 2007 on, six teams of local residents have been documenting various facets of the local social economies in the districts in which they live. The information here is largely the product of their work. These teams have documented the kinds of economic activities and institutions which exist in their communities, as well as the networks of authority, social influence, and political power. They have met with many different kinds of residents, observed many different formal and informal social gatherings, and spent long hours observing life in their districts from different locations and with different groups of local residents.

NORTH JAKARTA: FRACTAL SPACES AND POLITICS

Jakarta Utara (North Jakarta) is a highly fractal landscape of various kinds of ports, industrial complexes, small factories, shop houses, warehouses, theme and exposition parks. Its clogged arteries that run east–west across the long commercial belt articulate manufacturing, shipping, labor, and storage, elevated toll roads, the gated remnants of once thriving middle-class districts, and vast new residential developments, inexplicably overcrowded in some areas, vacant in others. As the site of the original settlements of Jakarta, the area is covered with residential and commercial histories that are densely burrowed into the territory and which make any alterations in the built and social environments difficult. There are also areas of substantial decline and disinterest as money and business move further towards the southern and western edges of the metropolis.

Much of the north is the domain of ethnic Indonesian Chinese, who largely remain the predominant commercial power. Even if their places of residence have been relocated to more prestigious addresses elsewhere, they retain their assets and psychological anchorage in the north, partly so as not to risk losing the place in the city that has long been consolidated as their particular sphere of influence. Another reason is because the proximity to ports and the airport permits a bit of security, since they know they can flee quickly if their long history of being scapegoats turns violent once again.

The city has long felt uncertain about what to do with the north. As the central business district continues to move away from the north across the region known as the Thamrin–Surdiman axis to the South, and as the content of economic power shifts from industrial production to services and finance, the North becomes the site of more individualized and scattered projects. These result in fluctuating land values

Map 2
Jakarta Utara (North Jakarta Districts)

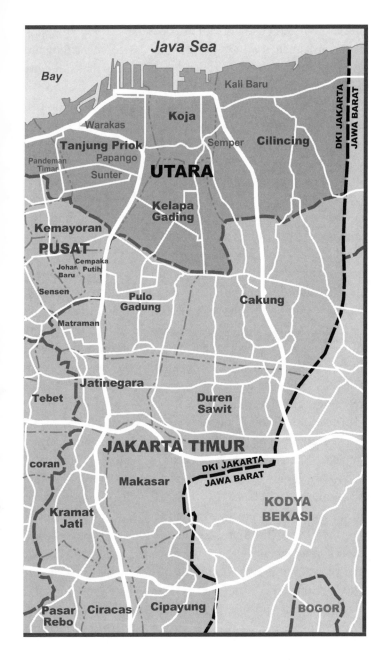

and more heterogeneous land uses. Several years ago the government launched a highly ambitious development program to reclaim two kilometers of land across nearly the entire city waterfront. The intent was to completely remake the look of the city. It was to be full of architectural fantasy, cosmopolitan populations, tourism, and high-end research and development projects. The idea was to enact a comprehensive vision of a new city over both pristine and waterfront land cleared of some of the poorest residents of the nation. The city thought it was too hard to disentangle and remake the built and social environments of the existing North. Instead, the authorities anticipated that most residents and commercial enterprises would have to relocate to the periphery in face of rising land values. This would then free up land to be incorporated into the activities of the port and port-related manufacturing, which would eventually be replete with new infrastructure, including a new network of roads. Given the complexity of the engineering work, the costs, and, more importantly, the predicted rising sea levels related to climate change, this ambitious program has been abandoned even as it remains the city's official vision and policy.

The major districts of the North—Kamal Muara, Muara Baru, Pluit, Grogol, Penjaringan, Kota, Ancol, Pademangan, Warakas, Sunter, Tanjuk Priok, Semper, Kalibaru, Cillindek— each have highly particular spatial layouts, legal status, and economic and residential histories. These particularities make it difficult to conceptualize any smooth way of interconnecting these areas into one coordinated region. The North is a region quite literally all over the place, or, more precisely, the site of many different discrepant places. While such dispersions characterize cities nearly everywhere, the intensive fragmentations and insertions of different kinds of residents with vastly disparate histories in the city seem particularly remarkable in this part of Jakarta. In part, this is because Jakartans in general live across what on the surface appear to be many discordant references. It is an intensely religious city with its authoritative rhythms of everyday personal regulation and moral comportment; it is a city severely lacking in well-elaborated regulatory frameworks concerning the rights and participation of citizens, basic planning, and the use and marketing of land.

It is city where the intense discrepancies between what is permitted, provided, and what actually takes place in the everyday behaviors of residents require a seemingly endless series of compensations. These compensations, in turn, generate basic livelihoods for many and sizeable amounts of money for bureaucrats. For example, not only is the informal selling of cooked food—an activity that involves nearly one million people—criminalized, but its consumption is as well. The utter impracticality of such injunctions ends up generating rents for those charged with "enforcing the rules." As it is, a series of unofficial fees—to sell, transport, rent facilities and carts, and use space—end up in the pockets of various brokers. While informal entrepreneurs may be protected, they inevitably become unwitting "foot soldiers" in extra-parliamentary political machines that enforce particular economic and individual interests that are not theirs. They can also be mobilized to fight off new policies and governance practices that might in the end better serve them. Yet, Jakarta largely remains a city of kampungs—small enclaves of entangled social relations, reciprocity based on ethnic origin, and mutual protection. Kampungs continue to persist alongside the widespread assumption that the critical world of belonging and dealing with others is found in the job that one does and not where one lives or comes from.

Municipal power remains overly centralized in the figure of a governor, who, in August 2007, was for the first time

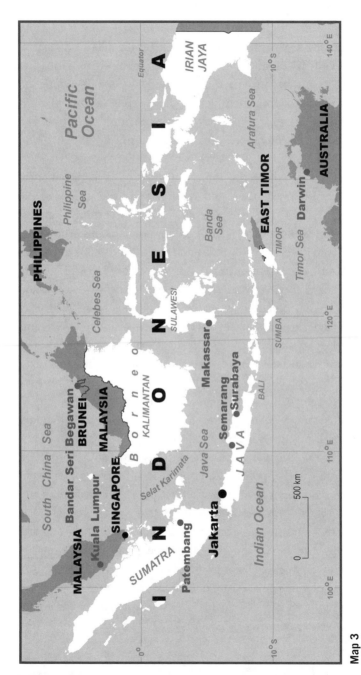

Map 3
Jakarta in Indonesia

chosen in a popular democratic election. The figure of an authoritarian strongman in face of social and urban complexity is a residual feature of Javanese political history. But it is widely acknowledged that such politics does not work well in negotiating the relationship between the now typical aspirations of urban officials for a successful global, world class city and the complicated interactions of highly diverse, multiethnic, and multi-religious populations. While nominally acting through a decentralized system of local governance, the only real decision-making power operates at the highest and lowest levels.

The crux of the local governance system is the *Rukun Tetangga / Rukun Warga* (RT/RW). As the basic administrative framework, Jakarta is divided into units of about 70 households; the RT, whose chairperson is a local resident, is chosen by consensus. The RW is made up of groups of RT and its officers are chosen by the RT chairpersons in a process that links neighborhood organization and territorial administration. As a hold-over from the three decades of military rule, the system of RT/RW incorporates residents into districts of 70,000 persons and ensures the proper registration (and surveillance) of residents in all domains—from births, weddings, Jakarta citizenship, schooling, and commercial licensing. The RT leader became the gatekeeper between the resident and the city. Ostensibly a network of local governments, *kalurahan*, was to be the mediation between these highly localized administrative systems and the municipal planning and service provision for the city as a whole.

But in actuality, there is little of substance in these interstices. As such, the authoritarian centralization of metropolitan governance ends up limiting available knowledge about what is taking place across the city. Thus, there is little ability to tailor planning, programs, and policies to the particular characterization of the hundreds of districts across the city. As one person in the governor's office puts it, "We wake up each morning hoping that the fires to be put out don't completely burn us." Subsequently, the governor's office ends up relying upon more drastic and arbitrary measures to reshape the built environment according to "canned" images of urban efficacy—i.e. large-scale evictions, overbuilding, over-reliance on questionable sources of financial liquidity, and on project development as an instrument for consolidating political status.

As a result, government is popularly perceived as powerful but more as a private actor than as something that embodies the interests of residents. It is commonly seen as acting in the interests of individual or syndicated commercial interests who are quite frequently public officials. In Kalibaru-Tanjung Priok, a traditional port for handling wood products, legal quotas have declined significantly in recent years and the port is increasingly dependent on handling larger volumes of illegal hardwoods. This necessitates frequently extortionist pay-offs that eat into the capacities of the port to employ local labor. Not only do much of these pay-offs go to Yusuf Kalla, the current Vice-President, but the subsequent ramifications of the port's decline have allowed him to acquire significant tracks of nearby land to develop new petroleum and chemical storage and car trans-shipment facilities. These are officially registered as government development projects but in the end are actually private assets.

In another example, the government, through its fisheries ministry, constructed a major industrial complex in Muara Baru, hosting over two hundred companies. These companies range from processing, canning, export and local distribution, warehousing, transport, large-scale corporate fishing, to the city's largest wholesale market. The market's customers are almost exclusively women fishmongers who sell catches to the city's local markets. The purpose of this development was to organize the various facets of the fishing industry—from the coordination of local city-wide consumption to international exportation—within the same spatial and administrative plant. This would then upscale the largely artisan dimensions of the pre-existing industry and promote enhanced backward and forward linkages, a strong regulatory framework, a more effective articulation of commercial actors, and an enhanced human capital base.

But this centralization contributed to the monopolization of resources and opportunities in the hands of fewer players. Spatial proximities resulted in greater opportunities for powerful individuals to dominate the ways different facets of the industry would be connected to each other—between docks, boats, catch, processing, storage, distribution, transport, financing, insurance, security, and so forth. In face of these trends, the government has acted as a private interest in this mix, largely through generating opportunities for rents. For example, all sellers in the wholesale market are required to purchase ice from a single company; porters within the market are required to don a specific uniform, which is sold at an exorbitant price by the regulatory authority; transport of a catch from a truck coming from the port to the stall where it is sold requires the accompaniment of a security official, whose services must be paid for. The government "inserts" itself into the marketing process in scores of arbitrary ways.

While appearing to significantly increase transaction costs, a part of these rents is redeployed to maintain and service the complex, although often only minimally. Another part "wedges" open rather opaque spaces of opportunity for residents of the surrounding local areas. The articulation of the various components and sectors of the fishing complex is brought into the ambit of a single, highly hierarchical corporate structure. As such, this monopoly would tend to reduce any concrete management role for government. The government instead concentrates its efforts on generating opportunities for rents that leak from the complex into a range of ancillary activities that the government cannot officially manage itself in its "public" capacity.

Rather, the money, when it doesn't go directly into the pockets of corrupt officials, is plowed into hundreds of small informal businesses, which are usually unrelated to fishing. These businesses attempt to gain advantageous spaces, rights, inventories, and information in several districts of North Jakarta, including Muara Baru, Pluit, Penjaringan, and Gogol, while retaining the bulk of their customers among the ordinary residents of these districts. This practice guarantees a continuous source of unaccounted income for the government officials acting in a private capacity. It also cultivates a network of clients in the local areas that can be mobilized by particular departments and cliques in the public ministries to fight off competitors, either in the private sector or in other sections of government.

WHO PLAYS THE ROLE OF "PUBLIC" ACTOR IN NORTH JAKARTA IF GOVERNMENT DOESN'T DO THE JOB?

If government is largely perceived as acting in a private capacity, or even as building specific constituencies of loyalty through acting as a private broker, who are the actors or forces that embody a more public character? According to residents across the different districts of the North, this more "public" dimension is spread across a variety of actors and modes of authority. For example, regardless of the participation of women in various kinds of work, their persistent role as household managers means that they cannot legitimately assume the risks of local political involvement. When this is overlaid with a conservative religious sensibility that is on the rise, with its prescriptions on female behavior, the space for women's involvement in community affairs can appear quite limited. Thus gatherings of women in frequent evening prayer meetings have become an important locus of women's mobilization. Those women able to legitimately develop and maintain a large network of such meetings are viewed as powerful leaders. They are able to shape women's collective attitudes through the information exchange and discussions that become an integral facet of these meetings.

Similarly, mosques, that continue to be built in ever greater numbers regardless of the economic status of a given community, are more than venues of worship. Because they are increasing in number they are more locally available to residents no matter where they live, and thus more convenient places of public gathering. Increasing the number of mosques also means theoretically increasing the opportunities that any given resident has for actively participating in discussions that take place within them. As more people are attending these discussions the importance of mosques as sites of information exchange and for shaping public opinion grows. Thus, neighborhoods organize different kinds of gatherings among the constituencies of different mosques.

In Warakas RW 14, for example, congregants of all 15 mosques in the area meet together once a month. But there are additional gatherings, such as an "exchange program" where individual mosques in the district will take turns hosting a weekly meeting for those who regularly attend the weekly meetings that individual mosques organize for their own members. So on some weeks, individuals might attend meetings at their own mosque or, alternately, go to meetings where there are people from several mosques. These movements give rise to new figures of religious authority who are considered to be not only highly educated, articulate, and devout, but capable of addressing different kinds of audiences in the styles and concerns particular to them. They, thereby, translate these specific realities to those in other mosques, identifying possible vehicles of commonality and reciprocity, while maintaining autonomy for individual mosque gatherings.

Jakarta neighborhoods long exuded both village-like features of residents tied together in close relationships of kinship and ethnicity and the more cosmopolitan interweaving of different histories, backgrounds, and sensibilities. Sometimes this duality has a tenuous existence, with neighborhoods in Tanjung Priok, for example, breaking out in protracted bouts of violence between residents from Makassar, Java, and the so-called indigenes of Jakarta, the Betawi. These fights inevitably have something to do with access to land, resources, jobs, and the tendency of non-Javanese to be forced to fight hard to consolidate territories of security near the few economic niches they enjoy in the city.

Many districts in the North are the products of self-construction and organization, with groups of residents staking claims on agricultural land and swamps, filling the land in, constructing their own homes, laying their own streets and drainage canals. As such, the collective framework of community development came out of these localities. They had to rely upon certain practices that could be brought together under a sense of common ethnicity, even when residents may have actually come from different origins. The process of securing a place and protecting the investments made in a place thus necessitated at least a strong local discourse of cohesion that could ward off external manipulation. So even when life in a *kampung* is contentious in terms of local social relationships and disputes, these tense realities are often underplayed in how the *kampung* presents itself to the outside world. The official RTs, civic leaders, and leading entrepreneurs will often act as if contentiousness simply does not exist, and as such, when things get out of hand, they are effectively unable to really do anything about it.

Instead it is often left to the figure of the *preman* (the freeman, gangster, the one unattached) to mediate and ward off disputes. This was particularly evident in the Pandemangan Timur district during the past years. Despite the fact that most residents possessed official certification of land ownership, nearly 10,000 were evicted in 1997. Nevertheless, the political and economic crisis of 1998 soon put to rest whatever plans members of the family of the ex-head of state had in acquiring the land. After the land had lain dormant for several years, a few residents from surrounding communities started to grow vegetables—not very successfully—and to claim various tracts of land. When unofficial land transactions began to take place at the end of 2001, 13 square meter plots were sold for Rp 500,000 (US$50), often to former residents of the area. The initial claimants implicitly knew how much land could be reasonably claimed without either having to risk local condemnation or, more importantly, having to fight to protect what would be considered an "unrealistic" claim and thus risk losing all.

Still, the first buyers of this claimed land had fights about how much they could purchase and, more precisely, how much profit-taking they could actualize given the intense demands on land. As both former and new residents were descending upon the area in larger numbers, how to weave together different aspirations, claims, histories, senses of entitlement became, at first, the job of the *preman* and not that of emergent local organizations. Forging some kind of harmonization of discordant factors requires an extensive knowledge of the different actors and stories involved. It was precisely this labor-intensive process of getting to know the different actors that proved to be the crucial element, and this is what, in popular understanding, the *preman* does best.

The contemporary position of the *preman* is largely wrapped up in the patrimonial character of Indonesia's New Order regime, which lasted for over three decades. Violence and extortion were largely normalized as state practice. The state cultivated extensive networks of gangs and associations to enforce its dictates and protect its economic interests, licit and illicit. When the Suharto regime fell in 1998, the logic of social organization did not so much change as it forced many to scramble for new arrangements. Particularly in Jakarta, the past years have witnessed deepening complicities among Jakarta's top property tycoons—who have largely made their fortune in gambling and narcotics—the regional governor, networks of martial arts clubs seeped in a belief of mystical powers (*pencak silat*) and linked to the Betawi Brotherhood Forum, specific factions within major political parties, and various networks of *preman* enforcing the illicit deals necessary to finance this articulation.[3]

The figure of the *preman* has a complicated history in Indonesia. They were once celebrated as well-trained martial artists willing to put their life on the line for the protection of their communities. Later on, they would be despised as criminals and thugs. These connotations intersect in various versions of the contemporary *preman*. The *preman* were the bandits and *jawara* (street mystics) making up the irregular militias, *gerombalan*, crucial to the anti-colonial struggle against the Dutch. They were then alternately depended upon and demonized as extra-parliamentary groups under Suharto's New Order. In past years, the emergence of large-scale organizations engaged in consolidating the collective aspirations of particular ethnic or religious associations through the control of informal businesses and racketeering are said to rely upon *preman*.[4] Many of these associations initially established themselves and maintain much of their continuous authority operating as local security forces. They incorporate the same *preman* that were otherwise their targets and, at the same time, attempt to combat the corrupt behavior of state authorities and police.[5]

Organizations such as the Betawi Brotherhood Forum, Pancasil Youth, and the Family of Tanah Abang Association—with thousands of members having *preman* "backgrounds"—may depend on a massive upscaling of activities usually considered the purview of *preman*. Yet, they present themselves as a guarantor of protection against *preman* and claim that what looks to be extortion and racketeering is based on specific moral and legal rights to ensure that specific ethnic groups, most often the indigenous Betawi, attain the recognition and security that they are due.[6]

As these large organizations gradually gained greater recognition from the government, demonstrated their capacities to protect individual members from police raids, provided a host of social welfare benefits, and seized control over large territories and sectors of informal trade, they became a major institutional presence throughout the city and an important form of mediation between neighborhoods and the state. At the same time, their control of specific trades and territories, as well as their increasingly pragmatic collaborations with formal state power, make them less adept at engaging complex local social dynamics, thus further remaking the role of the *preman*.

In Jakarta culture, the *preman* take the time to share cigarettes, tell stories and jokes, and suspend any feigned dignity in their willingness to talk to anyone. They listen carefully to the different sensibilities at work and are willing to fight, provoke, and shake things up as a calculated strategy to upend any status quo so as to have new opportunities to engage others. This "border crossing" is the source of power, as the *preman* embodies not only the aspirations of residents to operate beyond the space of the *kampung* and its mores, but the capacity to do so. This active process of translation—of how to translate a particular need, situation, and capacity into a concrete opportunity or resolution—became crucial in the land transactions in Pademangan Timur mentioned earlier. Thousands of people were quickly accommodated into an area that remained officially off the map.

Preman have no institutional authorization to impose or sustain specific negotiated settlements, as they can only shape the character of individual tendencies and decisions. Of course, sometimes they are eventually taken as a joke in the exaggerated way they may seek to curry political favor and join any organization in sight. Yet, they often prove to be an important intermediary force that gives time for new local associations to get off the ground and build upon local efforts at mutual accommodation. In Pademangan Timur, speculation on land and housing sales was held in check, even though the price escalation of the same 13 square meter plot to Rp 15 million within six years indicates how desperate people are to find places to live.

As mentioned above, the *preman*'s willingness to fight is an important feature of their consolidation of authority. During my interviews with *preman* across North Jakarta, long lists of fights were recited covering almost every imaginable particularity. Fights break out over the particularities of residential location, religious affiliation, ethnic identification, political party membership, and so forth. The sheer fact that people of different religions, occupations, ethnicities, residential histories, and political affiliations are living and operating in districts becomes the occasion of the fight, and an opportunity for the *preman* to demonstrate a willingness to fight for "one's own" regardless of the specific make-up of that "own"—e.g. family, region, or occupation. Perhaps more importantly, such fights become the vehicle through which individuals bring those differences into view, make them visible and significant in ways that otherwise could not be assumed. In other words, the fight reiterates the salience of divisions, boundaries, and ascriptions that otherwise are incessantly crossed, obscured, or confused.

In areas where there are intense concerns about access to work, resources, and opportunities, reiterating the salience of such differences becomes part of an overall social economy of deciding who gets access to what. But this process of re-visualizing the social field, of bringing specific differences into consideration, also reiterates the different kinds of elements making up the district. If you know that you live among people of different origins, ethnicities, and backgrounds, this knowledge is not only used to be wary of them. It can also be important that you assume that these residents have networks and information different from yours. These elements can then be combined in particular ways to extend the scope and efficacy of various local aspirations and projects. Still, in the everyday calculation of survival and social interaction, ethnic, occupational, religious, political, and regional backgrounds may be implicit, but these are not the main things on people's minds, as residents have to deal with all kinds of situations involving all kinds of people.

In my interviews with *preman*, they indicate that the fights put ethnic or area identity front and center so as to emphasize the fact that such differences may have important implications in terms of how particular kinds of residents are linked to the larger city—especially in terms of the kinds of authorities and powerful figures they have access to. For example, residents of Makassar ethnicity in Penjaringan may submerge this identity in terms of the day-to-day task of getting along with others in a multi-ethnic neighborhood. But they might also amplify this identification when it may have some use for getting work, services, or goods from other districts which Makassar residents dominate.

This process is demonstrated precisely in how stories about fights are told. While some fights may simply get out of hand or generate bad feelings that don't go away quickly, most are recounted in terms of what happened afterwards—i.e. where resolution and compensation resulted in a series of different events. At times, preman from other areas were called in to help settle things down and in the process new opportunities were identified and deals sealed. At other times, the fights rearranged the prevailing formulas for distributing jobs at ports, factories, markets, and construction sites. This was the case in Tanjung Priok when, for example, Betawi residents were given access to certain construction sites in return for an increase in the number of other ethnic groups in the street food trade. For while particular regional and ethnic groups may seek to consolidate their control over specific locations and economic sectors, there are also advantages to be gained by "spreading out"—i.e. having one's affiliates involved in a wide range of economic activities, work locations, and thus civic, political, and occupational networks.

BUT WHO IS A *PREMAN*, AND WHO IS NOT?

Yule is the grandson of a Betawi small businessman who left him some land in a kampung that was close to a market specializing in printing and the sale of carpets and tiles. The plot contained several houses which he reworked into rooms to rent. With this inheritance and the money generated through rentals, he received a loan from the bank to expand an ailing uncle's textbook production business. Presently, a large proportion of the kampung is involved in one or more facets of this business. There are small production centers where 10–20 young men assemble and glue sheets that have been photocopied from master copies that Yule secures from the agents representing different school districts across the country. There are hundreds of women who take these initially assembled books and work on the stitching in their homes. Many men in the kampung operate as sales agents, who attempt to drum up business across Jakarta and other cities.

They all operate as small independent units, sometimes integrated and connected as a single production system. But they are more often dependent on securing work from different sources and competing with other units involved in the same kind of work. At the most basic level, a small businessman will retain the services of his immediate women neighbors, paying them per book stitched. The quantity of work will vary according to how much volume he is able to secure from the different networks that he is a part of. Some will be content to take whatever comes their way based on the character of the social relations they enjoy in the kampung. Others will consistently try to reposition themselves across different networks in order to secure favors and opportunities that will increase the quantity of orders. When work is plentiful, the women will indicate their ability to take on more work. They will then pass it on to friends and associates in other parts of the kampung who work for "bosses" who either don't pay as well or who are having problems keeping up a steady volume of work.

In this way, investment in social relations across the kampung becomes a critical way of accessing opportunity and work at different levels. It operates as a way of smoothing out potentially difficult differentiations in opportunity and income accumulation within the *kampung*. But because almost all the different facets of this production system end up basically fending for themselves, it is difficult for managers, procurers, labor, and salespersons to predict how much work and income they will have on a consistent basis. Salespersons, often the husbands of the women who take stitching work into their homes, are dependent upon the specific seasonal patterns in which school textbooks are acquired. For other printed materials, such as bank ledgers, accounting logs, registers, or special editions of children's books or training materials, procurers may use different marketing agents. These agents outsource to different small companies. Some do the printing and reproduction, others do the finishing, and so forth, and so it is never clear with whom it is important to cultivate some kind of long-term relationship.

The disarticulations within such a production system introduce much flexibility. This keeps small-scale operations going in face of economies of scale in these sectors, in that they minimize sunk costs, labor, and marketing. The disarticulations enable a distribution of work and opportunities, but seldom at a scale that enables households in this *kampung* to really be able to save or get beyond being the "working poor." Nurturing social relationships is important but does not change persistent inequalities amongst neighbors, who are stratified in relationship to their history in the area, as well as their relationships to the offspring of the original landowners who retain their holdings and interests in many of these districts. These relationships are important in terms of securing work and mitigating glaring inequities. But while many neighbors are treated fairly by their "bosses," who are also their neighbors, these relationships often preclude the articulation of specific demands. Neighboring workers rarely group together to insist upon specific wage increases, for fear of unsettling these relationships.

Securing a location to operate in requires the cultivation and constant tending of specific relationships. This includes finding a job, selling things on streets or from store and house fronts, or offering services of any kind. These relationships are needed even when an individual gets a formal license or registration. Of course the issuance of such formalities largely depends in the first place on the kinds of relationships an individual enjoys in a given neighborhood or within a specific trade. At the same time, many urban residents know that they cannot afford to be "captured" by too many obligations in order to operate somewhere. This is especially true for those who do not have the means, knowledge of the city, or commitment to invest in long-term relationships in a given neighborhood. In other words, while social relationships remain thoroughly implicated in almost all attempts to generate livelihood, individuals know that they also must be able to get out of specific networks and arrangements if the cost, in terms of energy, time, and resources, outweighs the advantages.

Even though generosity and reciprocity remain strong in most neighborhoods, alliances and affiliations among neighbors may be volatile. Then from the top, from the vantage point of a local big man like Yule, these ambivalences are used as a tool not only for keeping his options flexible in terms of just who exactly performs a specific job for him at any specific time, but for manipulating the situation so that only he knows the entire "game." He will make sure that only he possesses the entire overview and map for the fabrication and sale of his product. By using the strong social relations that exist locally as means to access committed and low-cost labor and other inputs, and by manipulating the ambivalence individuals feel about "putting all their eggs in one basket"—i.e. investing in securing and maintaining a particular position in relationship to others—the big local men make the functioning of the overall system opaque to all but themselves. To a large extent, then, their power derives from this opacity. If only they know how the game works, they can ward off challenges and efforts others might make to learn the system.

Perhaps this is why most residents of these mixed neighborhoods also report having ambivalent feelings about *preman*. As the "free men," they are free from the game, able to insert themselves in the interstices of these relationships, beholden to almost no one, and able to extract a livelihood from staying outside of conventional relationships. They may gamble with the big man's money, they may threaten to upset the smooth functioning of businesses, or they may extort money from the bosses who make too big a show of their earnings. But now these practices are also a means of joining the game and of accessing positions of local power that come to blur formerly differentiated domains of influence and making things happen.

Preman in some districts become RTs and RWs, and use this position to run local rackets for selling the all-important Jakarta identity card that entitles residents to an official status and services. They formalize their protection rackets as the official administration of local security, as well as capture other fees for sanitation and street cleaning that residents pay as part of official local governance. The former Jakarta governor, Sutiyoso, appropriated the *preman* position in supporting the Betawi Brotherhood Forum (FBR) as a kind of extra-parliamentary task force deployed to keep tabs on what was taking place in certain districts and to intimidate local organizing efforts that were not perceived to be in the governor's interest. These forces have been maintained in many neighborhoods, and are now supplemented by associations nominally linked to the new governor, Fauwzi Bowo. Members of these groups appear official by wearing uniforms, but essentially participate in many of the same rent extraction activities as the *preman* many of them once were. In fact, the FBR has refashioned itself as a membership organization that provides individuals with the sense of belonging to a city-wide organization. For the many varied events and celebrations sponsored by the city, members have access to a wide range of small jobs, from parking cars, crowd control, to giving out flyers.

MANAGING DIFFERENCES IN COMPLEX NEIGHBORHOODS

In a city where large numbers live off minimal mark-ups and the complexities of making everything mesh in dense conditions—bodies, cars, trades, uses of space—differences are constantly a threat and opportunity, as well as a cushion. Being surrounded by those who are more vulnerable and destitute, more well-off individuals may exert greater effort protecting what they have. But they also know that the poor are in many instances more likely to be targets of overeager authorities and investment predators. Thus, the poor may act as a "running interference" with various authorities who may be too preoccupied with controlling them to take notice of how those with a somewhat better economic status bend the rules in order to get by. Being a part of strong family and neighborhood networks provides individuals with cushions of all kinds, as well as obligations.

In many working- and lower-middle-class districts of Jakarta, households work hard to attain a measure of security and development for their living spaces. This stability is sometimes accompanied by strong measures of implicit social control, where neighbors are expected not to make waves and are to conform to specific local mores. In neighborhoods where there is a mix of long-term home owners and more footloose renters, the renters are usually seen as embodying whatever is thought to go wrong in the neighborhood. In such circumstances, residents who have lived in an area a long time may have an enlarged space to do things under the radar that otherwise might be negatively scrutinized by fellow residents.

Differences participate in a vast game of costs and benefits. In Penjaringan, for example, there is a neighborhood in RT 12 that intersects the remnants of a once large informal settlement situated under the toll way. Streets are full of houses of various sizes, conditions, and ownership, and there are two distinct complexes of apartment blocks with some 500 dwellings. The largest of these was built nearly two decades ago by private developers to house low-income families but has in the interim been taken over by mostly lower-middle-class households. These are households where at least one member earns consistent wages as a store clerk, office worker, or shop keeper. These households are one step up from what would conventionally be designated as the "working poor" in that they manage to consistently cover the basic necessities without having to borrow money to get by.

Given the multi-tiered framework of Jakarta's land tenure system, low-cost apartment dwellings are sought out as an affordable form of security. As many dwellings are formally owned on leased land (hak guna bangunan), owning a low-cost apartment removes uncertainty and usually ensures more consistent and cheaper access to essential services. On the other hand, those with long-term leasing arrangements in the complexes have made substantial amounts of money selling the right to the leases to others who acquire them as a potential investment.

The second Penjaringan complex was also built for low-income residents by the North Jakarta municipal government. However, the price of a so-called registration fee and, more importantly, corruption within the authority responsible for the complex placed the majority of apartments in the hands of the lower middle class. Residents in the area claim that at an everyday social level these differences in the place of residence make absolutely no difference. After all, income differentials are not that substantial and the areas are ethnically mixed. Yet the differences come to mean something within the actual local arrangements of real governance. Even though residents within the complexes pay fees to their local RT for security, they have also championed a man, Buti, who operates as an auxiliary police official. He ensures that good relations with the police are maintained. One of the reasons for this support is that households are somewhat removed from the street since they reside in vertical arrangements. As such, they are removed from the circuits of information exchange, gossip, and mutual witnessing through which individuals gain a sense of what they can do and get away with. These exchanges are a kind of early warning system through which potential conflicts can be anticipated.

Residents of the complex champion an unofficial advocate with a relationship to the police in order to compensate for their perceived absence of "street smarts." When one becomes an advocate, however, it usually comes with other advantages, such as gatekeeping. For example, Buti controls who vends bottled water in the complex, who can sell prepared food at the complex gates, and who can repair the water-pumping system. These favors are distributed to those outside the complex in a game of trade-offs that enables the few households in the complex who own cars to not have to pay protection fees to local *preman*. These are fees that local residents outside the complex otherwise have to pay. So differences are constantly being marked and amplified as a way to create a space of interference, intervention, and deals. They introduce the possibility of threats where perhaps none really exist and compel protection from them.

There are more Chinese Indonesian households within the complex than in the surrounding area, although they are not the majority of residents. They have subsidized various deals Buti has made with assorted officials and *preman*, in order to use the latter's influence to keep the FBR out of the complex. These households are afraid that if the FBR gets any kind of foothold, they could extract various payments to not disrupt a water-supply system that could be easily subverted or to take control of various local concessions and small businesses within the complex. The Chinese Indonesians count on these concessions as more accessible and friendly public spaces than the surrounding streets in which to promote harmonious relationships with their neighbors.

The immediate neighborhood outside the complex recognizes that this concentration of lower-middle-class families provides a level of consumption that is advantageous for small businesses and services across the neighborhood. But since they are largely kept out of the two complexes in terms of everyday social transactions, these external neighbors are also suspicious about what is going on in them.

For example, many of the men in the neighborhood are employed as construction workers. They are recruited by a labor broker, *mandor*, who in turn is retained by various contractors to mobilize skilled and unskilled labor. For years, the most important *mandor* lived in a very modest dwelling in the neighborhood and was effective in generating jobs. But after he took an apartment in the complex, many skilled workers complained that they were not getting as many days of work, particularly in comparison to new pools of unskilled, recently arrived migrant labor. Rumors circulated that the *mandor* was now working for some bosses in other parts of the city who were paying him to recruit more labor from amongst residents in their neighborhoods. While there is probably no truth to the rumor, given the recent downturns in overall construction starts in Jakarta, it demonstrates again how minor differences become the stuff of economic consideration.

USING DISTRICT HETEROGENEITY AS A MEANS TO FIND NEW OPPORTUNITIES

The need to "spread out" is why many residents perceive certain advantages to living in crowded and insecure districts. Even when households may have enough money to rent decent accommodation in areas at the edge of the city, they may prefer to live in makeshift accommodation under toll roads, along creeks, lagoons, or rails because it positions them squarely in what they consider to be an information-rich environment.

For example, Penjaringan is a densely populated area just to the west of the historic Kota district. It is vulnerable to rapid flooding during even light rains, and is often difficult to navigate given its position under rail lines and freeways and between warehouses and industrial plants. The area houses a diversity of backgrounds and capacities. These include: lower-middle-class Chinese Indonesian residents who have always lived in Jakarta and are just barely holding on to their commercial assets and enterprises; Chinese Indonesians who are recent arrivals to Jakarta from other cities and who are trying to negotiate their way into businesses run by relatives and friends; skilled workers employed in nearby small factories, particularly shoes, plastics, and hardware; and unskilled workers employed in those same factories or involved more often in a variety of informal economic activities, such as waste-picking, prostitution, and cartage.

Most of the industrial plants in the area operate as

subcontractors for larger ones outside the city, handling special orders and niche markets, and therefore have oscillating production schedules that require the flexible mobilization of labor. Most seldom retain a substantial year-round labor force, instead depending on casual labor. Thus many workers in the area are not steadily employed by a single manufacturer, but instead circulate through a series of different jobs, and this entails both skilled and unskilled workers. In order to circulate, workers need to keep their "ears to the ground," to know who is hiring for what kinds of work and to maintain a foothold in informal work to smooth over periods when no jobs are available. When individuals live close not only to those who regularly search for new work opportunities themselves, but to different kinds of workers—i.e. skilled and unskilled workers, service providers, such as those who prepared cooked food, and the low-level management teams of the factories and warehouses themselves—different kinds of information are opened up that make it easier to get jobs.

Of course these circulations of labor in search of work can generate intense competition and conflict. Here again, the role of the *preman* is important. It is important in terms of judiciously working out distribution systems that make sure that work and opportunities are available to residents of vastly different backgrounds living in Penjaringan. It is also important in terms of securing an authority that is capable of representing and mediating particular interests—whether those interests are ethnic, occupational, or defined in terms of residential location. In Penjaringan, a sex district, consisting of about forty small shack bars and brothels built along both sides of an elevated rail track and in the residences immediately below, serves as an important context where different kinds of actors in the district, as well as outside, come together to negotiate such arrangements.

While the area experiences substantial environmental problems and insecure tenure, it is difficult to apply conventional community organization techniques or broad-based popular mobilization. Even though the local economy is able to work primarily by the ways in which different individual activities and skills complement each other, the kinds of exchanges and trade-offs they entail do not translate well in terms of the transparency, equanimity, and consensual participation usually valorized by urban social movements. Additionally, certain fault lines act as difficult boundaries when it comes to mobilizing the participation of residents for particular political tasks.

For example, Jakarta's most well-known organization acting on behalf of the urban poor, Urban Poor Consortium (UPC), had built up an effective organization of residents who were living under the toll road in Penjaringan. These are residents who usually purchased a site on an informal secondary market and then borrowed money to construct a small residence. They pay no rent, no local taxes, do not fall under any official local authority, but do have official access to electricity. On both sides of the toll road there are very dense neighborhoods of residents, who usually work the same jobs as those living under it. They attend the same schools, buy from the same markets, and socialize in the same places. Yet, these are residents who took out a rental contract for accommodation that most times was in no better condition than those makeshift shelters under the toll. Most do not know or have any contact with the owners of the accommodation and, instead, deal with an often confusing series of intermediary agents. Yet, they are convinced they have some formal status and security, no matter how tenuous it might be. UPC, through its local community organizers, has had absolutely no success in drawing these residents into their orbit, largely because they have not been able to convince them that the organization's largely rights-based approach to advocating for the interests of the urban poor is applicable to their situation.

Residents living on the side of the toll experience the same environmental hazards and income poverty. They confront unscrupulous agents that extract levels of rent that may often seem extortionate. But when it comes to representing their situation in the district to "a larger world," these residents feel that they have little in common with those living under the toll. In other words, at the level of everyday transactions—at the level of the street—a pervasive sense of commonality prevails, or at least a sense of widespread reciprocity. In identifying oneself to others and to the city, however, that sense of commonality falls away. For the terms of that commonality are based either in the very specific everyday activities of making residence in the district something that works or, more abstractly, in emphasizing a shared poverty. For the first, the everyday is too specific and intricate to elevate as a political platform. The second, a shared poverty, puts attention on a certain sense of weakness that residents find potentially debilitating when it comes to the local deal-making in which they must engage.

Residents living in areas next to the toll may feel that those under the toll face greater difficulties making ends meet that, in turn, result in their seeking accommodation where they do not have to pay rent. But, they often see these residents as having made a calculated decision to locate themselves in a situation where they do not have to pay in order to hedge their available resources in different ways. In other words, these residents, too, could afford to take out rental contracts but intentionally do not do so as almost a lifestyle choice. This choice, then, is what constitutes a kind of fault line and results in the belief held by non-toll residents that the UPC efforts can only be on behalf of those that have made this particular choice.

Throughout North Jakarta one can find districts that seem to work. They work in terms of the contiguity of different social backgrounds, classes, income groups, and ethnicities. They work for sizeable numbers of urban poor who live close to work and in information-rich environments where access to different kinds of opportunities is possible. While a multitude of complementary relationships exist among different kinds of actors, they may be functional but in no way are they egalitarian or necessarily just. Maintaining these spaces of social mixture is highly dependent upon the anchorage of one or several key sectors of economic activity. The efficacy of such activities may at times entail labor practices that are unpredictable and unfair. The only trade-off is that they help sustain a situation where middle-class and poor households are not only spatially close to each other but retain some form of constant interaction with each other.

In Pademangan Barat, a tradition of Javanese textile work has been transformed into hundreds of small-scale workshops producing clothing, primarily for the major market at Tanah Abang. Many of these are basically household operations that have been invested in by wealthier Chinese Indonesian entrepreneurs who live in the district. In some instances there is a situation of co-ownership where the provision of capital for equipment and stock entitles the investor to a share of the profits. This investment has also enabled these cottage operations to expand as space allows, and to hire local labor for a wide range of ancillary activities. These include taking goods to pick-up points where trucks can get through, running errands, purchasing cloth in bulk from markets, taking equipment for repair, and managing domestic economies as often entire households are involved in production work.

This niche industry, then, has brought together different socio-economic groups within the same sector and residential area.

Similarly, the area that runs from Mangga Bessar Raya to Jalan Jayajakarta between Mangga Bessar 3 and Mangga Bessar 9 is a complicated mixture of economic and ethnic groupings living in a diversity of domestic arrangements. Here, the poor work in the lower end of the vast retail, service, and warehouse complexes of Mangga Dua to the north, the lower end of the electronic markets of Glodok to the west, the night entertainment district of Mangga Bessar to the south, and the automobile parts retail and repair district of Taman Sari. These linkages to different sectors of work—retail, service, leisure, repair, fabrication—give low-income residents an economic foothold in the area. Perhaps more importantly, they enable groups of neighbors, relatives, friends, and associates in the area to forge an active conduit of exchanges between sectors, through the exchange of news and information. Then, by mobilizing their contacts in each sector as a resource for problem-solving, they maximize the advantages and competitive edge for a given operation in one particular sector.

For example, one resident's job is to haul garbage from the large retail market, ITC, to the loading docks, where it is carted away. He learns that the drivers are not satisfied with the way in which their present repair outfit handles the job. The resident informs a neighbor working for a large vehicle repair plant in Taman Sari, who in turn informs his boss of the situation, who then prepares an offer to do the job for a manager at the cartage company.

Equally important are the ways in which wealthier residents of the area depend upon conversations with their poorer neighbors in order to find out what is "really" taking place in the operations of their competitors. Middle-class residents demand particular kinds of amenities that practically have to be spread out to poorer residents, as they depend on their neighbors to provide cheap inputs that enable them to maintain certain levels of consumption. In many different ways these exchanges constitute a form of reciprocity, but it is difficult to concretize this reciprocity into clear policy frameworks and political practices.

On the one hand, Jakartan urban specialists, activists, and some local government officials talk about trying to preserve and better develop existing ways of life embodied by particular districts. The emphasis here is on how to sustain particular versions of the urban *kampung*, with its social heterogeneity, entangled residential and commercial spaces, and narrow lanes enforcing pedestrian sociality and fostering collective intimacy. While it may be possible to understand the efficacies and social coherence of individual *kampungs* and districts, it is much more difficult to grasp how they function as a collection of singular entities across an entire region. It is difficult to understand how specific development trajectories and regionalized governance frameworks might be elaborated through the articulation of these singularities. In other words, when one adds up the specificities of these districts, what does one end up with?

ANTICIPATORY POLITICS AND THE MANEUVERABILITY OF THE POOR

Arjun Apparadurai has written in recent years about the ways in which the capacities to aspire extend the horizon of what individuals believe it is possible for them to do and the kinds of practices, resources, and strategies that they may have available to concretize these aspirations. Because of the structural vulnerabilities in which they exist and the great demands placed on their energies and time to make ends meet, the scope of the poor's aspirations is usually highly constrained. Within this reduced sphere of aspirations, the kinds of collaborations, abilities, and imaginations that they are able to put into motion are also constrained. This in turn reinforces a limited world of aspirations and thus the reproduction of impoverishment.[7]

Apparadurai goes on to talk about interventions aimed at emphasizing concrete opportunities for aspiration through incremental developments of land tenure, self-constructed housing and the acquisition of assets through savings. These trajectories of eventual accumulation over the long run specify concrete steps the poor can take both to work toward specific aspirations and to expand the horizons of what can be aspired to. They can be effective political strategies, but they also need to be complemented by a more textured depiction of how different individuals and households may calculate their possibilities and make decisions as to how to use available resources and time.

Here I want to talk about a politics of anticipation. This entails a way of thinking about what is taking place, of positioning oneself in relationship to events and places in preparation to move quickly, to make one's situation and actions more visible or to maintain them under some radar. It is a way of reading the anticipated maneuvers of stronger actors and forces and assessing where there might be a useful opportunity to become an obstacle or facilitator for the aspirations of others.

Such anticipation entails the ability to see the loopholes and unexpected by-products in the intentions and plans of more powerful others. Then the trick is to use those gaps as a means to become important compensations; in other words, to become resources for helping those plans attain their eventual objectives or, alternately, to use the moments when these more powerful actors are distracted to win limited gains, such as moving to better locations or taking steps to better consolidate an individual or household's present bearings.

Many of the poor recognize that they operate in a "game" where they have limited power to set the rules and agenda, or to guarantee a stable place from which to operate. While the rules, players, and procedures may be well known, there is little access to the game, little opportunity to demonstrate any capacity to know how to play. But the poor also know that occasionally the game, with its competition and complicities among clearly delineated economic and political interests, plays to an inconclusive resolution. Or the conventional rules are suspended for a brief period of time in order to determine a winner or a specific decision.

As one resident of Penjaringan once remarked, "Our world is that of injury time in football." We watch as the game plods along to an increasingly frenetic endgame, and as official time runs out, there is that small gap at the end, those few minutes of extra time that have been accumulated only because the game had been momentarily stopped to deal with the various wounds of the players. Then, in these few minutes, one tries to frenetically do what one can. You know that the real game is not yours—with its rules and time frameworks—so you know that there isn't much time. You also know that it is not precisely clear what amount of time you do have. So anticipation entails both the sense of looking for those moments when the conventional games break down or go into an overtime with their own procedures and the sense of knowing that whatever one decides the clock will soon run out.

In some instances the eventual gaps, inconclusiveness, or unexpected outcomes of the conventional games of economic accumulation and political management are internalized by individuals as the main way in which they look upon their daily lives. In other words, they are always anticipating that the unexpected will show up somewhere and that their job is to be prepared to find some way to take advantage of it. This anticipation also involves a certain resignation that individuals can never know the entire story about how decisions are made, how the economies that shape their lives really work, or where the key powers are actually located.

So living in a partial world means somehow living through what might otherwise be considered to be either hegemonic or comprehensive—as a form of rule or economic logic—as if it were full of potential holes capable of providing, albeit always temporary, shelter and maneuverability. As nothing works out precisely as it is planned, there is always the possibility to find some way to keep going under difficult circumstances. So if the government declares that a community will be evicted, it probably won't happen according to the announced timetable. If a large development is scheduled to replace the area in which an individual has worked some informal job, then it probably won't take the exact shape and space planned. And even if it does, there may be delays and problems that make other opportunities visible.

So anticipation does not so much entail an orientation to a future that evolves along a clearly discernible path; it is not about anticipating the fruits of one's efforts or the attainment of a better future one day. Rather, it is about mobilizing one's energies and attentions to minimize disappointment when preferred ways of doing things do not work out. It is a way of sensing when things are about to take unexpected turns and being prepared to abandon what one is doing in order to change gears. It is sometimes the ability to rehearse the state of suspending hard-won stabilities in order to better test out what may be really going on in the place where one is working or living. In other words, when there seem to be major changes immanent in the conditions under which an individual lives or works, the poor are usually in no position to get the information that would clearly tell them what is going on. So sometimes they disseminate specific impressions and rumors across different circuits of information, far beyond their control, in order to see what kinds of responses it may stir up. In those responses, then, they may get a better sense of what is likely to happen to their community—in terms of new developments, infrastructure, or agendas—so that they may know better how to act.

This politics of anticipation is not just a form of resistance or simply a politics from below. It may contain aspects of these formulations, but it is also a calculated risk on the part of the poor since these very anticipations can be also used by the more powerful actors and forces around them. In some situations, these more powerful actors wait until the poor make the first move in order for them to gain a better sense of how easy it may be to force through evictions, appropriate land, or pay off particular leaders with specific amounts of compensation. As a strategy that looks for things, plans, and organizational efforts to break down or veer off into unexpected directions, the same orientation also finds itself sometimes applied to the collective organizational efforts of the poor themselves.

For example, the poor are sometimes reluctant to change or improve their living environments even when this is plausible. They too often invest in maintaining the status quo as if it were something more than that. In other words, the poor may cling to keeping things the same, not only as a form of security but as the only real condition of a possible way out. Sometimes they think that improvements in living conditions would likely raise lots of problems that the community doesn't have the resources to deal with. So in many respects, the politics of anticipation is a politics of irony.

What is most critical here is perhaps not the tactical orientations of anticipation—maneuvers with which urban theory is well familiar—but rather its concomitant practice of discrimination. What discrimination means here is nothing less than a turning of what has been lost—the old mediation, the old sense of belonging and orientation—into an opportunity. This is an opportunity to reclaim various forms of paying attention to things and of being receptive to what is all around which circulate through the city as bits and pieces of different knowledge many different kinds of residents have brought from various elsewheres, times, and circumstances. Often reduced to the status of being "distorted traditional practices," "magic," "intuition," or "street smarts," to name a few, these operate as tools of inventing and implementing specific ways of thinking and feeling. Discrimination thus entails how one learns to pay attention to and engage the forces of family influence, social affiliations, local and distant authorities of various kinds in ways that circumvent the reiteration of easy divides and oppositions—"us versus them," "here versus there."[8]

Usually individuals and households have particular ideas, norms, and cultural rules about people and things that are to be considered close or distant: people and groups with whom one can exchange things, lend things, as well as forces and people that must be resisted. But here, discrimination is a way of paying attention to what one's neighbors or associates, coworkers, friends, or acquaintances are doing, not with the familiar conceptualization of what a neighbor is or should be, but through creative conceptualizations that enable a shift in the conventional patterns of how distance, proximity, reciprocity, and resistance among people are orchestrated. As such, it becomes a way of anticipating what might happen if a person takes a particular course of action. Most important, it is a means of inventing a field of probable outcomes in everyday life situations that no longer have a strong relationship to reliable institutions for interpreting what is going on. Discrimination thus seeks lines of connection among disparate actors, domains, and ways of doing things that open them up to the possibility of different affiliations. Thus anticipation is something that exceeds simply "trying to get one over" on the more powerful or of sneaking one's clearly or not so clearly defined self-interest under the radar. Rather, it entails small experimentations that enable people who share an environment to concretely do small yet different things with each other.

Perhaps some would argue anticipation is not a politics at all. But what I want to explore here are some examples of how these practices of anticipation "cut both ways." In other words, how they constitute a game of transactions that propel different kinds of residents into varied forms of contact with each other and that result in different kinds of benefits and constraints for all of them.

The poor may not march forward with a series of clear victories toward greater justice, rights, and opportunities. But they do, in many instances, create new positions and opportunities to keep specific advantages and places of operation. Often they simply reproduce a situation where they become a "problem" that needs to be dealt with or an impediment to be overcome. But even here, the extent to which they generate new dimensions to this problematic status, as well as their capacities to extend it and change the terms of how it is problematic in specific contexts, keeps them in view and in play.

WHEN THE POPULAR ANTICIPATION BECOMES EVIDENCE FOR THE BIG URBAN PLAYERS, WHAT DO THE BIG PLAYERS DO?

As indicated earlier, North Jakarta is an especially jumbled-up landscape of ports, warehouses, industries, dense residential areas, overcrowded feeder roads, decaying infrastructure, and new project development. Much in the region is in need of significant repair, and its vulnerability to flooding requires massive engineering works that will inevitably disrupt existing commercial and residential districts. It is a region in need of effective planning as its current fractal landscape tends to enforce too many enclosures and a de facto enfolding of activity and attention, making flows and linkages across the region even more difficult. A critical question about North Jakarta, then, is whether a politics based on the defense of place makes sense given not only the needs of the North Jakarta region, but the city's obsession with becoming a functional global city. This question goes beyond whether the way of life to be defended is particularly just or equitable, or even if such a thing is really identifiable.

In a recent spate of evictions that have displaced thousands of households across the region from their locations under the toll road—that runs horizontally across the north—it is clear that the intent of the municipality is to basically "warehouse" the poor in large residential complexes at the periphery of the city. It is easy to forecast that such warehousing will produce greater difficulties and costs for the city in terms of social control. Many residents will either not be able to afford the nominal rent or will choose to seek out residential locations both more central and more out of view. This is likely to produce severe overcrowding in already overcrowded districts and increase the vulnerability of already precarious environmental landscapes.

It is clear that discourses which emphasize the right of the poor to the city and their right to make a viable living within it have little traction as the competition among cities grows more intense in terms of the pressure on cities to offer cutting-edge imaginaries and amenities. Economic cost–benefit analysis becomes necessary to demonstrate that keeping the poor in more central locations goes a long way to maintaining a diverse urban social economy and, thus, a well-funded city. But such arguments are often difficult to make and require not only intricate research but ways of presenting evidence that make sense to government officials who insist on versions of economic efficacy that are usually much too narrow in scope.

It is true that the hyper-visibility of North Jakarta's toll way residents made them an easy target. As a series of fires, popularly believed to have been intentionally set, damaged parts of the toll road's structure, it was easy for the municipality to claim that it had to act in the interest of protecting the integrity of a major infrastructural resource. These toll communities are usually the most spatially and economically marginal in the districts to which they nominally belong. Yet, the Urban and Regional Development Institute (URDI) estimates that almost 30 percent of North Jakarta's residents live on unsecured land with no official certification.[9] Even in areas where the majority of residents do have long-term title, they are vulnerable to the manipulation of powerful interests who use rumor and promises of large pay-outs to acquire land, prompting a kind of domino effect. Particularly as once viable manufacturing and port sector jobs continue their downward decline, the strategic advantages inherent in particular residential locations also diminish. In many neighborhoods there are intense arguments concerning what really does constitute a strategic location. Many residents have indeed moved further south, opening up the region to more transient flows of nascent inward migration.

Again, the question emerges as to how specific ways of life, with their efficacies and social heterogeneity, might be concretized in ways that do not necessitate the defense of particular places. While some architects and urban specialists in Jakarta have long played around with ideas about how to translate the horizontal and street-level dynamics of complex social transactions into vertical spatial arrangements, the proposed scenarios are usually too radically disjointed from what is acceptable in terms of appropriate housing and commercial space. While some residents of both Penjaringan and Pademangan have been calling for on-line facilities for information retrieval and communication to both mirror and extend street-like social interchanges, there are few strategic formulations available for how to really use information and communication technologies (ICTs) as a way to approximate the information-rich environments of district streets. Clearly applications of these virtual tools will be necessary. But it is a major leap to go from the way these challenges are being experimented with in the worlds of urban design, ubiquitous computing, and planning to the reconstruction of entire local social worlds.

Familiar models of community and political organization face great difficulties operating in situations where the entanglements of affiliation, loyalty, and power are complex. As such, it is difficult to foresee the concrete terms of an anticipatory politics. We can understand many of the dynamics involved, and a more complicated representation of how local power really works theoretically does fit well with the use of certain virtual tools and on-line networking processes. A major difficulty is that the street is still viewed by many residents as a powerful instrument for negotiating spaces of operation.

Even if they were well versed in the use of various ICTs to communicate, get needed information, and transact across a wide range of spaces and sectors, it is still this use of the street as a kind of political weapon that they would find difficult to let go of. For example, as we have seen, the districts of Muara Baru and Kalibaru sit next to major industrial and port facilities. No matter how sophisticated the security operations managed by the major companies in these facilities may be, there is no guarantee that trucks, ships, and labor will get in and out. All can be subverted and disrupted. No matter how well guarded certain facilities may be, there are still leakages, people who can be paid off, and ways in. The street continuously presents itself as a potential weapon.

This is why in Muara Baru, for example, the primary economic player in the government-sponsored fishing complex, Ah Hong—with his factories, his fleet of 150 boats, his 35 warehouses—brought *preman* like Bang Juned, Bang Cipto, and Bang Oca into his operations. He made them the final arbiters and managers of labor. Juned controls all of the work on ships, Cipto in the market, and Oca in the security operation. They are the ones who control access to work, who make sure nothing is subverted, and who, according to the popular belief of many residents, hold both Ah Hong and the government captive. They are the ones who micro-manage particular situations. They create more jobs than are perhaps necessary, and even if they pay less than what others might have got in the past, they always throw in lunch and free cigarettes.

What cements a particular attachment to place, especially in these districts, is participation in a system of "power-sharing" that residents believe to not only provide a platform for livelihood but also to make them really "count." Of course, these mechanisms, based on a seemingly anachronistic politics of patron–client gridlock, are not the only ways in which such residents could count for something. Other forms of valorization are both well known and even available. But residents claim that this is a situation that they can see play itself out on a daily basis. More importantly, it provides the critical social infrastructural element in a wider practice whereby different actors in the district are forced to take each other into consideration, regardless of who they are and what they do. This practice opens up the space for residents to have many kinds of compensations and adjustments available and which are necessary as prices rise and fall and needed services come and go.

Thus what presents itself as a particular way of life may indeed have its discernible and measurable practices and representations. But much of what it does in the end is to keep a sense of the virtual in play. In other words, the transactions, hedges, exchanges, negotiations, fights, and subterfuges of daily life in districts don't so much produce a steady state of clear-cut, predictable resolutions as keep open a sense that many different outcomes are possible and workable given the specific problem and history at hand. It is not that residents are dependent upon a specific formula, image, or scenario of what is needed or what works. Rather, they are prepared to believe that different formulations might indeed work in their interest. So an anticipatory politics is in some way already in operation. If one doesn't get a specific job or piece of land or selling space as part of a resolution deal for a particular conflict, then the very nature of who has been involved in the negotiation makes it quite likely that several different work opportunities will be opened up.

It is thus important to better understand the terms and operating procedures of the anticipatory politics already being concretized in specific districts. Particularly crucial here is some sense of how far the networks mobilized to participate in various instances of local deal-making extend into other parts of the city, and how varied their operations are in different districts. Of course there are limits as to what can be done with such an anticipatory politics. In significant ways this resource for residents can also be turned against them.

Earlier, I mentioned Kali Baru-Tanjung Priok on the northern coast of Jakarta. This is an area that has been settled for a long time due to its proximity to the sea and to a deep harbor that has long been the site of trans-shipments not routed through the major port of Tanjung Priok. Much of the local economy has focused on artisanal fishery and, in recent decades, the importation of wood from Kalimantan.

Given the character of the area, it has been one of the most important districts for the Bugis in Jakarta—a traditionally seafaring people that have been historically concentrated in Northern Sulawesi. Kali Baru was the site of the first major modern fish market in the city and continues to be the chief supplier of dried fish products. Although the bulk of the region's fishing operations have moved elsewhere, most of the residents remain involved in either fishing or port-related activities. The majority of residents live on state-owned land where their tenancy is formally registered. There is also a densely populated quarter, Kabu Linda, which sits on abandoned private land next to a vast area of chemical storage plants and whose residents have no formal status.

Kali Baru seems situated in a prolonged period of uncertain transition. At the peak of the logging business, its many large warehouses were full of wood and its streets clogged with trucks, buyers, and carters. While the wood port is still active, national controls have attempted to place strong restrictions and quotas on the trade—given the alarming rates of deforestation in the province of Kalimantan. It is a barely disguised secret that the business largely circumvents these restrictions and that each boat load that arrives in Kali Baru mixes both legally and illegally obtained wood products. The artisanal dimensions of the trade, relying on the mixture of big patrons and their fleets of large old wooden ships and the highly decentralized networks of longshoremen, woodcutters, carters, warehouse owners, brokers, truck drivers, and middlemen, is particularly adapted to its increasing illegal character.

This system has existed for a very long time, and was suited to a trade that constantly had to make deals to access forest lands, build access routes, and negotiate with multiple "fiefdoms." But it has also lacked the ability to consolidate resources and efforts to improve the overall working conditions of the Kali Baru port, and it is clear that little investment has been made in maintaining the conditions of the harbor and the infrastructure of roads, docks, and warehouses.

Now the absence of investment is compounded by the uncertainty of the trade itself. Volume has clearly declined. Although the wood business remains protected by very powerful individuals and the dilapidated conditions of the port itself—making it difficult to apply strict accounting procedures—there is widespread worry about the pressures being exerted on the Indonesian government to clean up the business. Rumors circulate that the government will simply construct new facilities far from Jakarta through which they are most assured of being able to apply strict controls. But there are other pressures as well. The area has a lot of advantages. It is close to the main port, is a key site for industrial storage, is close to the emerging export processing zones to the east, and anticipates the construction of new arteries to the regional transport network. Given these advantages, many initial overtures have been made on the part of some major industries to acquire large tracts of land in the district. If this would be the case, not only would the major residential areas be greatly affected, but a large portion of the current port facilities dedicated to storage and sales would have to be relocated.

Even though Kali Baru retains the largest dried fish market in the city, the majority of the facilities for drying the fish are no longer located in the area of the market, as this land was sold and developed for residences attached to some of the recently developed industries. As mentioned earlier, the country's former Vice-President, Yusuf Kalla, is one of the largest investors in the area, with the construction of a Mitsubishi carport, and there are reports that Humpus, the shipping company belonging to Tommy Suharto, son of the former head of state, may acquire a large amount of land in the area. As the economic character of the district changes, so does the intimate relationship that has been developed between residents, labor, and local politicians.

Fishing and logging were activities that brought in large numbers of outsiders as customers, transporters, and often brokers. A wide range of ancillary activities grew up around this transience. The alliances between local leaders and gangsters who largely administered these activities plowed an important portion of the proceeds into the area, enabling residents to assume powerful bargaining positions with the regional government, planners, and local economic bosses.

While these relationships remain important, they are disrupted as the area becomes a site for large industrial plants and is targeted for more. The residents of the areas that abut the Mitsubishi carport, for example, have grown concerned over the limited influence they have had in winning jobs at the carport. The frustration has been expressed in some symbolic acts of vandalism that have prompted Kalla to use ambiguities in the community's tenancy status to threaten the residents with eviction. These maneuvers have been extensively talked about across the district. Gestures on both sides constitute a kind of "trial balloon" through which to read what is likely to happen elsewhere in the district.

The development trajectory of Kali Baru is further complicated by the uncertain plans for just how major road systems will be extended across this area of the North. It is clear that major improvements are required in order to better circulate the traffic that connects the port at Tanjung Priok to the emerging industrial areas in the east, as well as to the major commercial centers to the west and south. But how these changes will actually be routed remains an area of controversy. Major storage facilities, factories, and container docks would be displaced—and so part of the overall task is how to minimize such collateral damage by cutting through residential areas.

The climatic conditions related to all of these "projects" are becoming an important issue. The north coast of Jakarta experiences rising tides that flood many areas along the northern coast. Many infrastructural improvements are necessary, including further dredging of the harbor, the repair of existing seawalls, and the construction of new ones. Given the massive repairs, improvements, and new construction necessary across the entire northern part of the city, there is much debate among planners, national and municipal officials as to the formulation of priorities and where the money will come from. None of the major political or economic actors is making clear moves. Those involved in transportation planning and investment appear to be watching to see what moves the industrialists will make, as the latter, in turn, wait and see what kinds of plans emerge from various ministries and municipal authorities to mobilize the investments needed for new roads and coastal engineering works.

Situated in the midst of these hedges are the residents of Kali Baru themselves, many of whom expect to be forced to move within the next two years. These expectations are stoked by various rumors which are intentionally circulated by local strongmen signaling their availability to deliver particular pieces of land for new economic uses or to mitigate possible resistance to them. Some *preman*, labor brokers, local bosses, and municipal officials, expecting major transitions ahead, try to position themselves to cut the best deals in terms of favorable relocations for the businesses they are involved in or in terms of winning new positions, markets, or labor quotas for new projects and industries. Although the district's reputation as a place of illicit commodity chains, questionable business practices, prostitution, extortion, and transient customers would seem to leave it vulnerable to redevelopment, this reputation also implicates some politically powerful individuals who profit from prolonged and uncertain changes.

A critical question in all of this is the history through which residents became convinced that they had to move and that specific acquisitions, deals, and development projects were in process, when actually very little has been concretized. In other words, residents have been cultivated to anticipate that a specific future is imminent. This anticipation limits their options and takes away any negotiating leverage they might have. Here, anticipation acts to constitute residents as those who will make the first move, who will decide that they will have to move and that they must get what they can now in terms of compensation before it is too late.

At the same time, more powerful actors can then sit back and hope to minimize the costs of their own maneuvers through a cheap displacement of residents. But, this is matter that goes beyond simply manipulating the dispossession of residents. The powerful actors trigger the anticipations of the residents and watch just how these residents think about and concretize their own next moves. How far are households willing to relocate; how adept are they at finding other jobs, and how much are decisions collectively deliberated, among neighbors or individuals working in the same economic sector? In this process, interested parties get a better sense of what the likely ramifications might be for their own possible plans. They get to know where possible points of resistance might come from; they get to know the extent to which an existing labor force could be rearranged and redeployed for new uses; how residents are connected to local power brokers; and how far their influence runs across a larger spectrum of political and economic spheres.

Again, North Jakarta is an area of great uncertainty in terms of environmental conditions, future investments, the functionality of the built environment, and the configurations of deal-making among a very diverse set of economic interests and actors. Economic development requires the ability to develop new businesses, provide secure working conditions and reliable transportation of goods and services coming in and out, and piece together a network of small producers, casual labor, and ancillary services that keep production, labor, and storage costs low, as well as minimize the pay-offs often required to keep the "wheels going." All of this necessitates fine-tuned assessments about the "ins" and "outs" of a district. These assessments entail more than demographic information and more than a reading of the local political and social dynamics.

Instead, knowledge is required about what people living and operating in a particular place are willing to do, how they get things done, what they are prepared to do to with each other, and how they are continuously positioning themselves for alternative futures. Here, then, the anticipations of residents become a resource for others, a resource which does not necessarily work in the interests of the residents themselves.

In sum, then, anticipation is a two-edged sword. But this is what is implied by the notion of the crossroads. Many urban residents operate in spaces where many different things could happen, but where in the very public choice they make to take a specific course of action they can never control who is going to follow and what the implications of that following will be. No matter what "road" is followed, no matter what choices and calculations are made, there are always other crossroads ahead. And there will again be the need to incessantly revise and take new decisions and risks. For the majority of urban residents, it is never clear what will be asked of them and how the rules of the game will change. But it is only at the crossroads where the marginal and disenfranchised have some kind of opportunity to remake the city. As cities invest in flyovers and freeways, fast conduits and high speed communication networks which would seem to filter out interruptions and constitute smooth pathways for big and well-financed aspirations, more ordinary residents, then, have a reason to turn as much urban space as possible into crossroads of all kinds.

But it is precisely these crossroads that fight a battle against being made peripheral. In the following chapters, I want to extend this metaphor of crossroads and talk about the importance of *intersection*—a crossing of paths, histories, and ways of doing things among people of various backgrounds, statuses, and capacities. The vast body of Richard Sennett's work has focused on the ways in which the city is place of diversity; where diversity strengthens individual capacities and generates new forms of thought, feeling, and action. As a place of strangers delinked from ties to clear pasts, traditions, and a well-organized universe of beliefs and behaviors, urban dwellers have to find ways of making use of the relative anonymity and autonomy that urban life affords, as well as to continuously adapt those uses to the ones made by others with whom they also share tenuous social ties.[10]

Many of these assumptions have been criticized by those who emphasize the increasing individualization of urban life and the fact that the process of establishing social relationships takes place more through various networked media and dispersed work careers than it does in specific places and neighborhood of urban residence. People can then lead functional urban lives without ever having to take others with whom they nominally share living and public spaces into any substantial consideration.

What residents of these districts are enacting is not the dream of urban cosmopolitanism. It is not simply a crossing of paths, histories, and ways of doing things among people of various backgrounds, statuses, and capacities. It is not a *cityness* which focuses on the ways in which the city is a place of diversity; where diversity strengthens individual capacities and generates new forms of thought, feeling, and action. Rather, intersection is a machine-like process that appears inevitable when relationships, economies, and ways of doing things become so densely entangled that it is difficult to talk about a formal versus informal economy, adult versus youth, citizen versus stranger—whatever terms you want to use. Residents, relationships, ways of life are forced out of their particular identities because they have to deal with an enlarged world of causes and effects, powers, influences, and considerations. How in this era can one draw a line between what is relevant or not, what is a causal factor or not?

Intersection, in the use I make of it here, doesn't assume that the city is headed for any new kind of social harmony. Rather, a certain dystopian dread will always hang over the city, always make it seem that cities are veering off the tracks as well as building more secure walls behind which its residents must hide. It is a matter of looking at the different potentialities that are produced when bodies, feelings, and ways of doing things are no longer tied to any particular meaning, even if this comes perilously close to their conversion into disposable commodities. These "social machines," whose components are shed of specific meanings and values, are never built to last, but take those who live in cities to places and experiences that are yet to be conceptualized or mapped. It is difficult to see these "machines" as households, groups, or institutions, but they are collectivities of some sort. We have to remember that by definition the city goes toward many different futures at once, it is not hinged, not anchored to any specific plans, economies, or future—no matter what residents or powerful players and money may do. So in part, these machines are "brought to life" only because they have to deal with the unexpected crossings of noise, information, people, and materials that such a city brings. In other words, the very lack of "real" social trust and conviviality can be the basis for ways of "being together" that are potentially productive and dangerous at the same time. While urban policymakers have always warned against messiness, the breakdown of social cohesion, and the dangers of an ungovernable city, there is much within these apparent dangers which are the very resourcefulness of urban life.

It is only by seeing urban life as a context for intersection that we can understand how those with few apparent resources can act with a heightened sense of resourcefulness. In the following chapters we will see that urban life does include numerous situations where different kinds of residents are trying to figure out what to do with each other, and where no one has enough power and money to impose their stamp on the situation, and where there is no ready-made map or policy that dictates the kinds of accommodations that should or will ensue. Those who rely on a capacity for anticipation then have an opportunity to affect the course of events, and the question of what urban residents can do with each other remains an open question.

Three

The discussion in this chapter is organized around a simple but fundamental aspect of urban life: What can people do together and under what circumstances? From this question stem the critical dimensions of urban policy in terms of who residents have to deal with, talk to, be intruded upon or intruding: who does space belong to, who has access to what kinds of space for what purposes? As soon as these considerations are opened up a wide range of political, administrative, and technical considerations about how cities are run also become more contestable and specific.

We know that cities are full of people doing specific things with each other, both voluntary and involuntary. The necessities of economic life mean that there are many people one would prefer not to be in contact with but one has little choice but to do so. There are many people and stories we would like to become part of but feel that we have no basis or points of entry. Cities are full of discrepant eligibilities and statuses, codes and requirements for accessing particular experiences, places, and opportunities.

WHAT IS AN URBAN PUBLIC AND WHY IS IT IMPORTANT?

Yet cities are also about publics—i.e. about forms of being together or of being connected that go beyond the specific details of what a person does, where he or she lives and comes from. Rather, to be conjoined in a public is to be part of a larger audience or convocation that is the addressee and witness of a particular communication, address, or appeal. It is the assumption that one shares a common space of concern that is generated from the production of a specific event or communication. It is something anchored in the experience of a specific part of the city or groups of residents within the city but which communicates to have a response, an audience, and a consideration that goes beyond the specific character and identity of this group or place.

In a specific urban locality, association, or institution, where people are in some form of direct contact, people try to work out ways of dealing with others based on selectively incorporating or ignoring various dimensions of their backgrounds, everyday life situations, personalities, and so forth. But they find ways to deal with these specificities, even if relationships are argued about and broken off. What people can do with each other then is the product of those everyday negotiations and the prevailing codes, rules, norms, and implicit assumptions operative in the contexts in which they actually try to do things—whether it is in the workplace, civic associations, religious institutions, or informal affiliations.

What is important about the sense of a larger public is that the ideas, actions, questions, and provocations communicated by a specific set of actors can be potentially opened up to a wider set of uses than that imagined or possible within the specific known situation from which these ideas and communications originated. They can be potentially "put to work" in many different ways. They have effects upon the specific ways of thinking and living in a wide range of contexts. As such, they are a form of connection, a way of feeling that people are operating in a larger common arena of life without specific criteria of membership and belonging needing to be precisely identified, measured, or referenced.

Therefore, the public becomes a vehicle through which diverse facets of urban life can intersect—a way, as Le Gales puts it, of people coming together without having to be integrated.[1] Instead of people coming together to consensually decide the markers of identity and common rules necessary to recognize common participation, the public is a matter of projecting a way of talking and regarding that goes beyond the specificity of one's life situation. It is an appeal for a consideration of how that specificity may be something that can be recognized by someone else's specific situation. In other words, it is an act or speech that is produced with the openness to be translated; it advertises its very existence to be something other than what it may appear to be. It is an appeal to be linked, grouped together with something else.[2]

For example, central Brussels is a city full of volatile interfaces. It is full of tightly bounded and controlled ethnic communities, such as the Moroccan neighborhood Molenbeek, where an outsider could be easily fooled into thinking that they were in Casablanca. Relations between Flemish, Walloon, Congolais, Turks, Moroccans, Albanians, Afghans, Poles, and the large number of middle-class Europeans who fill the European Union bureaucracy are often very tense and contested, particularly around spatial claims and cultural sensitivities.

For example, in a bar popular with many people, including young Moroccans who sit drinking juice or even older Moroccan men sitting with a beer, and situated just across from the main entrance to Molenbeek, a Moroccan man passes the bar several times before taking a trash can and smashing a window because a group of young white friends is sitting in the bar with a young baby. The city is full of events like this, of situations that are interpreted as offensive or improper. Yet, when a group of Turkish and Moroccan imams hold a press conference in the center of Brussels on the afternoon of

Eid al-Adha, one of the holiest days of the Muslim calendar, and collectively speak of the possibilities of a renewed urban life in Brussels, of the need for more coordinated municipal spatial planning and its relationships to building civic trust, and how Muslims want to and should be involved in the municipal affairs of Brussels, this speech and event go beyond the complaint of how Muslims may be treated. They go beyond the specificities of a particular confessional or ethnic community and appeal to a process which others could become a part of.

This speech by the imams doesn't mean that the discrimination felt by Muslims ceases to be important or that Muslims are being asked to not be sensitive to what they perceive to be the improprieties all around them. Rather, what is being appealed to is the right and opportunity for a specific confessional community to have something to say about the city as a whole. In order to do so, they have to go beyond the specificities of the Muslim community's hurts, slights, and moral priorities in order to make a range of unspecific others feel that they are being addressed in a way that they feel part of; something with which the specificities of their own different lives and values can intersect.

KINSHASA

I want to talk about some of these notions of the public as a reflection of what people can do with each other in the city through the example of Kinshasa. By any measure, Kinshasa would appear to be a dysfunctional city. In fact many commentators use it as a typical example of just how bad urban life can get. I don't want to play down the severity of Kinshasa's situation. But I want to talk about it in a way that demonstrates just how many different things it is possible to conceive of people doing with each other in a city—how creative and imaginative these things can be—but at the same time how limiting this richness is without a dynamic sense of publics being made and remade. As such, this notion of a public may be crucial to the viability of urban life.

Although no one knows for sure, since no recent census has been taken, Kinshasa probably has a population of nine million people spread out over a metropolitan region that extends nearly 100 kilometers to the west, east, and south of the city center. There are probably more people living on less than $1 a day than in any city of the world.[3] In Kinshasa the overwhelming impression is of a city that doesn't work, that is broken. While the center is equipped with several large supermarkets and department stores, most of the city is dotted with tens of thousands of barely discernible small businesses, usually no larger than a big closet, which, nevertheless, advertise themselves as *la référence* (the best) or the result of divine inspiration.

The logic of such commerce rests in the attempt to capture a local moment—a passerby, an immediate need on the part of someone situated in the immediate proximity. In other words, the commerce attempts to intensify and concretize a highly localized possibility. These businesses open and close, hundreds on a daily basis, yet, if possible, households located on any viable artery will attempt to build one in front of their house. Some of the most successful businessmen in Kinshasa are those who have lined streets across the city with what looks like an endless string of small motels.

For example, there probably are more pharmacies in Kinshasa than any other city in the world. Sometimes one finds 70 along a 2 kilometer stretch of road. As they basically function in the same way, it is not clear which ones will make it in the medium to long run, as if the crowding itself takes place in order to generate a reality where success or failure

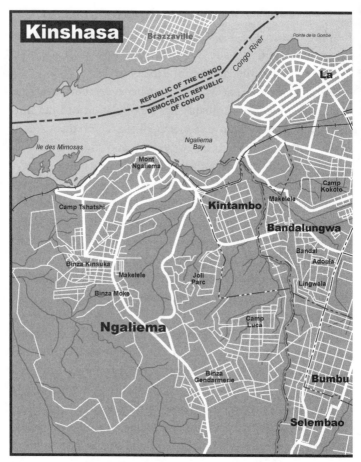

Map 4
Central Kinshasa

becomes something arbitrary or simply a matter of luck. While certain customers will intentionally set out from wherever they are to buy medicine, the logic here seems to be that the sheer excess and concentration may impress upon a potential customer the need to acquire medicine right then. Conversely, the stores try to capture the sudden and often arbitrary

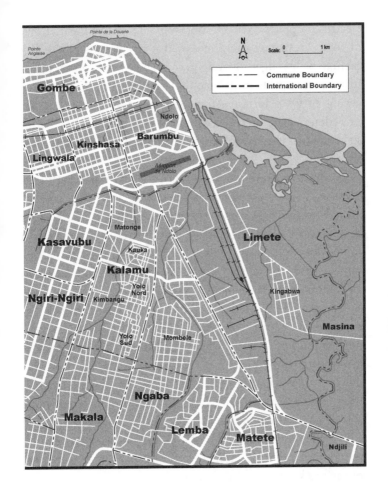

ability of a customer to make a purchase—an ability that often cannot be anticipated in advance, as it is often unclear just when a certain amount of money will actually be in a customer's pocket.

These kind of spatial arrangements and commercial logics have something to say about infrastructure. For the dynamics of infrastructure don't rest just in the fact that water and electrical supplies are scanty and sporadic, or that the majority of roads are barely navigable, or that many parts of the city seem to be literally drowning in shit. The usual focus on urban infrastructure rests in its technical features. While the engineering of what infrastructure is supposed to do must take precedence, it is in cities which so substantially lack infrastructure that it is possible to discern its impact on how people are able to use it.

For infrastructure is a medium of conveyance and articulation. It establishes a concrete framework for how residents are able to reach each other, how they are able to think about how they are positioned and located in relationship to each other. Through roads, wires, conduits, grids, and pipes, infrastructure establishes particular forms of individuation and autonomy. If the essentials of everyday sustenance assume a particular form of delivery into the intimate spaces, for example, of a family compound, the need for interacting and negotiating with others is lessened. They won't have to wait at a communal pump or negotiate to make sure that someone delivers the right amount of water from the vending truck. If transportation opportunities are provided in sufficient volume and efficiency, residents are able to design more personalized approaches to the navigation of the city, potentially expanding the territory covered and, thus, the availability of resources of various kinds.

WHEN PEOPLE ARE INFRASTRUCTURE

In a city like Kinshasa, people themselves are the important infrastructure. In other words, their selves, situations, and bodies bear the responsibility for articulating different locations, resources, and stories into viable opportunities for everyday survival. In a city with few ready-made formats capable of specifying just how individuals are to obtain shelter, food, money, and status, the particularities of an individual's family and ethnic background, their personal character and style, and their location in particular arrangements of residence and circulation with others all become the stuff of shifting circuitries of connection. Information, cash, obligations, possibilities, and support pass along these circuits. In such an existence, it is difficult for individuals to think of a life only for them, to plan a specific trajectory, or to know in advance just what implications a particular course of action might produce. At the same time, there is little else to hold individuals "above water" except for the personal effort they make to decide to take a particular course of action. This does not mean that there isn't discussion, counsel, or advice. But in the end, this effort is the propulsion for an existence and the engine that drives a resident into tomorrow.

Even in the everyday expenditure on basic necessities, it is not clear for many what the household might be able to eat by day's end. Streets are full of people on small errands; as a little bit of money comes in, a family member is immediately sent to buy a small quantity of cassava powder or even rice, cooking oil, or bits of meat. At the same time, streets are full of people milling around, taking a beer here and there, calling out to acquaintances, as most flows of passage, here to there, are interrupted. Although the interruption can be a source of frustration, like the interruption of water or electricity, it becomes a necessity for everyone in that it provides a mechanism for people to switch gears, to consider other options, to take on needed information about what is happening in the neighborhood or city. In neighborhoods full of residents struggling to make ends meet on a daily basis, and without effective laws, policies, or institutions capable of imposing functional maps for how people should act with each other, such interruptions, such incessant checking and conversations, become the mechanisms for keeping things from getting out of hand.

Where people are the important infrastructure, the value of an individual existence rests less in the elaboration of a "meaningful" life or a coherent story about a person's character. What is important is an individual's ability to be "hooked in" to different daily scenarios, dramas, networks, and affiliations that provide a constant set of alternatives for how to put bread on the table or how to become a person that can be taken seriously. As a "piece in a mutating puzzle" or a link in a chain, people are also more readily expendable. At times, they simply acquire a history of having participated in different situations and for which there is no overarching logic that enables them to make sense of this accumulation of experiences. The person, him- or herself, becomes the intersection, rarely able to take the things he or she brings together and then use them as a platform or as material to develop a story of individual development or change.

These practices take place against the backdrop of a former colonial city that in nearly fifty years of independence has been not only badly run but administered in a despotic and bizarre manner. The years have been punctuated by war and massive corruption. As a colonial city, the racial divides between populations were spatially marked. The Belgians constructed a sprawling garden city for themselves along the east–west axis of the Congo River, extending into the verdant hills to the southwest. Densities were kept low, except for the indigenous populations crowded into quarters safely kept at arm's length from the white quarters.

The residual complexion of this spatial logic has been carried into the city today. The bulk of the population is scattered over a large territory. The lack of municipal finance maintains the majority as a huge rural population. For hundreds of square kilometers, Kinois live across valleys, ravines, slopes, creeks, riverbanks, and gullies with little hint of urbanization except for the sheer population densities.

What is called the *cité*, the town itself, varies between administrative and residential districts set on wide expanses of land, commercial landscapes, many of them long abandoned, and densely populated quarters such as Lingwala, Ngaliema, Matete, Kasavubu, Kitambu, and Bandalunga. Most of these districts contain entirely broken, nearly impassable streets, few if any urban services, and far more people than the existing built environment can safely bear. Even Bandal, the historical quarter of the *evolué*—i.e. those Africans "cultivated" as functionaries, teachers, and other professionals by the colonial regime—and now the key residential district for what exists of a lower middle class, is separated from the central city by a 4 square kilometer military camp, most of which consists of empty space.

The current municipal budget of Kinshasa is around US$23 million, barely enough to cover administrative salaries and not much else. National legislation granting Kinshasa the power to generate and retain its own finance was only passed in 2008. While democratic elections in 2006 instituted some limited institutional development and accountability, much of politics is run like an extended extortion racket. The governor of the city is not directly chosen by the population but by the parliament, and constitutionally mandated local elections have now been held up for two years. When the governor of Kinshasa, for example, attempts to allocate a certain amount of money for the repair of the city's primary schools, the parliament decides that it needs new cars. The majority in parliament basically bought their seats, including the governor. When he refuses to use the city budget to fund such purchases, the members of parliament threaten to vote him out of office. In July 2008, a cabal sought to remove him by making it seem he was behind the assassination of an important politician.

EVERYDAY URBAN LIFE AS THE BALANCE OF OPPOSITES

The point I want to make here is about the extent to which residents live a life "in between," where contrary dimensions of urban life would seem to come together but, in a fundamental way, do not. In other words, residents appear to simultaneously live in seemingly very separate realities that don't come together to produce the possibility of something else. Here, the individual, him- or herself, is the intersection. They bear the full brunt of absorbing these contradictions, of cushioning their impact, and of deflecting them onto someone else. Everyday life then becomes a game of constant deferral, of putting off a task or obligation to another time, of making someone else also responsible and implicated in whatever is going on. Perhaps more importantly, it is about coming up with the right approach to various situations confronted on a daily basis and on the verge of getting out of control.

This sheer volatility is itself an important game because it signals that there is space and opportunity to make things happen. Even in situations where people have taken strong offense at something, at some intrusion, some violation of perceived codes, or where greed or desperation lead some individuals to grab onto a particular happenstance and milk it for all it's worth, there seem to almost always be opportunities to steer what is going on in a different direction. This capacity doesn't easily translate into any clear evidence that long-range problems are being solved or that people or neighborhoods are being better prepared to cope and build something new.

But the ability of people, who often do not even know each other, to ease a situation away from the brink depends on the fundamental ability of all involved to translate the present situation into some other possibility. There might be a dispute over prices or proprietorship, an attempted shakedown, or a person who ends up being in the wrong place at the wrong time. The willingness to be convinced to take less money, to pay an unfair price, to wait for another day, to let someone else have the advantage—all are predicated on emphasizing the flexibility of a situation, of folding it in to other relationships and events where the participants see that it is worth "letting things slide" for now.

But in the long run, it is not clear what such capacity produces. Most of Kinshasa spends a lot of time literally living between work and home. Distances are great, as the majority of the population live 3 kilometers on average from the nearest available road serviced by motorized transport. The demand for such transport far outpaces what is available, and so walks to key terminals where space on vehicles can be found are often long. The absence of any significant development money means that salaried work, quality schooling, and important commercial and market activity still take place in the city center. Hundreds of thousands converge upon a small administrative and commercial territory on a daily basis, often leaving before sunrise and returning late in the evening. The resulting traffic congestion means a variety of staggered hours and thus the productivity of people's work and commercial activities is greatly reduced. Even though a new market was built in the major population center of Messina some 15 kilometers from the central city in 2001, it has barely made a dent in the practice of people descending upon the central market—a point I will return to a little later.

Similarly, most Kinois live between the urban and the rural. While household compounds may seem to be located in a pastoral setting, the absence of the coherencies of village life regarding land use, social responsibilities, cultivation, and long-established frameworks of social relationships make everyday life that of the urban. At the same time, the lack of services, infrastructure, and institutions maintains the population in a rural-like mode of existence. The overall experience, then, is one of being neither rural nor urban. Whereas the sheer act of crossing the metropolitan region might expose residents to experiences of being both rural and urban, the difficulties entailed in transportation mean that individuals are rarely in one place long enough to really experience this diversity.

Kinois live between veracity and exaggeration, the empirical and the baroque. As everywhere, many topics are not easily talked about, and allusion and euphemism abound. But there is also a pervasive matter-of-factness and precision in people's speech. A woman will quickly tell you the number of loaves of bread she has sold in the past six months; a resident in Bayamu will point out the overcrowded tenements on a random street and tell you the various prices of the rooms without hesitation. Minute details are invoked with great confidence. Whether the content of the assertions is really true is not the point here. Rather, it is the attention to detail. How many sticks of cigarettes is a child street vendor selling on a particular night on a particular block in comparison with the ten other kids working the same turf? How many glasses of whiskey did the commanding police officer buy the night before for the relatives of the *chef du quartier*? What is the exact time the manager of the warehouse for the beer company Primus arrived at the house of the sister of the head of state?

A drug wholesaler in Matete, in a matter of fifteen minutes, identifies the different routes by which heroin, cocaine, and amphetamines enter the city, with an outline of the prices entailed in the many transactions along the way. He can recite the consumption patterns of each of his 657 clients and generate a rapid analysis of exactly how his prices have fluctuated according to different supply trajectories over the past three years, as well as the full names of hundreds of people associated with the various policing authorities he has had to pay off.

All of the details are recited without emotion or hesitation, as if whatever is being spoken about is fully within the natural order of things and could have easily been spoken about with equivalent authority by anyone else. Everything that occurs may somehow be important, if not now, then later on. In a city of few luxuries, and where survival requires constant decisions as to what in the hundreds of conversations, events, and words that surround the individual on a daily basis is important, this almost promiscuous attention to the mundane would seem to be impractical, if not impossible. In a city of incessant trickery, where everyone is trying to take some advantage of each other, it would seem more rational for people to ignore much of what is going on and focus on what really matters—i.e. on the specific details of their current situation. But where individuals are implicated in the lives of both so many known and unknown others, and where it is difficult to get a handle on what is likely to take place in the very immediate future, this kind of paying attention is a constant means of hedging one's bets. It is a way of finding new angles to earn money, get information and opportunity.

This approach to the empirical, of a taking into account the smallest details of transactions of all kinds, makes it possible for individuals to also act as an authority in many matters. It is the basis from which people can speak to various situations, on the street, in the bus, bar, or office, so as to possibly shape the outcome. In this way they do not leave themselves vulnerable to the impact of other people's actions. It provides them a basis to intervene in situations that on the surface would not seem to be their "business" or concern. This is not the act of nosey arrogance, but stems more from the uncertainty as to what one's "business" really is after all. For the boundaries between matters that concern an individual directly and those that may have only a tangential relevance are often fuzzy. No matter how distant they might be, it is often not clear what events will come back to haunt one. And so it is often better to be proactive in advance—not with the speech of opinion but with "facts," which in the end may be nothing more than speculation rendered with cold calculation.

At the same time, Kinshasa is renowned for being a city of exaggeration. Despite the capacities for resilient interactions with others, for changing gear, and finding new opportunities in new affiliations and scenarios, the daily grind for most Kinois is a repetitive search for small money, for drinking beer, and going to church. The details are banal and there is not much basis to make claims for anything else. The precariousness of existence would seem to indicate an overarching need to be precise, to keep things focused and functional. But this is where the exaggeration kicks in. What could be expressed in a simple phrase becomes a highly decorated discourse full of ironies and *double entendre*. The movements of the body, particularly the hips and the ass, during dance, exaltation, and everyday meandering, are accentuated to the obscene.

Music is everywhere, and is perhaps the one constant of Kinois life. Rooted in the rumba, it changes only slightly as it becomes the key instrument of what residents have in common. Thus, it is the backdrop against which Kinois can safely display a sense of singularity and express the raw desire to exceed whatever individuals experience themselves to be. For in the daily grind of looking for money, of dealing with hundreds of others where words must be chosen carefully, of boarding overcrowded vans, and carving out small spaces of safety and health, individuals are always having to "rub shoulders" with others, always having to signal that one knows one's place, even if there are no clear maps to refer to. And so always the obverse is not far away in this practice, the sense that all of these bodies in close proximity—barely arranged and activated in ways that provide a functional separation, a set of functional roles and responsibilities—could converge in some wild assemblage.

Thus the exaggeration of the body and speech—particularly the exaggeration of the sexual—becomes the mechanism to handle a permanent state of excitation that the city offers by its very definition. When the reproduction of family life becomes increasingly difficult; when the assessment of one's life chances basically entails the necessity to leave the country and go somewhere else, and when working hard at school or work promises almost nothing, then the available mechanisms for domesticating this desire to exceed all that one is seem to have little efficacy. At the same time, the dangers of physical desire are well known. The seemingly endless stories of jealousy and witchcraft, the rampant problems of sexual abuse and HIV, and the long history of the use of physical violence in the city on the part of authorities of all kinds make the expression of desire dangerous. So personal expression often assumes baroque forms, particularly in front of the music, as a way of dealing with this dilemma. But the vitality of such expression doesn't necessarily need to have anything to do with personal efficacy, talent, or skill.

For example, Werrason, a.k.a. the King of the Forest, remains Kinshasa's foremost band leader—a position he has maintained now for over a decade. By all conventional aesthetic parameters, Werrason cannot really play musical instruments, dance, or sing—yet he is at the top. While there is a long history that can be told about this, nevertheless Werrason conveys the rawness of that expression of desire, full of its complications, full of its burdens. Yet, it remains a powerful evocation of something that cannot be captured or tamed, something that cannot be made into aesthetics, even if the image of Werrason has been used in all kinds of advertisements. It is an expression that ends up counting for a lot in Kinshasa because it can't be counted. It can't be subsumed as a social event or a pure uninhibited cry for life. Rather, it is full of the detritus of the city, and yet, it doesn't care, it proceeds to act as if there is nothing in its way.

Increasing numbers of Kinois dedicate their lives to the church. With the endless prayer services and financial obligations of the church, it seems as if the majority of the population have tied their existence to a millenarian struggle with the forces of good and evil. They have effectively decided either to hold their aspirations in abeyance to a time of future redemption or basically to accept that God has asked them to be successful in this life no matter what it is, and that he will show a way even in the belly of the beast. But in the exaggerated style of the street, the bar, the terrace, the dancehall, and the weddings, funerals, and graduations, what is conveyed is the extent to which the city is always something more than it is. To be an urban citizen carries with it the responsibility to get "carried away," to show that there is a way of living beyond redemption, correction, policing, sorcery, negotiation, and subterfuge—all of which are practices common to Kinois life.

Of course such exaggeration is itself exaggerated and commoditized. A clear example of this is when individuals hand over wads of cash to have DJs call out their names in the nightclub or on the radio. Even Werrason holds weekly audiences when he is in Kinshasa to lines of people wanting him to call out their names on his records or concerts, all for a price. At a certain point, no matter how sensuously the hips and ass may undulate, the sheer repetition becomes boring. It becomes part of the banal landscape of quotidian activities, and the ability to stand out becomes more difficult. In response, entire imaginary worlds have been created, where the navigation of the local terrain, all the familiar spots and activities, now becomes part of another world.

For example, the young gangsters that gather in the empty market in Matete in the middle of the night believe that they are guarding Area 51 outside of Roswell, New Mexico—the top secret purported landing place of aliens in 1947. They can recite with amazing detail all of the circumstances surrounding this event and the subsequent reports over the years by the U.S. Air Force. They claim to be the descendants of these aliens. This mixture of public delusion with comprehensive knowledge places these gangsters at the intersection of both the real and the imaginary but in a way where neither takes precedence over the other. In order to gain the knowledge they have, they would have had to spend long periods of time poring over documents available on the internet. At the same time, they do not perceive themselves to be researchers carrying out a particular investigation but situate themselves at the heart of the event, at its very beginning. When they go home to sleep at sunrise, a different scenario kicks in because it is only in their relationship with each other that another zone, that of Area 51, is reachable and lived—and, as such, this exaggeration is only really for them.

WHEN CONFIDENCE AND FEAR, PRECISION AND EXAGGERATION PROVE TOO DIFFICULT TO RECONCILE

In a less extreme way, the continued association of the "real city" with the former colonial city and with Europe leads many Kinois to assume that real urban life is located only in Europe. Over the years this has led to an almost cultish obsession with traveling and the subsequent status of the voyager. The airplane has attained iconic status as the instrument of travel, as well as the visa—a document increasingly difficult and expensive for anyone to obtain. Families go to great lengths to find a way for at least one of their members to leave. Those who have an opportunity to study abroad and then make the decision to come back are usually treated with utter derision. How could they possibly, once away, dare to return? At the moment it is especially difficult for the young to travel, even if they have the means, since the government has largely stopped printing passports due to their cost.

For the vast majority who will never go anywhere, then, the imagination is used in order to fold Europe into the everyday life of the neighborhood. The most fortunate and sometimes the most devious go to elaborate lengths to obtain the latest and most expensive clothing fashions which they parade in, constantly pointing to the label. European locations are frequently attributed to a local place; they now become part of Europe and require particular ways of speaking, gesturing, and dressing. Purportedly "white" postures, gestures, and modes of comportment are incessantly imitated. Specific neighborhoods cease to exist as parts of Kinshasa and instead become a European neighborhood requiring the display of specific signs, gestures, and speech in order to gain entry.

On the other hand, it is also important not to stand out. In the everyday life of the neighborhood it is critical not to show that you have money or opportunity. Friends of mine make sure to wear the same shirt for one week in a row to display their limited quantity of clothing. Often homes remain unrepaired so as not to signal an infusion of cash into the household. Initiatives to clean up the street in front of one's house or to improve the general environment are frequently met with trash piled in front of one's door. This hovering around a generalized bottom or the precedence of the least common denominator—i.e. the shared shit of everyday existence—not only makes things seem worse than they are but also makes people have to work harder in terms of making everyday conditions of living somewhat possible.

Whereas it would not take much collective effort to clean the mounds of trash from neighborhood public byways, or clean drainage ditches, or make small improvements to urban services, years of administrative corruption have left neighborhoods feeling that there is no one they can trust to manage local funds collected for these purposes. When the motives of those who take the initiative are suspected, nothing ends up being done, however welcome the intention of the initiative may be.

Another factor here is that Kinshasa is a heavily policed city, and the police have a very visible presence nearly everywhere. What the police actually do, as well as who the police actually are—when considered in relationship to the profusion of private security agencies, government militias and security personal, and the army—is another matter. All of these personnel, as in many countries, are woefully underpaid, and earn their living through extracting bribes and pay-offs. A shifting terrain of legality prevails, as sometimes street trading is tolerated and other times not. Infractions are invented for transport vehicles, which, because of the horrendous road conditions across most of the city, can never maintain the condition that is officially demanded. Complicities with local gangs are rampant, and the police let the gangs do most of the dirty work and then extort a certain percentage of the proceeds. In a country that long tolerated absolutely no dissent and enforced a shifting series of mandatory comportments, attire, and even everyday language, it is nearly impossible for individuals to identify even a limited space of freedom which is theirs. As a result, autonomy is often a negative autonomy, expressed through the refusal to comply or to attend to matters where planning and follow-through are required.

Residents sometimes go to great lengths to dissimulate in order to deal with the omnipresence of surveillance. For example, in order to win some space of autonomy residents will invent certain codes so that they can sell their wares at prices that are not inflated in anticipation of having to pay off the police or to hide the fact that money is being exchanged for a particular service. For example, days of the week will be invoked as representing a particular amount—Monday, 500 Congolese francs; Tuesday, 1,000; and so forth. So, to say, "I will come by on Monday, if you come by on Tuesday" may mean a loan of 500 Cf at a daily interest of 100 percent. Of course, the references are always being adjusted in this cat and mouse game to stay one step ahead of the cop's comprehension. In many ways, Kinois live between the need for veracity, precision, and forthrightness and the need for dissimulation and trickery. People have no choice but to make demands and requests of others.

Before, I indicated that the proficiency of Kinois in speaking with a highly empirical discourse enabled them to act with a certain authority in different situations that come up in everyday life. But, even so, they always face the problem of their own legitimacy—i.e. who are you to make this request; what can you offer in return? In such a scheme, all kinds of deals are made which generate various equivalences—where perhaps radically different amounts, items, favors, and activities are brought into some kind of equation that then allows people to seek assistance from each other or make certain demands.

Sometimes, the problem is that the urgency of the situation forces a person to give up something that goes beyond the value of that which is being asked for. To borrow school fees to get through a month, for example, may require having to devote unpaid labor whose monetary equivalent would otherwise be worth six months. In the proliferation of these deals, then, it is difficult sometimes to calculate what some action or object is really worth. To circumvent having to inflate or reduce otherwise conventionally accepted values, trickery comes to the fore—i.e. to get someone to do something, lend something, or give up something by making them anticipate that they are going to get a good deal somewhere down the line. Trickery is thus everywhere, which in turn heightens the desire for some kind of truth. But at the same time, it is difficult for people to have a sense of what the truth really is.

THE PRACTICES AND IRONIES KINSHASA UNDERTAKES TO LIVE WITH UNCERTAINTY AND THE ROOTLESS

This is a city where the institutions of mediation are weak, where relationships between family members grow more difficult, and where economic needs grow more acute. As such, which authority can be relied upon to convey a sense of truth, especially when many people believe that any claim to authority and legitimacy is invalid simply because a claim is being made?

As Filip De Boeck has so powerfully pointed out, even the definitiveness of death becomes a vortex of confusion regarding what is real and what is not.[4] As he points out, death takes on a carnival atmosphere where those who are supposed to have no role in the rituals of death—the youth—often end up hijacking the proceedings. Funerals become lewd displays of carnal acts and songs, and insults to the older generation, to whom the responsibilities of burial usually belong. Cemeteries become open air markets, with the buying and selling of used coffins and plots, and the demonstration of all the demeanors that would otherwise be prohibited. But for many youth death is simply without any particular truth, and truth without any particular finality. Whatever surrounds it, particularly the pretense of supposedly sacred order, can be upended, can become the object of ridicule as well as invention. Death is the greatest trick of all, played on everyone, and there can be no particular truth associated with it.

De Boeck's work on Kinois funerals also points out the dilemma individuals have regarding the family. Family relations remain potent, all encompassing, and the anchor of everyday urban life. But their power largely rests in their sheer factuality. Kinois often speak about the absence of rapport in families, the speed with which estrangement and reprisals can take place. It is common for family members to disperse and not know where the others are located. Yet mutual obligations remain strong, especially financial ones, and individuals feel they seldom have any choice but to keep the needs of a large number of relatives in mind, even if emotional ties are weak. Family members are quick to accuse each other of sorcery when things go wrong, and their demands are frequently extortionist. Yet, they still provide a kind of hierarchy which people can fit into, a way of finding a place in the city, even if the relationships do not have much content to them beyond their instrumental character.

This is not to undermine the importance of that instrumentality. Kinshasa is a dangerous place, with little recourse to justice of any kind, and residents need protection. If families are a protection racket, so to speak, then they play a crucial role. The irony is that much danger rests within the family, in part because of the intensity of dependencies that take place without a very functional way for family members to talk to each other. This is one reason why the thousands of neighborhood churches across the city play a mediating role between the dangers of the family and the dangers of the street. But again this role is only played implicitly as the overt focus of the church tends to be somewhere else and does not usually explicitly address the dilemmas of either the household or the street.

In fact, Kinois life is replete with false dichotomies and oppositions. No one has any faith in politics—viewing it as a corrupt game that has little to do with the everyday realities people face. As such, there is little popular mobilization or use of politics as a way of disciplining the social body and organizing it for particular ends. One of the few forms of organizational life, besides the church, that has traction in Kinshasa is football. The passion for football is sufficiently intense to mobilize people into large-scale affiliations with particular clubs. The matches sometimes turn into intense fights between rival fan clubs, but more often they channel the passions aroused into a kind of disciplinary force. Fans clubs are expected to demonstrate a capacity for organization and discipline in the public displays of their support, even if at times conflicts are settled in the streets.

Because of the capacity of football to mobilize the youth, that part of the urban population always the most feared by the Congolese rulers, politics depends on football. Important politicians acquire football clubs, and owners of football clubs use their proprietorship as an entry into politics. The potent dissimulation here is that football creates an experience of popular opposition. Youth can be affiliated with rival football clubs and live out this experience in ways similar to that of belonging to a particular political party in opposition to others. While Congo has a formal multiparty democracy, there are no clear ideological or policy differences among the parties—rooted as they are in particular regional and patronage identifications. All parties are generally viewed as corrupt, and there are as many significant internecine battles within parties as there are between them.

Even though football conveys the impression of opposition, with even politicians of opposing parties owning rival clubs, the world of football becomes a vehicle through which these opposing politicians are largely enjoined. For example, two major rival military leaders during the civil war of the past decade acquired rival football clubs in Kinshasa. But they acquired these clubs largely through acquiescing to cooperate with the regime in power, which facilitated the acquisition as a reward for this cooperation. What then looks like the appearance of "real" opposition within the only "game" where seemingly real opposition is permitted turns out to be a kind of ruse to cement political ties.

Again, Kinois seem to live at the intersection of veracity and dissimulation, where even the relationship between the two is a matter of constant trickery. This relationship in the end becomes a kind of public secret, since almost everyone knows exactly that this is the way the "game" (politics and football) is played. But everyone cooperates in maintaining the ruse so as at least to have the sense that somewhere in daily life there is the experience of a "real" collective struggle.

LOOKING FOR THE PUBLIC

Still, the aspiration for something more continues—for the ability of residents to effectively reach each other, mobilize each other beyond their albeit enormously creative capacities to affect each other in the wide range of specific situations they confront day by day. As mentioned earlier, tens of thousands of Kinois converge on the central market on a daily basis. There are many historical reasons for this. Some have to do with the residual insistence upon using the market as a means of making claims on the center—on the right to operate in the center, to be close to what is perceived as the critical nexus of power, and to be close to where the main wholesaling activities were located—in other words, to be closest to the best possible price for particular commodities. This sensibility persists even though many efforts have been made over the years to decentralize the marketing and distribution systems.

Thousands of people operate in the markets with nothing either to sell or to buy—simply taking their chances to make something happen given the sheer density of people from different parts of the city. They act as steerers, carters, rumor mongers, thieves, and facilitators. They act as if they have special information about particular deals or favorable transactions. Because they circulate around and pay close attention to what is happening, to who is trading what with whom, they try to piece these observations together and act as go-betweens among different sellers and customers while taking a little something off the top. Because there are so many things taking place that have nothing directly to do with the actually marketing of basic goods, much of the market has the appearance of complete anarchy. Indeed, any commercial operator who can afford security personnel displays them in great numbers. Even while the getting into and getting out from the central market, let alone navigating its interiors, can prove exasperating and sometimes even dangerous, people continue to pour in.

When people are asked about this, the initial reactions are almost always in reference to finding the best deals, but in further conversations this sense gives way to the conviction that only through the central market will something be put in motion that will change Kinshasa as a whole. This is not to say that people believe that new policies, governments, or infrastructure will emerge from the market itself. Rather, it is only in the market that people are able to get a faint glimpse of an urban public, a Kinshasa that both exceeds the sum of its various districts and operates as a collective force where residents do not have to continuously renegotiate their own individual participation in it. So while the market—replete with competing commercial interests and often exploitative relationships—is not in itself a fully realized public, it is in the market that Kinois are able to concretely maintain an imagination of what a public might be. This is a public that would exceed the highly parochial ways in which the city is governed, the official indifference to the wellbeing of the vast majority of its residents, and the seeming official cluelessness the government demonstrates about how the city actually works. Media are tightly controlled; it is difficult for associations to put their messages out or for there to be any creative displays of provocation, challenge, debate, or even artistic reflection on people's urban experiences.

Over the coming years, any regime that so fears ten million people residing in the capital that it acts in a way that makes it more difficult to really know who those people are and what they are doing will defeat itself. Yet, at the same time, there is very little that takes place in the collective life of urban residents who live through and embody the collision of all these seeming contradictions that prepares it to effectively run the city. Local associations and the trappings of a "real" civil society—in contrast to the proliferation of NGOs that are mostly small-time swindlers—painstakingly work at the most grassroots level with groups of households. They work on how decisions are made and resources used. While this is important work, it is a long way from the world of running municipal institutions, whose existence in Kinshasa has for long been mostly in name only. Still, this is the divide that must be crossed, the divergent logics and ways of being in the city that must be somehow intersected.

IF KINSHASA LACKS INFRASTRUCTURE THEN WHAT DO INFRASTRUCTURE AND TECHNICAL SYSTEMS ACTUALLY DO?

Again, the usual reaction to cities like Kinshasa is to attribute much of what goes on to the lack of infrastructure and functional technical systems. While we have seen that people are the important infrastructure in Kinshasa, technical systems do have much to do with the possibilities of what urban residents can do with each other. In order for there to be productive intersections of people, materials, information, and viewpoints, it is necessary that there exist conduits, routes, circuits, and pathways through which things reach, pass through, and affect each other.

So even if urban technical systems may, on the surface, largely concern the provisioning of water, sanitation, power, and communications, these become matters of concern in that they facilitate specific possibilities of social activity and social relations. They are the precondition for economic life, in that they generate the material conditions through which certain kinds of productive activity are possible. These activities in turn then become the platform through which urban residents mobilize specific resources that they "bring to the table" as inputs in prospective collaborations with each other.

Infrastructure does have specific characteristics which not only join the activities of residents to each other but also establish sometimes rigid parameters as to exactly what people's activities will look like and accomplish. They go a long way to defining what an urban public will look like. The problems of service coverage, affordability, and efficacy are directly related to the specific ways infrastructure and technical systems define the connections between people and space. For example, in order for provisioning systems to attempt universal coverage of water or electrical power, residential and commercial spaces had to be organized in ways that corresponded to the linearity of the pipes and cables that would branch off of major trunk lines.

Certain proximities of residences and commercial activities had to be maintained in order to reduce the costs of carrying underutilized loads over long distances. As Torrance points out,

> every physical infrastructure produced and used has a complementary social infrastructure that is constitutive of a particular system of social relations underpinning the spatial practices producing and using this infrastructure in the first place. This social infrastructure regulates how the infrastructure is planned, built, financed, and maintained; it provides the means to produce the necessary scientific and technical knowledge, as well as the management techniques that not only run the systems but which collect, store and communicate information relevant to the many different facets relevant to the functioning of the systems.[5]

Because of the need to supply materials and services critical to people's domestic lives and the economic survival of a city or region, the organization of technical systems were thought to have an essentially monopolistic character not subject to market forces and which necessitated public regulation. The initial sunk costs of accessing raw supplies, building treatment plants, laying out grids, managing repairs, subsidizing and recovering costs were thought to be beyond the possibilities of profitability for private enterprise, or at least demanded the active intervention of public authorities to mobilize finance and regulate complex systems.

Because the grids, pipes, switching systems, power plants, generators, highways, trunk lines, reservoirs, and most of the components of infrastructure and technical systems lasted a long time, the institutions that were responsible for overseeing them tended to settle into often highly sedentary routines for managing these systems. These routines were not responsive to changes in use or for developing anything more than small incremental innovations.

Because policymakers thought that infrastructure was only viable through economies of scale—where smaller networks are progressively incorporated into larger ones until a designated territory is saturated with the coverage of water, transport, or power—the various public authorities responsible for managing particular infrastructure tended to think of the use, consumption, and consumers of infrastructure in largely global terms. As such, ideas about urban economy and what people did with it were often based on "factory models" about the nature of urban work, household, and domestic life. These ideas reinforced rigid spatial distinctions between the worlds of work, domesticity, leisure, administrative, and public life. Activities had to be located somewhere and there had to be some kind of corporate structure that was to be accountable for the consumption and use of specific resources. As such, there had to be identifiable points of delivery and ways of accounting for specific levels of consumption that could be costed. There had to be transparent records that counted essential materials such as water and power in specific units that were to be provided in specific volumes to identifiable customers.

In the past several decades the concepts and modalities of urban infrastructure provision have changed substantially, and with them notions about urban consumers. This is the result of the fiscal burdens faced by municipal and regional authorities, the increased competition between cities, the heightened emphasis on the management of decentralized components of production systems, concerns about the environment and the ascendant ecological understandings about material flows, and changes in the conceptualization of public authority and its role in provisioning systems. As a result, notions of provisioning and technical systems were differentiated into a greater variety of products and services, managed by private corporations, and set in competitive relationships with each other.[6]

Diversification meant that it was now possible for particular quantities, qualities, and guarantees of services to be provided for specific kinds of customers at a particular price by private companies. These companies would manage a particular portion of either a public good, such as water, or specialized technical goods, such as components of information and communications technologies, through licensing arrangements with states or municipalities. As Offner indicates, technical systems increase the "available stock of geographical levels from which various social, political, and economic players can draw their supplies, according to their own rationale and strategy."[7] If this is the case, then the provisioning of infrastructure no longer need be associated with the political institutions of a particular city.

As Torrance points out, the character of infrastructure as linked into and managed by a single political territory is increasingly unbundled and inter-linked internationally through various investment funds that acquire different infrastructure assets in different parts of the world as a way to spread financial risks. Through the use of contractual obligations that public authorities enter into with private investors and which govern the management of a highway, sanitation or water system, investors are given the opportunity to invest in urban assets that are now managed outside of the local political sphere yet still impact upon the city.

Additionally, in Europe and North America municipal utilities and regional suppliers form strategic alliances in order to negotiate cheaper purchases of bulk supplies of water and energy. These alliances assume that commercial actors, public institutions, and households within a city will require different kinds of services, depending not only on the specific form of their activity but also on where it is taking place. Since the materials that go into provisioning systems are not drawn from within cities themselves, different cities will find ways of collaborating in the management of these resources. As Monstad et al. point out, the components of technical systems have spatially expanded and grown because the technologies that manage them across different territories and regions now converge. They converge through transnationally valid norms and standards, the physical links of diverse networks, and the role of international companies in managing them. At the same time, through the development of low-cost innovative technologies—such as gas turbines, steam, small-scale fuel cells, and renewable energy generating plants, and membrane technology–technical networks and supply systems can also become decentralized and insular. Such decentralization can either promote ongoing innovation and greater efficiency in resource use as supply and demand are more effectively matched, or result in leaving certain urban areas under-serviced or overpriced.

The importance of these comments on infrastructure is to point out how technical and provisioning systems put in place certain possibilities for what urban residents can do with each other and how they can connect and see their lives as either conjoined or separate. Public action and space are dependent upon the kinds of enabling materials that are provided and the ways in which provision is managed. Many claims have been made about how diversifying and respatializing urban service provisioning and corporatizing technical systems fragments and polarizes cities—how it further disassembles their public character. Although in many cases it is clear that residents can be pulled apart, there are other potentials that also could be at work.

It would seem that changes in the provisioning and management of essential infrastructure and urban services make the ways that people live, work, and collaborate within cities more flexible and varied. Urban management need no longer be bound to economies of scale. Both management and technical systems may now be better equipped to put together innovative ways of building residences, expanding what activities count as work, and re-arrange the social ties between people operating near and far from each other. Changes in infrastructure provisioning and management would also seem to bring residents spread across different cities into closer political ties. These ties could, in turn, achieve more effective environmental regulations.

Yet, infrastructure services developed as commodities paid for on the basis of recorded use and targeted access raise the specter of how water and power were provided in many colonial cities. Here, service provision was used to mark fundamental differences in the status and rights of residents. For example, the provision of piped water was frequently used as a political instrument to signal specific urban populations as sufficiently worthy and responsible to be considered legitimate urban residents.

Even to this day in many cities of the Global South, the poor, often highly dependent upon water vendors, spend a disproportionate amount of their daily income on water in comparison to other urban residents. Even when the per unit costs of piped water are substantially less than vended water, meter fees, annual charges, storage costs, and the often exorbitant connection fees make the total cost of water unaffordable for urban residents. Even when they are willing to absorb those costs, they still find it difficult to do so in places where tenure is insecure and the implications for making upgrades in rental accommodation remain uncertain. In many cities, even when contracting out to private operators was done in the name of securing universal coverage, pricing contracts tended to be calculated in terms of the unit of volume of water delivered to the distribution network rather than in terms of the billing revenue. As a result, municipal governments continued to bear the responsibility of cost recovery. These arrangements, in combination with lack of political commitment, the spatial orientations of existing supply systems, and poor management, are significant disincentives to providing essential services to the poorer segments of cities.[8]

For the poor, the search for water and power takes up time that could be devoted to other economic and social activities. Also, local competition over scarce resources gets in the way of cooperation among neighbors. For example, in a neighborhood with both flat and hilly terrain, low water pressure may mean that piped water is only delivered to the lower terrain of a community, giving a specific advantage over access to the people who live there. This advantage can then be parlayed into a larger economic advantage when these residents sell portions of this water supply "upstream." In crowded neighborhoods, certain residences may have opportunities to store water that others may not have. In neighborhoods where most of the area is impassable by truck, those living by passable roads then have opportunities to hoard water as they are at the first point of contact. In addition, certain powerful figures, such as a local businessperson, politician, or religious leader, may exert sufficient influence to divert and accumulate supplemental volumes of a given resource that are then parceled out as a means of mobilizing loyalty.

An interesting dimension of this process is the extent to which residents are captured by their specific positions, proximities, and relative privileged positions in relation to a particular resource, such as water, or whether they are able to do something else. There are times when residents will "trade" on their positions—i.e. use them as chips in a larger game. In other words, residents who may be adept at managing the carrying of water across a neighborhood, or have room to store water for others, or who may live next to points of easy access, may use these positions in transactions having nothing to do with water *per se*. If a neighborhood is full of practices of compensation that are continuously being put together and remade in order to maximize the volume of water that any single resident can get their hands on, then the brokerage that takes place around the supply of water can also be converted into other economic activities. As a result, residents do not either feel trapped in having to continuously re-secure their privileged positions or feel trapped in not having them. It is precisely this kind of deal-making that not only enables better access to limited services but begins to tie together different facets of local economic life in ways that not only keep debilitating competition within tolerable levels but sometimes produce new synergies among discrepant people and their activities that otherwise might not be possible.

IF INFRASTRUCTURE ESTABLISHES A PLATFORM FOR MOVEMENT, HOW THEN DO PEOPLE MOVE AROUND THE CITY?

What people in cities can do with each other and how their lives and actions intersect of course have a lot to do with how people move around and through the city. We are well accustomed to experiencing cities as an amalgamation of different spaces, histories, functions, and possibilities. Although for a variety of reasons some urban residents may always stay close to home, it is increasingly difficult to conduct one's life in narrow territories of operation. This does not mean that efforts are not made to try and make the things we must do and their locations seem close to home. We usually try to make the discrepant places we must cross and perform particular activities within familiar. At times, we might assume that all of these different spaces, histories, functions, and possibilities are held together by some overarching force or rationality; that somehow whatever makes them different—by virtue of the particular character of people living or operating there and the activities that take place—is not sufficiently distinctive or powerful to override a dependence that each different district in a city has upon the others. And just in case, there is the insurance offered by integrated scales of governing and accountability, where decisions made at the levels of nation, state, and city governments would seem to structure the relationships different parts of the city have with each other. The transfer of funds, the enrollment of resources and residents in various modalities of participating in the urban system as a whole—through citizenship and other forms of belonging, through the cross-subsidization of public goods and services, and through the use of infrastructure—would seem to guarantee coordination of differences and their ultimate coherence.

Even the customary spatial layout of the modern city in its logic of grids enforces the sense that distinctive locations are clearly recognizable in terms of their relationship with others. Grids are a means of designation, registration, and accountability. They specify routes of access and exit, and make possible the clear definition of sectors and zones. They offer a particular calculation of distance that is self-referential in that it can overshadow other perceived or felt measures of how close or far things are to one's experience. It becomes a way of making "locational decisions"; in other words, decisions about where to put things such as particular businesses, services, public facilities, or residences based on a seemingly transparent overview of where things are in the city as a whole. Grids permit the calculations of population densities and spatial use patterns. They are an important tool in decisions about what makes up legitimate and viable uses of the spaces in the city.[9] Even when layouts don't consist of straight lines, like many suburban developments with their circular drives, they remain coherent enclaves with clearly designated connections to the rest of the city. They are embedded within easily mapped frameworks of use often aided by the sheer sameness in the way residences and businesses are made to look.

Certainly there is a substantial thickness to the relations among all the different things and persons that compose urban life. There are many places within the city to which residents will seldom if ever go, and many reasons available for them to justify these decisions. It is easy for us to think that people who live in certain places are not within our personal or professional networks. There are always territories of people who belong to cultural and social categories that are different from ours. Additionally, there are similar services and opportunities that can be found closer to home or in areas more compatible with or convenient to our lifestyles and schedules. Just because residents may often not know much about the spaces of the city beyond where they live this does not constitute a factor for them questioning the "integrity"—the overarching order—of the city as a whole. When people don't know much about each other, they are often tempted to impose their interests, values, and ways of doing things on the larger city. They do so by trying to shape the city's policies, rules, and regulations. Yet, most residents seem to realize that such impositions are not practical, or even desirable, and accede to the fact that large levels of uncertainty are a fact of urban life.[10]

The location of key institutions, entertainments, public facilities, and shopping areas within a city's downtowns, central areas, and feeder areas has traditionally brought diverse urban populations together in a kind of mutual witnessing without making it incumbent upon them to constantly work out the details of their being together. The dispersal of residential opportunities far beyond the city center, and the subsequent dependence on automobiles, diffuses the tensions and conflicts produced by the proximity of urban differences.[11] At the same time, the profusion of media—newspapers, television shows, internet sites and blogs—creates a sense that the city, in all of its aspects, is available. Media heighten local knowledge about the city and enable residents to more proficiently zero in on the kinds of experiences they desire regardless of where they might be located.

In other words, navigation does not depend very much on making generalizations concerning specific territories within the city. Rather, what is more important is a sense of location that is much more site-specific. Particular things can be experienced or consumed regardless of how much people may know about the specifics of the place in which these sites are located. Restaurants, galleries, clubs, small businesses, boutiques, and so forth then can search for financially advantageous conditions in places that are not necessarily known for housing their particular kinds of activities. Those who start these ventures realize that it is possible to cultivate a more "knowing" clientele amongst a wide span of the city's population. The search for cheap rents, properties, labor, and costs drives certain businesses to margins of all kinds and to locations that otherwise would not be necessarily compatible. But once they occupy these spaces they then engineer these compatibilities. As a result, the connections between these areas and the rest of the city become much more extensive. Usually, over time, each district of a city becomes increasingly more complex in terms of the kinds of activities taking place within it. Of course districts have their own particular histories of ascendancy and decline. There are areas that lose substantial proportions of their population and businesses. But in some cases, depending on their locations and proximities to places of some economic vitality, these districts become readily available to various forms of renewal.[12]

Of course these decisions about where to locate residences and businesses often come down to a matter of different preferences. For example, some people prefer lots of space around them and are willing to put up with driving long distances to work and other places in order to act on this preference. Others prefer to have a lot of amenities and opportunities around them and are willing to forego space and cars. The expression of preferences is constrained by a spatial structure and built environment that endure and are not easily changed, thus limiting the numbers and combinations of preferences that can actually be acted upon. Additionally, as Storper and Mandaville point out, certain expressed preferences really don't fully capture a resident's intentions or aspirations, but sometimes are seen either as the lesser of two evils or the necessary baggage that comes with another set of preferences. For example, a family may not really want to live in the central city but do so for the range of educational choices such location may offer.

Just as cities bundle particular configurations of housing, transport, services, and work locations in different ways, so too are people's preferences bundled. As a result, there will be particular components and aspects of such bundles that people won't prefer, and points of tension will always arise.[13] But it is these points of tension which contribute to keeping cities dynamic and policymaking significant in terms of shaping the contexts through which different preferences can be acted upon. Just as individual lifestyles and livelihoods are partly built on a bundle of different preferences—some of which, in Storper's terms, are un-preferred in and of themselves, and thus become a matter of trade-offs—many relationships between urbanites are also built on trade-offs. Therefore, much of what urban residents do with each other is based on a series of trade-offs and sought after complementarities among different kinds of enacted preferences. The more that different kinds of preference can find concrete expression, the more basis there is for people to collaborate in some way since no set of preferences can be comprehensive—be everything someone needs or wants.

GIVEN INFRASTRUCTURE AND MOVEMENT, WHAT ARE THE TRAJECTORIES OF URBAN DEVELOPMENT?

In the discussion on Kinshasa, I talked about the way in which residents seemed to live along multiple instances of parallel tracks, tendencies, and trajectories, and the difficulties entailed in putting together urban publics. In a not dissimilar way, across the cities of the world, two trajectories of urban development seem to have been happening at the same time. On the one hand, cities grew more complicated, with residents more activated and even vociferous in their demands for specific services, affordances, and opportunities. The field of consumption becomes more differentiated as urban economies generate accumulation based on the proliferation of niche markets. As such, residents gravitate toward specific lifestyles in a place where they are surrounded by others like them. Rather than defend rights over a district shared with many different types of residents and of commercial and administrative activities, residents increasingly "find their own space" in the development of new residential areas beyond the central city or in the recuperation of economically and socially marginal areas within it.[14]

On the other hand, the disentanglement of diverse populations and sectors of activity is seldom comprehensively complete or total. Different settlement histories are at work and intersect in different ways. Within these histories are different capacities for making things happen. New ground is charted. Sometimes, different ways of life seem to condense in that they "hold their place" in more narrow, sometimes stereotyped, versions of themselves. Particular kinds of neighborhoods, with particular kinds of residents and ways of doing things, may extend themselves across the city. They may disappear in some places and reappear in others. They may fracture and regroup as smaller enclaves in different parts of the city, or simply integrate themselves into other more predominant forms of social identity. A highly mixed neighborhood of different kinds of residents and activities may simply become available to mixtures of a new kind. What starts out as a highly homogenous area may over a matter of decades become highly mixed or vice-versa. In other words, gentrification, decline, sustainability, diversification, and growth—to name a few of the keywords attached to critical urban processes—do not necessarily take place in stable and clearly recognizable ways.[15]

What this means is that it may be necessary to shift our common understandings about the relations among differences in the city. Instead of assuming a fundamental field of thick connections, aided by frameworks and practices of governance, spatial arrangements within the city may also take on a much more fractal dimension. They are fractal in that they posit ways of being in and navigating the city largely rooted in the specificity of a particular district's own singular ways of doing things, rather than adhering to an overarching logic of urban civility and communicational practice.[16] In other words, we are used to thinking that different areas of the city negotiate or "buy into" a consensually determined way of dealing with each other. We assume that they communicate their realities to one another. That they use the political and administrative processes supported by municipal government to "put their case on the map" and determine how the different areas of the city are to be linked to each other. Instead, when we see this as a fractal process, it means that the different areas of the city use what they recognize as their own particular ways of doing things as the method through which they act on the city as a whole.[17] This means that a sense of an urban public becomes much more complex. While notions of citizenship and rights to the city may remain important, they may no longer adequately cover all that needs to be thought in terms of the making of urban publics—the sense that people can exceed the particularities of their everyday situations and be part of something larger.

Particularly in many cities of the urban South, the conventional frameworks of organization, such as the preponderance of the grid, were not extensively present. This didn't mean that without the grid these cities didn't experience a powerful sense of interconnectedness or that their subterritories were simply small bastions of singularities that had little to do with each other. In many cities built or substantially remade for colonial economies, the imposition of grid systems did take place. But these grids then often existed only for areas of the city designated for European settlers or in cases where the spatial configurations of the city appeared so complex and opaque that grids were forced to be partial.[18]

The histories of many Global South cities document the absence of systematic zoning laws and cadastral systems designating property ownership and use. Additionally, there are usually many different and competing frameworks of land ownership, tenancy, and use. The major metropolitan areas of

Asia and Africa tend to remake the central city by displacing poor residential districts, small- and medium-scale industrial and service enterprises to the periphery of urban areas, and installing what is by now the familiar array of premium commercial, tourist, and service infrastructure in the center.

Even so, the massive growth of the periphery takes on a highly differentiated composition of residential, agricultural, leisure, industrial, and service activities, all with different economic capacities. In other words, the periphery becomes perhaps even more conventionally "urbanized" than the center.[19] With this shift of complexity to the periphery and the overall difficulties entailed in re-imagining the ways in which viable urban publics might be made, there is the temptation to avoid the problem altogether and think about urban development in other ways. This avoidance of the "real urban problem" has been partly demonstrated through what might be called the financial models of urban development—to be taken up in Chapter 4.

Take the situation where you arrive at a party with a friend or partner. After a few minutes, having grabbed a drink, you announce to the person that you came with that you are now going to circulate. And so you proceed to go around the space of the party talking to people already situated in different combinations of conversation that are likely to rapidly change. You move from one set of conversations to another amongst groups of shifting composition. You never really stay very long in any one place and don't dwell intensely on what anyone is saying, since prolonged conversations limit your ability to exit and move on to the next one. In such a situation, people and their stories and situations seem to rapidly bounce off each other. Although many convergences are possible—i.e. reports about mutual friends, movies everyone has seen—this is not a context in which people's situations really intersect. This is not a context for reflection or deliberation, or of experimentation or provocation in anything other than a perfunctory or easily playful way.

In the past two decades strong emphasis has been placed on circulation as a way of producing value and as a means of remaking cities. The idea has been to bring a lot of different things together that have no long or intensive history of being together and to quickly see what comes out of it. Since whatever is brought together—people, materials, things, backgrounds, instruments—has not settled into a particular style or mode of being together, it is never quite certain what can happen. But it is this unanticipated, volatile process that is viewed as having value because it potentially produces something unprecedented—i.e. some critical innovation, or something that no one else has done before. Bringing highly discrepant ways of doing, calculating, and valuing things together is imagined to open up various unforeseen opportunities for each component. These relationships can be volatile—given how little the different things brought together may have in common. Since there may be difficulties to smooth over and work out the tensions and incompatibilities that are likely to ensue, here a lot of time or commitment is probably not going to be invested. So circulation is a matter of "hit and run"—see what happens and if there are not quick results or profits then things must move on, circulate to the next round of relations.

In this chapter I want to explore this notion of circulation and the way it puts aside certain notions of intersection and the role it plays in maintaining the dynamism of urban life. Since circulation has been a critical linchpin in the growth of finance capitalism, much of this discussion will center on the relationship between cities and finance economies, particularly on the financial instruments that have been invented to attain new forms of circulation. Particularly in the major cities of Europe and North America, it has been the circulation of money, credit, and other financial instruments that has shaped urban economies, with profound spin-offs on cities across the world, as we can see by the severe contraction of this circulation in the deep recession of 2008.

CITIES AND THE MODELS OF FINANCE

There are many different pulls on how urban space is shaped. Certainly the applications of finance capital have produced some of the most sweeping and visible changes in cities. Massive construction projects of commercial and residential units in remade downtowns and central cities substantially inflate the price of land. Because finance capital is not rooted in the concrete processes of making things, of organizing specific practices of labor, or having to engage the contextual specificities of particular locations, it is easily shifted across different sites and applications. The way finance circulates through cities and concretizes particular uses of urban space is key to the possibilities of profit making.[1]

The emphasis in past years on derivatives, commercial paper, and credit default swaps demonstrates that a substantial proportion of the accumulation of financial resources centers on the conversion of one form of finance capital to another. In other words, while "real" things continued to be produced—wheat, oil, steel, for example—at specific costs, under specific conditions, and then sold for specific prices—there are a wide range of financial instruments in play that basically make money from the anticipations, hedges, and manipulations of how those costs and prices might change. Since production units must pay for depreciation and pay shareholders as well as interest on loans, wages in circulation are never sufficient to consume all that is produced. New consumers and new consumer needs have to be produced in order to absorb all the goods and services that are in circulation.

In order to afford these goods, consumers have to borrow money from the future. Banks create money by the creation of liabilities (debts). These debts are then paid off using a portion of the anticipated proceeds of future production. Maintaining a high rate of profit in the present becomes tied to attempts to fix just how much of future production needs to be dedicated to paying off debts in the present. As a result, a wide range of mechanisms are used to control risks which are seen as impacting upon what is likely to happen in the future. These mechanisms include locking the purchase of future supplies to a specific price, specifying the conditions under which certain prices of commodities and services will be available, generating various options to acquire materials in the future, or "rolling over" debt repayment to some future time. The mechanisms are organized by contracts that are themselves bought and sold like money. As such, it largely doesn't matter if these contracts originally had to do with some specific product, like wheat or rubber.

Additionally, differences in tax exposures, accounting requirements, production schedules, currency rules, and liability structures on the part of companies operating in specific countries and regions can be "packaged," bought and sold, as speculations on what is likely to happen in the future to various economic transactions. These are essentially bets on the probability that certain events and processes will either disrupt or make possible continuities in the supply of food, oil, manufactured items, pharmaceuticals, or water. It is common to have contracts such as the following: a major bank agrees to pay a Mexican investor 7 percent on a deposit of 100 million pesos every day that the national Mexican interest rates remain less than 3.2 percent and, conversely, accrue 9 percent of the deposit when those interest rates exceed the 3.2 percent benchmark.[2]

Yet profits have depended upon these volatile movements of prices—of currencies, insurance, shares, interest, and debt—up and down. It is a situation where all assets act like money. Their value is not predicated on what these assets are supposed to be used for or what function they are made for. Rather, their value is calculated in terms of the price movements of different types of assets with which they have no intrinsic or obvious relation. Wheat is tied to rubber, rubber is tied to optic fibers, and optic fibers are tied to pharma-ceuticals, simply because their price histories and fluctuations are brought together in a single financial instrument.

WHEN URBANIZATION GOES BEYOND THE CITIES

What is important to this discussion is the way in which this process of circulation becomes a form of urbanization. In other words, ideas about the remaking of actual cities have recently been quite limited in part because finance economies have themselves become a way of urbanizing relationships—an urbanizing less dependent upon the concrete realities of actual cities. We know that the production of commodities has been dispersed all across the world. Resources to make things are sought from areas where supplies are plentiful, labor is cheap, and long-term claims to inputs and markets can be more easily solidified and defended. But this exposure to a large world comes at a price. For example, the money a com-pany puts into a particular location and the marginal increase in living standards attained by workers in a factory, sweat shop, or mine will eventually broaden the local demand for things to consume and, over time, raise the price of doing business in this location.

Since there are always other places where the cost of labor and the costs of dealing with government tax structures, bur-eaucracies, and transportation systems are lower, the issue for investors is how much money they should put into developing a specific site and operation. How prepared should they be to have their sneakers or circuit boards, for example, made somewhere else, or their phones answered or basic paperwork processed in another city? Then there are issues about the volatility of climates, civil conflicts, changes in governments and rules, and increased competition among firms wanting to lock down particular supplies and advantages in a particular place. All of these factors affect the costs and thus the profits that can be expected.

As such, firms attempt to protect themselves against these uncertainties by trying to tie down and lock in the prices they will pay for specific amounts of goods and services in the future, or specify the conditions under which they will honor contracts or pay for particular services. Of course, actual conditions of production and trade still will be subject to many uncertainties. Costs, prices, profits, and consumption will rise and fall according to these uncertainties. It is also difficult to determine all of the factors that will affect what food, oil, and consumer goods will cost in a particular location as events near and far and the behavior of untold others come into play. Usually, as firms begin to operate in much more expansive global arenas, the factors that impact on local conditions are not necessarily very local.

Tens of thousands of firms are also seeking more solid guarantees from a future that their own larger exposure to the world itself makes more complicated. As such, any single firm's efforts to tie this future down—to be more flexible and mobile; to distribute the different facets of making things and running the firm across more supposedly advantageous sites—end up making the present more volatile. Movements of prices up and down may be more accelerated; smaller increases or decreases in prices and costs may take on greater significance. As a result, firms rely upon financial instruments to try and make the future more certain. They hedge against the risks of working in places where social, transportation, political, and climatic conditions are either not well developed or unstable—but where the possible profits are high. If attaining high profit margins requires firms to be opportunistic in taking advantage of unforeseen opportunities—i.e. to acquire particular goods and services or to operate in particular markets—firms also don't want to necessarily be tied down to the investment, insurance, or borrowing instruments through which they have tried to tie down the future. So these instruments also change hands in a wide range of swaps or are traded in markets, used as securities in deals that have nothing to do with the conditions and motivations that were at play at the time a firm had originally pieced them together.

What then occurs is a more extensive and intensive circulation of bonds and securities, interest rate swaps, collateral debt obligations, and other derivatives of all kinds. All of these varied ways of trying to simultaneously specify the conditions—under which firms will do something, make something or pay for something in the future, and be more flexible and footloose in how they can operate—end up in more complicated and provisional relationships with each other. In other words, bonds, securities, debt obligations, and derivatives circulate and pass through each other.

Firms still have clear indications of the profits they are making and the extent to which the goods they produce continue to have viable markets. However, the overall value that is generated by what a firm does in a particular place and time becomes less and less clear. In other words, the impact of the goods and services a firm produces on all other goods and services in existence becomes increasingly difficult to assess. The interest rates on the money they borrow, the ways they seek to make their workers' pension funds more profitable, the way they try to lower transaction costs of all kinds—all of these facets of the firm are also being bought and sold, changing hands and being repackaged. They become instruments of speculation, where money is to be made through making prices more volatile, of manipulating small differences between prices and costs in different locations.

For example, in the most basic and safe version of "selling

short" an investment firm might borrow or rent a certain quantity of stocks from another company and sell them off at a particular price. By thus anticipating the probable fall in the price of these stocks, they then buy them back at the lower price, return them to their original owners, and keep the money they made through manipulating the difference in prices.

It is thus possible to think of an increasingly "urbanized" world of abstract, even ephemeral, financial instruments through which value circulates in highly dense relationships almost impossible to map. Unlike a real city, where for all of its complexity and sometime chaos it is possible to identify real actors and real places with clear differences, agendas, roles, and territories of operation, this kind of urbanization tends to operate with great opacity. It also brings together places, conditions, circumstances, ways of life, and materials that otherwise maintain a great distance and high degree of separation in the "real" world. Derivatives can attempt to secure, insure, hedge, leverage, or speculate on a particular price and cost for a firm, and then can be repackaged with the efforts of many other discrepant firms trying to do many different things with their money and opportunities.

Through these derivatives, for example, the coltan that is used for cell phones and mined in highly informal and dangerous conditions in Eastern Congo and which must travel great distances on bad and insecure roads to get to often inefficient ports in Mombasa and Dar es Salaam can be lumped into a relationship with the circuit boards made under usually stable conditions in the Eastern Seaboard Region of Thailand to be delivered just-in-time to Taiwan and China, where they will be assembled into a wide range of electronic products. Two commodities, one sourced from usually stable conditions and the other from usually unstable ones, and from two very different parts of the world, are brought together. They pass through each other with the use of an abstract financial instrument that seeks to mix different kinds of values and motivations as a way of apportioning risk. In other words, it uses risk as something to be defended against and, conversely, sought out for the high profits that it might bring. As such it reflects the willingness of some economic actors to pay to take a chance to get advantages that others then will not have.

It is of course possible over time to trace out the various ways in which Eastern Congo and Thailand have "real" relationships with each other. But, in this particular version of an "urbanized" world of financial relationships, these "real ones" are made more peripheral—their histories and concrete ties are basically irrelevant. For if highly dense relationships among very different places, conditions, and materials can be engineered at great speed, and if the specific distances and differences that otherwise would keep places apart can be overcome or made immaterial, what are those "real relationships" now? How do they count and what do they count for?

In light of the massive world financial crisis that started in 2008, there is likely to be a substantial return to past realities. But it will be difficult to completely change or circumvent the fascination with circulation and the idea that circulation is about things simply passing through and passing by, intersecting only in highly abstract ways, and where the conditions that defined the places, sectors, products, and circumstances to intersect really didn't matter.

WHEN CITIES BUILD FOR SHORT FUTURES

With this logic of circulation, companies, investors, and service providers have often implanted themselves in cities where they otherwise really had no historical relationship. Places can be remade rapidly without regard to how they then subsequently relate to the economies and cultures of the rest of the city. For example, insurance companies may rush into Phnom Penh simply because banks, tourist agencies, venture capital firms, and engineering companies are moving in, and not because there is any clear history or current tendency for residents and local commerce to buy insurance. Some companies are there simply to service each other, and end up paying little attention to the context in which they are implanted.

The monumental dimensions of "big projects" seem to demonstrate a new form of efficacy through which all facets of urban life are to be compared, and thus seen as lacking something. Real estate, architecture, engineering, spectacle, and media combine in projects intended to draw new lines between commerce, entertainment, culture, finance, tourism, and residence. Instead of organizing space into discernible and thus predictable territorial, social, and economic relations, these speculative products depend upon and mark a sense of fragmentation and temporariness.[3]

This temporariness stems from several factors. First, many investors in these big projects simply acquire commercial or residential units in order to sell them off within a few years before any assessment can be made about the long-term viability of the project. They capitalize on a certain "herd mentality" whereby groups of companies and investors converge on particular sites simply because everyone else is doing so. Second, many of these projects are initiated and developed not with any immediate sense of the markets they're supposed to work in or any sense of their short- and medium-term viability, but simply because these projects claim space. They consume prime, high-value locations and build major shopping or commercial complexes in order to keep others from staking their own claims. So even if subsequent occupancy rates remain low, investors remain convinced that, at some point in the future, the infrastructure they have put in place will inevitably be used for something and generate value, even if it is not for the purposes intended.

Additionally, these interventions into the built environment are a means to launder illicit money and for illicit economies to gain access to the formal financial system. Regardless of their veracity, rumors, for example, that the megalopolis of Dubai is largely being built with Russian mafia money point to a widely held assumption that big urban projects put illicit financial capital to work.

Perhaps more importantly, finance capital requires architecture in order to circulate. Money must be put to use in order to cultivate opportunities to spread out and be applied to a wide range of situations—which is why it must be placed somewhere.[4] Efforts to use big projects to bring together different kinds of actors—politicians, architects, consulting firms, engineers, lawyers, accountants, public relations, media in a multifaceted interaction of labor, infrastructure, and technology—are meant to cultivate capacity and knowledge that can make things happen beyond the city. On the one hand, it takes time to develop such capacity—even when so many resources are brought together in highly advantageous conditions. On the other hand, there is also the pressure to act quickly, given the competition amongst cities, and to exert a force with wide-ranging effects even when knowledge is a scarce commodity.

This need to operate with speed thus limits the scope of what all of these actors can actually do with each other. Extra-economic dimensions, such as creativity, cooperation, and trust, remain key elements of any effort to bring actors, things, and decisions within the orbit of a specific city. Their value, however, is calculated in terms of how they make the city more competitive—not in terms of what the city is actually capable of doing for its residents—but in a mostly abstract sense of how much inward investment the city can attract and hang on to.

BIG PROJECTS AND THE ROLES IN BUILDING BIG URBAN ECONOMIES

Big urban development projects provide the concrete opportunity for financiers, politicians, engineers, planners, developers, and corporate consortia to come together and try to make the city a place that enables their operations to circulate widely across the world.[5] States invest heavily in projects aimed at revaluing urban land and producing substantial rent income which it is thought will translate into a higher tax base. Because the apportionment of responsibilities and accountability among partners is rarely well defined in many of these project developments, it is unclear whether public authorities and the city as a whole really benefit from them. As a result, states are often left holding the bag in terms of covering deficits.

Part of this opacity stems from the often irregular ways different streams of finance come together. This represents relatively new forms of cooperation between actors that have little prior experience with each other or, alternatively, require these projects as the very means through which their different interests can converge. These collaborations usually prove immune from public scrutiny and are, in fact, aimed at excluding real public participation.

Many big urban projects are meant to be fungible. In other words, the projects can be financially and spatially connected to uses that have nothing to do with their original intent. As such, these developments don't so much "exist for themselves." Rather, they aspire to become valuable facets of larger packages that bundle together real estate, financial instruments, and shifting trajectories and forms of investments from which new conditions of management, urban politics, and taxation schemes become inevitable. Bringing all different kinds of actors and money together in dense spatial arrangements acts as a way of visualizing uncertainty since spaces can be developed for users and purposes that have no clear historical or economic connection to them. Territorial claims become "bets on the future," hedged to the eventual remaking of anything that exists.

Of course, there are other logics and developments at work in the cities under consideration besides these big projects and the finance model of urban development. This is not to say that such big projects, by absorbing substantial municipal resources and attention while enrolling the cooperation of key politicians and administrators, do not inevitably exert considerable power over the city. But the persistence of other trajectories of urban life means that a more "fractal" city is produced—one that compels new behaviors from its residents.

The fragmentation of urban space is also promoted by the particular ways cities connect to globalized economies. Saskia Sassen's well-known thesis on the importance of cities to the making of global economies emphasizes the challenges of exerting centralized control over economic activities that are intentionally dispersed across the world.[6] Firms look for cheaper labor markets within which to make their products, manage their accounts and bureaucracies, and store their supplies and inventories. Continuous innovations in information and communication technologies make coordination possible across geographical distance. They enable the activities of the firm to "hang together" without depending on the physical proximity of a firm's various functions and departments. Yet as this dispersal takes place across many different locations coordination is no easy matter—as each location has its own particular histories, politics, regulatory systems, and ways of doing things. As Sassen points out, central control over dispersed activities requires more complicated forms of management and thus expansion of headquarter functions. Locations will shift, as will the rules of the game, the legal frameworks, the transportation routes, and the political and economic conditions. Relationships between sources of supplies, suppliers, transporters, financiers, managers, politicians, distributors, and retailers will also change as each looks for more advantageous positions. Long-term contractual relationships between firms fade into more short-term deals.

Given this situation, there have been enormous increases in the number of corporate service firms that provide a range of specialized skills to firms on various occasions. These include special financial and legal services, accounting, public relations, international arbitration mediation, and media that enable firms to maximize the benefits of technological connectivity and act decisively and coherently across discrepant settings. It is not just information per se that is important. If a firm making cell phones gets important materials from volatile political environments such as the Eastern Congo, manufactures high-tech components in Malaysia and Taiwan, assembles products in Vietnam and Mexico, and then forges various deals with service providers in countries across the world, the critical information required is not easily generalized from other histories and situations of manufacturing. The context-specific intersections of many different kinds of assessment, data, styles of interpretation, and corporate experiences must be analyzed and used as a basis for action. This kind of knowledge is facilitated through the synergistic effects of having many different kinds of capacities, knowledge, and operating procedures available in dense relationships with each other in a single city, often in a single district.

At times this density will manifest itself as central business districts. At other times, depending on the kind of products or activities firms specialize in, centrality will take place in specialized research and development zones, science and technology parks, or specialized "cities" devoted to particular sectors, such as Dubai's "Media City" and "University City." Centrality is also constructed through premium spaces of interchange networked across cities, such as ATT's business networks, which provide a specialized series of support services for participants which, in turn, allow continuous interactions among them. These forms of spatiality are connected to material arrangements which are inter-territorial or trans-territorial. What this means is that activities which "occur together" depend on a flow of interactions across varied distances, i.e. circuits of exchange and movement, nodes or hubs, and locales of support and social cohesion for the dominant players.[7]

A trans-territorial city is made possible through the connections among telecommunications and customized communication, intra- and inter-organizational communication networks, business class air travel, networks of hotels and business centers, conferencing, cultural networks of museums, galleries and performance centers, entertainment districts, university research centers, and exhibition places. Accordingly, the connections among these domains in New York, London, Paris, Frankfurt, Los Angeles, Singapore, Hong Kong, Rome, São Paolo, Mumbai, Dubai, Sydney, Mexico City, Amsterdam, Beijing, and Moscow constitute a new urban territory whose various individual components have more to do with each other than they do with the regional territories in which they are individually located. As it comes to embody the command functions of global capital and social power, this new trans-territorial city—constituted as a network of large urban areas—is an object to which all other spaces and territories must relate.[8]

Even in the most volatile and dangerous of cities, such as Bogota, Manila, Caracas, Karachi, and Johannesburg, a tightly secured urban space mediates relationships between national, regional, and global economies for the major politicians, businesspersons, and professionals. At the same time, these zones, and the functions they serve, have less and less to do with the rest of the city of which they are nominally a part. Yet, an inordinate share of a country's budgetary, material, and symbolic resources is deployed to make sure these zones operate with security, efficiency, and comfort.

At the same time, the majority of residents of these cities are weakly supported by low-income and casual labor largely taking place in thousands of small informal settings. Large-scale industrial production and manufacturing have either been shifted to more advantageous locations or rescaled so that the fabrication process—taking raw materials and turning them into finished products—no longer occurs in a single place, operation, or firm. Rather, different stages of the production of electronics, plastics, clothing, foodstuffs, and other consumer goods are completed in different smaller plants, workshops, and households by temporary labor, and in specific batches and orders. Workers then are not likely to have full-time jobs, or, if they do, are paid according to the number of items they handle.

This trend reflects not only efforts to reduce labor costs, but also the inability of many industrial districts in cities such as Mumbai, Cairo, and Manila to effectively reinvest in equipment, human resources, and management systems. It also reflects the frequent mishandling of efforts to transform production systems—i.e. introduce new technologies, upgrade skills, and make production systems more flexible—and provide existent work forces with new opportunities within these changed systems. Rather, the prevalent practice was to reduce the power of labor. The task here was to seed divisions within the labor force, reorganize production units into smaller sizes, staunch new labor recruitment, speed up attrition, and retain jobs without amenities or welfare measures.[9] All this was done in order for owners to substantially remake and reduce the costs of their businesses or turn their land over to more profitable new commercial and residential developments.

WHAT IS REGULATION FOR CITIES WHO NOW DEPEND ON EXPANDING CIRCUITS OF CIRCULATION

In part, urban residents were linked together through consumption of the basic services required to sustain habitation in the city. The public character of the provisioning of water, power, sanitation, and telephonic communication once constructed an implicit platform of intersection. Urban physical infrastructure enabled a "thickening" of the city's social field. This thickening enlarged the spatial scope of possible social projects among the city's diverse populations. It also anchored those same actors to the semblance of a collective fate. As indicated earlier, this infrastructure and the modes of provisioning connected to it have been increasingly particularized, both in the institutional forms responsible for the production, delivery, and valuation of urban services and in the character of the infrastructure itself. Disaggregating the components of provisioning systems into separately administered domains has subjected different actors to varying prospects and futures. The cultivation of new supply, guarantees of continuous supply, service upgrades, and enhanced efficiencies are now usually available only to those able to pay premium surcharges.

Urban residents willing to pay a premium for greater access to and quality of a particular service can use this advantage to pursue economic activities and lifestyles that have little do with the rest of the city. Urban space becomes a series of archipelagos of varying capacities and potentialities. Graham and Marvin, in their seminal work *Splintering Urbanism*, argue that unbundling infrastructures allows "valued" or "powerful" users and places to be connected while, at the same time, bypassing "non-valued" or "less powerful" users and places.[10]

When public infrastructure is dismantled into an assortment of varying gradations and delivery systems, specific parts of the city become de-linked as new infrastructures, custommade to the new economic and social requirements of highly capacitated domains, circumvent the existing grid. With access to power, water, and communications minimally linked and minimally dependent upon pre-existing infrastructure, these urban domains can "go their own way" without having to take into consideration the rest of the city's realities.

Conversely, unbundled infrastructure and provisioning systems are used to enforce spatial segregation of urban populations,[11] as valuations of land and the built environment within the same metropolitan area also become more disparate. Municipalities may attempt to impose minimal standards of equity in terms of access and pricing. But they usually have limited resources to oversee the complex operations of infrastructural systems whose profitability is partly contingent upon enlarging the scale at which bulk supplies are sourced. Profitability is also contingent upon using sophisticated informatics to ensure that provisioning takes into consideration the particularities of the context in which a resource is consumed. Municipalities also use the guarantees of premium provisioning systems as a way to secure inward investment.

SERVICING CIRCULATION: WHEN DIFFERENT KINDS OF RESIDENTS COLLIDE

The city is made up of more than premium users. As Sassen points out, corporate command functions and complex organizations require a large pool of relatively low-paid labor. This is often made up of immigrants and women of color, who work as information processors, secretaries, messengers, guardians, cleaners, and office assistants. Thus, re-centralizing the city is also part of an ongoing process of re-localization, as divergent patterns of investment, speculation, and divestment put together new forms of segregation and zoning.

This re-localizing is not simply a matter of dispersing or controlling where the disadvantaged and low-paid will live. For, re-localization is not only a process which creates gentrification, business districts, or residential ghettos. It is also a process which elaborates new spaces between communities of the poor, the rich, the business center, and the small workshop or light industrial districts. Distinct groups continue to fight over how the city is to be used. For as Henri Lefebvre speculates, the multiplication and complexity of exchanges necessary for the global command function cannot take place without privileged places and moments freed from the constraints of the market.[12] Whether such spaces can actually exist as freed from the market may still be unlikely. However, ambiguity and indeterminacy remain regarding how certain places are used and by whom.

The contemporary urban situation is thus characterized by the competition for scarce space, the deployment of excess liquid capital in land acquisition and new construction, policies which enforce exclusion, and diminishing access to the social supports and training necessary to maintain viable footholds in cities. Nevertheless, an important informal sector of service provision, light manufacturing, and craft work incorporates many urban residents into an economic system with great inequalities.[13] In other words, providing for the local demand which accompanies the re-centralization of the city—e.g. niche markets for the particular, often idiosyncratic, consumption styles of the varied white-collar workers with expendable incomes—is best accomplished through vibrant informal or small formal business sectors. These are forms of entrepreneurship that occupy the vestiges of former industrial or commercial zones or produce from homes. On the other hand, as financial markets shrink, these informal sectors will be particularly hard hit, even if they provide cut-rate services to an urban population whose disposable income takes a big hit.

These production sectors frequently become the domain of immigrants, who convert networks of social relations and familiarity in delivering specialized products and services to an immigrant community into an ability to service emergent niche markets. The lifestyles of the "rich and famous," the new breed of young financial whizz-kids and entrepreneurs, or, more recently, the hard hit urban middle class, are often serviced by African immigrants crafting clothes and furniture in conditions that do not vary greatly from those of their "fathers and mothers" back home.

Immigrant communities may hold on to small pieces of territory within the central city, but they are increasingly forced out to various suburban estates. While solidarity is broken up, new forms of cooperation must emerge, which, in some ways, have the advantage of being forced to take place across larger portions of the city.

Still, the cultivation of premium spaces, viewed as necessary for developing the centrality critical to managing global economic activity, tends to make many central districts across the world look the same. The architectural designs, the construction practices, the organization of infrastructure, the ancillary services, including shopping, entertainment, and leisure zones, appear to be the same everywhere. So do the synergies among information and knowledge formation, management and coordination, marketing and communications, which are seen as crucial to effectively running global economic activities.

Yet, as Sassen emphasizes, the key question is what does a particular city or region bring to the table of a continuously changing and networked global economy? What do a city's particular geographical location, history, and position in a larger context of international political and economic relations enable it to do well? Accordingly, some cities will have lots of experience dealing with particular sectors, such as agriculture, steel manufacturing, or the trans-shipment of goods. This experience enables its firms and other institutions to acquire expertise that detaches itself from the specificity of prior economic histories, and is reapplied as specialized skills to new globalized demands and opportunities. The formation of specially serviced, high-tech, premium spaces of centrality may be evident across the world's major cities. Even so, the ways in which they are spread out and located in a given city will vary according to particular services and functions that become the city's primary connections to the global economy. Thus, apparently homogenized built environments can house many different kinds of economic activities and operational styles.

The urban majority in cities across the South have invested in many residential and occupational niches. Spontaneously constructed neighborhoods have been upgraded and serviced by various combinations of resident self-provisioning, government and private funding, and external assistance. No matter how simply constructed, homes across neighborhoods in

Jakarta, Bangkok, Dakar, Lagos, and Karachi are continuously repainted and replenished with greenery. No matter the municipality's infrastructure capacities, mechanisms to access water and manage sewerage are renovated. While slums and urban poverty continue to grow, cities do demonstrate an often remarkable and continuously understated capacity to sustain sizeable numbers of dense but environmentally, economically, and socially viable districts.

It may be true that most instances of self-provisioning of essential urban services and the wide range of actions undertaken to compensate for limited income generating opportunities are both cost ineffective and labor intensive. But what is often obscured is the continuous reshaping of many low-income localities and their particular capacities for driving and adapting to new modalities of urban existence.[14] The compositions, histories, spatial characteristics, economic complexion, and political contingencies of low-income communities in the Global South are inundated with their own particularities, sensibilities, and potentials. Yet, they often exude a dynamism that reflects a mostly implicit collective efficacy to sustain the affective vitality on which cities must continuously draw in order to productively make use of the natural, technical, productive, and symbolic resources it has available to it. In other words, cities must continuously rework how people, things, infrastructures, languages, and images are to be intersected and pieced together. These are efforts that self-conscious planning may provide representations of but which are generated by maximizing the vast potentials within the city itself for relations among all kinds of things for which there exist no prior maps, inclinations, or even apparent possibilities.[15]

The logics of intersection connoted by high end production systems also find their correlates in zones of economic specialization that have emerged from the ground up. These zones have relied upon the consolidation of completely localized investment and skill. Benji Oyelaran-Oyeyuku describes in detail the development of the Otigba Computer Village in Lagos. From a street of several photocopy, camera, and printing shops in the mid-1990s, a thriving computer district consisting of 2500 shops developed in less than a decade. Relying on more horizontal forms of knowledge transfer among local university faculties and graduates, businessmen, artisans from non-related mechanical sectors, self-taught computer engineers, and entrepreneurs familiar with various Asian markets, the district has put together dynamic complementarities among branded computer sales—both foreign and local—computer refurbishment, accessories and components, maintenance and repair, peripherals and ancillary equipment, products and installation, and computer cloning. Specialization in the cloning of computers using non-standardized components proved particularly important, not only in terms of adapting hardware to the specificities of Nigerian and West African users and conditions, but as a step to the formation of specific Nigerian brands capable of adhering to universal standards.

While many participants in this sector are well-trained technicians, the success of the district was also dependent upon a wide range of technical skills that were honed by non-formally educated technicians working in other sectors. This background instilled flexible and innovative approaches to problem-solving. Apprentices working in various domains of the computer business also proved important to the circulation of information and skills. The entrepreneurial skills of businessmen in other sectors were enrolled to help develop networks with 800 different international suppliers. What is important here is how knowledge is not just the purview of formal training. Rather, it is a capacity to adapt flexibly to changing conditions and act decisively even when one might not have the apparent "eligibility" to do so.

More importantly, collaboration among the main actors was substantial. This collaboration took many different forms: joint marketing, sharing storage facilities, joint actions around quality improvement and control, training and skills upgrading, technological improvement, inter-firm credit facilities, shared management of local security, and the use of industrial associations to exert political leverage on issues important to the district, such as tariff levels and transportation infrastructure.

Here, critical dimensions of any business could be addressed through a concentration of capacity and a continuous sharing of information. This allows individual enterprises not only to devote heightened attention to the specific features of their core business specializations but also to construct a culture of experimentation. This culture enables discrete enterprises to go beyond what is familiar—in terms of production formats, customary markets, client needs, conventional uses of products, and trade networks. In the process, they become more versatile in how they do things, capable of greater specialization, and more expansive in what they pay attention to and the territories they serve. Not all firms may do these things equally well or devote equivalent attention to each of these dimensions of innovation. But here, too, new complementarities emerge which deepen the relationships amongst firms even as each strives to maintain its competitive edge.

As we have seen, the massive redevelopments of the center compel new logics of urban regulation. Rich and poor have to be brought together and kept apart. New ideas must come from underdeveloped spaces that soon get overdeveloped, and so the center always struggles with an uneasy balance between the temptation to try and control everything and link it to ever larger arenas and the need to cultivate spaces of singularity, where creativity can emerge.

The new logics of regulation also imply an increasingly difficult process of attempting to understand and manage relationships between the core and a periphery whose social dynamics are increasingly difficult to understand and predict. This is particularly the case as urban work for the majority tends to be broken down into smaller jobs, tasks, and sites. Workers end up doing many different things in different parts of the city and through this process engage the city and act on it from more points of view. The now dominant economic motivations which operate within central cities produce more substantial connections to exterior economies and cities. Here, there exists a heightened dependence on dynamics over which any individual city exercises limited control. If this is indeed the case, then the additional disjuncture between central and peripheral urban areas, as well as the divides between different categories of urban actors, perhaps introduces a large measure of vulnerability to these big urban development projects over the long run.[16]

MOVING AWAY FROM THE FINANCIAL MODEL: THE CHANGING SPACES OF URBAN LIFE

In part, this issue of the relationship of the periphery to the city stems from the fact that economic development and accumulation, as well as governance and regulation, have in the past several decades been framed and managed in terms of urban regions. This is a process which entails various modalities of articulation among discrete cities and conventionally non-urban areas of various sizes and histories. As a result, notions of urbanization, entailing changes in the characteristics of a given territorial entity—the city—are displaced toward concepts of the metropolitan, entailing the realignment of a plurality of territories and institutions in relationship to each other.

Within this process of "metropolitanization," the heterogeneity of socio-territorial mosaics, once the predominant feature of core cities, is pushed out into the regional periphery. The periphery increasingly becomes an arena to accommodate discrepant urban challenges. These include housing poor populations displaced from the city, providing premium living spaces for middle-class families, developing campus-like spaces for research and development sectors, and exporting environmentally precarious industry to the fringes of the urban system. As these challenges are usually not viewed as connected to each other, it is increasingly difficult to bring the periphery into some functional domain of administrative coherence.

Given the heterogeneous composition of the periphery, there are frequent conflicts and competition over resource allocation, fiscal exploitation, and the claims of residents engaged in different forms of livelihood and with different historical relationships to a given territory. Additionally, complicated negotiations between the core city and the periphery about calculating the costs of services provided by the core further fragment relationships among diverse districts in the periphery. Although national legislation in many instances does aim for inter-communal fiscal equalization, the infrastructure to facilitate such lateral articulation remains limited. Rather, the economy of spatial distribution still centers on cultivating pockets that specialize in particular activities—for example, in Greater Paris one finds a university research center in Marnes la Vallée, research and development centers in Saint-Quentin en Yve and Plateau de Scalay, and administrative centers in Saint Denis, with little sense of potential complementarities or conflicts.

Although metropolitan frameworks tend to emphasize polycentric layouts, particularly as a way to manage urban sprawl, minimize environmental hazards, and develop pockets of complementary specializations across a region, there is much ambiguity as to what this actually means in practice. Much effort has gone into trying to spread people, their work and activities more evenly across wider territories. However, in Europe, for example, job creation has not attained the levels anticipated, as volumes of commuter flows to core areas remain unabated, and the bulk of economic development attaches itself to already established urban areas, leaving large swathes of territory to remain as interstices with uncertain futures. As mentioned before, there is also the trend to re-centralization in the core city occasioned by the density of linkages across various sectors of the service, information, and media economies occasioned by globalization.

All of these trajectories tend to leave the immediate peripheries, most usually the domain of those who cannot afford to live in the core cities, in a more tenuous position, particularly as poorer residents are pushed into former industrial areas. Rather than being more fully incorporated into development scenarios that extend themselves from the core city, development instead "leapfrogs" over these near-peripheries. These areas no longer constitute a physically spatial periphery to the city, but enter into a new system of proximities where they become problematic "in-betweens" situated between differentiated growth poles.

Despite the trend toward "metropolitanization," the centers of cities like Jakarta, Bangkok, Karachi, Bombay, Cairo, Lagos, Nairobi, Abidjan, and Dakar are replete with heterogeneity. In their centers one finds various kinds of ports, industrial complexes, small factories, shop houses, warehouses, theme and exposition parks. They contain densely populated residential areas of extensive social mixture, land-fills and land clearance, condominiums and colonial heritage, lattice-like extensions of makeshift barely constructed shelter fixed on poles over highly polluted creeks and bays. Clogged arteries articulate manufacturing, shipping, labor, and storage, elevated toll roads, the gated remnants of once thriving middle-class districts, and vast new residential developments, in-explicably overcrowded in some areas, vacant in others. Mega-projects, premium end residential and commercial zones, research and development districts, info-tech, bio-tech and university centers, and upscale leisure areas are not seam-lessly integrated with one another. They inevitably produce a wide range of "shadow spaces" necessitated by the practical-ities entailed in laying out road systems, technical and engin-eering "dead zones," parking facilities, and conduits for bringing things in and taking things out.

Cities contain areas of residential and commercial entrench-ment whose historical weight makes them very difficult to dislodge, as well as areas of substantial decline and disinterest as the money moves further towards the edges of the metrop-olis. Old developments coincide with new, and this contiguity may mean different things. It could rejuvenate the old or could limit the prospects for the new, or these trajectories may have nothing to do with each other.[17] Yet, the uncertainty can be the occasion for getting things to move within and between cities in a much more dynamic way.

For what is important here is that many of the ways in which urban development has attempted to use the city to speed up and extend the circulation of people, money, materials, and information have not only slowed things down for many resi-dents but have limited the circulatory system of the city as a whole. While big projects have attempted to fulfill big agendas, they end up creating a rather narrow universe of operations.

Movement is not just circulation but the dynamic that is created when different histories and logics of urban operation are allowed to work. What we saw in Jakarta was the way in which different tensions, aspirations, calculations, and ways of doing things rubbed up against each other and were always having to be re-aligned and shifted. This bouncing off things is movement, and it is a rough-and-tumble game, and not the smooth fantasies of easy circulation where everything blends and moves on.

The development of residential and commercial projects connoting an "extreme modernism" across urban systems may, within their specific orbit, enforce a unified approach to managing everyday life, including specific calculations as to what is possible, valuable, and viable. Yet, while these big developments do take up more and more urban space, they do not crowd out or entirely displace older commercial areas. Here, available infrastructure, services, and levels of profitability are, even if at times highly problematic, still adequate for many urban residents to survive, even thrive, for now.

If the financial model for remaking urban life takes the "juice" out of the city, as well as having run out of juice itself, then what is likely to happen in cities, particularly those of Africa and Southeast Asia which have been the primary focus here? In this chapter I want to return to the notion of intersection as a way to rethink the possibilities of urban life and what urban residents can do and make with each other. Through this discussion I want to also re-link the notion of circulation to intersection, and talk about the importance of movement—movement at a crossroads, movement for intersection.

Intersection is about people and ways of doing things coming down to a crossroads, not knowing what else is going to be there, and no one being able to completely dominate what takes place there, since there are many different ways to get there and get out. Whatever happens, people coming to the crossroads are changed. They may come with specific ideas about what they are and where they are going, but the intersection at the crossroads can change everything. It doesn't necessarily mean that that change will happen, but it is an inevitable possibility. We are familiar with crossroads—cities are full of them. But it isn't just a spatial notion. Anywhere can be a crossroads at a particular time. The key is how spaces get turned into crossroads—points and experiences of intersection. The key is how any place in a city can become a moment and opportunity to create the experience of a crossroads where things intersect—in other words, take the opportunity to change each other around by virtue of being in that space, getting rid of the familiar ways of and plans for doing things and finding new possibilities by virtue of whatever is gathered there.

I will start with some examples from Jakarta and Abidjan, which demonstrate some of the same capacities to circulate different kinds of materials and ways of life that made up an important piece of the logic of the financial model. But they stick with the concrete practicalities of fitting things together in a specific place over time. Based on intermixing different kinds of local skills and backgrounds, local district economies in these cities are simultaneously close to and far from the logic of circulation talked about in Chapter 4.

Here, the emphasis is on how districts, with diverse populations and economic activities, attempt to adapt to changes in the larger city context, and how they use their diversity as a resource to develop new engagements with the larger urban space. Sometimes these new engagements are forged through the use of what on the surface might appear to be rather parochial and narrowly drawn institutions. Certainly there are many tendencies on the part of urban residents to re-establish tightly drawn forms of security.

But I want to discuss how sometimes apparently conservative forms of social affiliation are used to support innovative and risky experiments in social collaboration and investment. Then I want to consider the notion of the street both as an actual place of intersection and as a process of bringing various dimensions and ways of doing things together in ways that are not obligated to always produce some specific goal or product, but as a "field of rehearsal"—a mechanism through which the city continuously opens itself up to new ideas and provocations. Finally, I end the chapter with a discussion on

Johannesburg as a way of talking about the difficulties in actually trying to manage intersections among the different aspirations, efforts, and initiatives that residents set in motion.

INTERSECTING THE INSIDES AND THE OUTSIDES OF DISTRICTS

The Kali Baru-Senen district of Jakarta is strategically located at the intersection of important train lines and highways in an historical commercial district of the city. (See Map 2, pp. 64–65.) There are over 600 small enterprises that have something to do with printing and digital reproduction. For the most part, owners and workers live in the area. Thus, there is a mixture of highly developed residential blocks and poorer quarters, all attached to several large markets that bring in large numbers of consumers not necessarily linked as clients to the printing sector.

For much of their history, districts such as this relied upon local authorities that embodied their particular ways of doing things. These authorities connected the district's labor, craft, and social mores to a larger world of clients and politics. These local authorities often assumed positions within municipal government, particularly when the running of cities was decentralized to local levels. Yet, there was not usually a strong relationship between local municipal positions—i.e. mayors and councilors—and those of the "real" local authorities, who remained outside of administration and often even of municipal politics *per se*. Rather, such "real" local authorities would broker the terms of the relationship between local dynamics and those at the municipal level, within the framework of prevailing municipal law and policy, but also with flexible measures. These authorities were deal-makers, and the deals aimed to exempt districts from certain taxes, rules, policing, or other municipal obligations. They also aimed for at least some unofficial recognition by the municipal government of local ways of doing things—e.g. managing property, running businesses, organizing local associations—that acted as a compendium of "local law" and was applicable to just the district itself.

These patterns of brokerage continue to exist along with heightened participation in municipal administration—and thus more harmony between local practices within municipal policy. But there is also a shift in the character of the articulation of districts like Kali Baru to the larger municipal space and even to spaces beyond it. This is not only true for mixed-sector, mixed-income districts like Kali Baru, but also for other localities made up of different mixtures of the "urban poor" or the "middle classes." Operating costs are increasing for small- and medium-scale businesses. This is even true when labor and production are informalized to keep costs low. There is increased competition, not only from local competitors, but from those operating at larger scales who can afford continuous technological and marketing innovations. This means that keeping a business afloat may require new abilities to identify and sustain niche customers. These customers would include those who are not only interested in basic technical proficiencies at a good price, but who can request outputs better designed to recognize the special character of their needs, who can enter into flexible payment plans, and who feel like they have a good rapport with the business.

Now the workers who clean the offices, or repair the machines, or who make tea or fetch snacks for the customers, or who guard the facilities at night, or who deliver finished jobs or make sure that the business has the materials it needs readily available when it needs them, they can no longer necessarily count on patron–client relations, or common belonging to a particular ethnic group, family, local history, or religious organization. Not that these affiliations don't count.

In fact, common membership in something remains a key way for someone to get a job. But their status as a kind of guarantor has diminished, and therefore lower-status workers, along with even more technically proficient semi-professionals and professionals, have to be prepared to do more in terms of both the kinds of work they imagine possible and the locations in which that work might take place.

In a district like Kali Baru there are many ancillary activities attached to the formal printing industry. Because it is a dynamic area, there are many informal economic activities that attach themselves to it, from food vending, automobile repair, and the marketing of all kinds of consumer goods. These more "informal sectors" have also become overcrowded, with too many people selling the same goods and services. Thus, informal workers also have to be more flexible and mobile in face of shifting conditions. When workers of all kinds flexibly respond to larger numbers of particular situations and preferences, they, in turn, face a greater particularization of their own needs and practices. If they have to design special services and bundles of things for their customers, they seek out special brands, parts, and components. Taken as a whole, these practices of adaptation and flexibility introduce a large measure of volatility into economic life. This volatility, in turn, has to be compensated for with even more flexible measures.

As we started to work in the district, we of course were interested in interviewing owners, managers, and workers in the printing industry. While the presses were always rolling, initially the operations seemed understaffed; managers were often not around, workers took frequent breaks to "run quick errands," and still a steady stream of people, few of them actual customers, would come and go from the shops. If we would spend a day observing several shops from the street, workers, managers, errand boys, cleaners—the whole array of staff—would come and go, hopping on to motorbikes or marching toward the large nearby market, and for mostly short periods of time. We began to be interested in what people were doing, where they were going. Often it entailed a spur of the moment discovery of a new place to buy a special part cheaply, or acting on a tip or even a spontaneous hunch that a funeral taking place a few miles away involved a group of school officials who might be interested in a new style of textbook.

In other words, it was an incessant acting on information that came to the attention of not only the managers, but different kinds of workers. This led us to pay further attention to the amount of time residents in the district seemed to spend outside it—not to go to work or tend to family or social network responsibilities, but in a wide range of small actions—to join a card game, watch a local sports competition, attend a prayer service at a mosque, to eat at a distant street stall—all things that could be easily done locally and with more apparent affective ties and interests. In talking to residents about how they spent their time and how they decided to use whatever resources were available to them, we became increasingly aware of the chances that they took and the degrees to which they looked for new possibilities to be a part of stories and events outside the district.

These ventures could become a prelude to highly speculative investments for even those with little money—who wanted to get a "piece of action," some kind of small asset somewhere. Instead of a pool of people who basically share the same area of residence and similar kinds of jobs, experiences, incomes, and access to savings and resources, collaboration was developing among people who knew each other but often not for long, and who envisioned the possibilities that could emerge from pooling not only their money but their different networks, experiences, and skills. For example, two friends who worked as freelance machine repairers in Kali Baru would often travel to a market on the other side of the city to find parts that were heavily discounted. There they would go with one of the salespersons to eat in a small restaurant down a side lane; next to the restaurant was a small paper-cutting warehouse that had just been abandoned. Through the restaurant owner they met a former foreman who still had the keys. Together the five of them over the coming weeks scraped enough money to pay off the owner for one year in order to see if they could supply paper to a sufficiently large number of print shops back in Kali Baru, using their current connections. They also moved some of their younger relatives to temporary accommodation near the paper warehouse in order to try and save on initial labor costs. Ventures such as this are risked as potentially important ways of attaining assets that existing levels of household income and savings could not otherwise access. Here, more conventional instruments of investment either do not generate sufficient earnings in the short term or are not readily accessible.

Thus Kali Baru operates as the intersection of many different kinds of actors and activities. Now there is no preconceived way available to make this intersection work. It has to be negotiated in order to keep competing claims—for space, customers, services, and prerogatives—from getting out of hand. Streets must not be too clogged with hawkers to make it difficult for trucks to come in and out with essential supplies and to ship out merchandise. Security must be maintained in order for customers to feel safe. A reworked framework of belonging has to be continuously reapplied in order to cultivate and stabilize particular affiliations and loyalties, and in order to guarantee some predictability in the relationships that residents, workers, business owners, service providers, and various community leaders have with each other.

At times, resources, equipment, space, and labor have to be shared either when particular tasks are larger than usual or where markets contract and people have to smooth over the situation in order to last until conditions improve. All of this means that districts come up with particular ways of doing things that combine historical memory, religious sentiments, entrepreneurial styles and customs, and a set of tactics honed in the contingencies of specific problems faced by the district over time. Here, the particular setting gives residents, workers, managers, officials, and authorities a framework for dealing not only with themselves but with the larger city.

This process of intersection doesn't necessarily mean that everyone and everything taking place within these districts has to take each other into consideration. It doesn't mean that they have to meld their actions into some kind of hybrid way of doing things that incorporates bits and pieces of the actions and interests of everyone. Part of every intersection is the prospect that things will not come together and take something from each other. Some fundamental divides and impossibilities of translation will remain. The idea of local intersection among heterogeneous actors here means that accommodations—in the form of giving rise to new consensually determined ways of relating, deciding, or sharing—do not necessarily take place. This absence doesn't mean that people don't pay attention to each other or take each other seriously. Rather, the differences of others don't mean that any particular group now has to start living in a substantially different way.

People do seem to often act at cross-purposes. But it is these very cross-purposes that provide a concrete demonstration of the different things that can be done and anticipated in any given place. This is a materialization of different possibilities, different routes in and out toward the rest of the city. It is a reiteration of the possibility that specific prospects can be pursued by individuals and groups without them being perceived as threats and competition to others, and that their effectiveness need not be predicated on having to somehow appeal to or subsume what others are doing.

This proximity of different daily performances doesn't mean, obviously, that fear and anxiety about others simply disappear. Rights and resources will be contested, as will access to opportunities and privilege. There will be times when it seems that one's way of doing things cannot proceed without the other being eliminated in some form—even if symbolic. The aspirations of residents for more space, resources, time, support, and opportunities will often diminish the capacities of others. Conversely residents will completely ignore each other, and not consider what the other is doing as having any importance whatsoever to anything. People will just get on with what they are doing, heads down, mouths and ears seemingly closed. The density of diverse residential and economic situations is never a guarantee that everyone will take each other into consideration.

The point is not that intersection is some kind of a cure or developmental resolution for heterogeneous actors and activities operating at close quarters or that fights and contestation are a reflection of the inadequacies of intersection. It is not even a matter of intersection having to come up with some consensus about how things will be done from now on in order for everyone to get along. Rather, these possibilities exist side by side and in different kinds of relationships with each other—ones that go beyond cause and effect, or compensation, or development. They constitute a kind of material force that pushes residents along varying lines where life becomes predictable, but not too predictable, stable but not too stable, and so forth. So in complex urban environments linked to a larger urban world in many different ways, residents always have options.

MAKING THE LINKS ACROSS PARALLEL WORLDS

Here, I want to take the example of Abidjan—a city that in the past decade has had a turbulent history reflecting a national

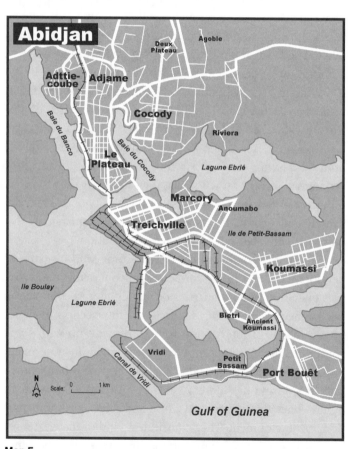

Map 5
Abidjan

conflict over citizenship, political power, religion, land rights, national identity, and postcolonial affiliation. This is a city that once was considered the most cosmopolitan in Africa. The economic vibrancy of the country, Côte d'Ivoire, attracted migrants from Mali and Burkina Faso to work on large agricultural estates, as well as migrants from Guinea, Senegal, Mauritania, Ghana, and Nigeria to work in a growing urban commercial sector. While many settlements retained an exclusive ethnic character, the rapid growth of the metropolitan area resulted in many mixed communities.

Over times replete with various economic crises and declining investments in urban infrastructure and public services, as well as shrinking employment, Abidjan experienced an increase in criminality. Many areas became insecure, replete with gangsterism and illegal activities. Local residential quarters looked for ways to secure their homes and persons against outside incursions. This was done through the formation of local management committees, twenty-four-hour security patrols, affirmations of the particularities of regional and ethnic identities, and even the re-design of traditional residential compounds to privatize formerly communal space. The measures taken varied according to the income levels of the particular quarter, with richer areas like Riviera becoming almost self-contained mini-cities, and poorer ones, like Port Bouêt, using a highly militant form of ethno-national youth politics to protect their "security."

Since 1998 there have been escalating battles over what constitutes an authentic "Ivorian"—someone entirely committed to the independence and integrity of the land and the solidarity of related people across territories. This is a struggle that simultaneously excludes others and becomes a vehicle through which minorities claim to act as a majority.[1] The intensifying political and economic divisions in the country—between different regions, ethnicities, and religions—were reflected in the city. Over the past twenty years, Abidjan has acquired the reputation of being a highly fractured place. It is a city full of contentiousness—within the political class, between neighboring districts, between long-term Lebanese residents (who have greatly profited from the recent ten years of political strife), Ivorian entrepreneurs, and Dyula traders (an amalgam of West African Muslim trading groups), and between religious sects and criminal syndicates.

Spread out along a finger-like lagoon system that snakes its way from the coast, the geography of the city facilitated the development of discrete enclaves to go along with the conventional divisions in colonial towns between the "real" city of the Europeans, the Plateau and Cocody, and the "popular" city of the Africans, Treichville and Marcory. Thus, Abidjan has been a growing patchwork of highly differentiated settlements and markets.

These localities served as enclaves for the growth of particular economic interests and statuses, political and cultural projects, and the consolidation of particular ethnic identities in the city. Each of the city's major ten districts, however, also had pockets of informal settlements, particularly within the physical recesses and fringes of the developed land, of which there were many given the terrain. So every locality was highly diversified despite the specific approaches to consolidation at work. Every locality also had to find its way in terms of connecting to the larger city. During the economic good times from the 1960s to the mid-1980s, public employment was a large sector and consumption was buoyed by the availability of goods and services provided by residents coming from all across West Africa. As the economy declined and competition for resources grew more intense the relationships of localities to the city became volatile as the institutions of mediation grew weaker in face of diminishing public expenditure.

As such, residents needed to put together their own platforms for reaching and dealing with the larger city—its resources, opportunities, insecurities. In prolonged political and economic crises the youth in particular perceive themselves to be cut off from a viable future. Where once urban households readily took in and educated relatives from other towns and rural areas, this practice has greatly diminished during the past two decades. But this does not necessarily staunch the flow of youth coming into the city. Households, pinched for resources, must often choose which of their kids will go to school in face of substantially escalating fees, as well as demands for these kids to find money to earn their keep. As households tend to reside in more individualistic spaces, with a lessening of the shared responsibilities and reciprocities which embedded individuals in a wide range of supportive relationships, domestic life has become more volatile.

In times of crisis, the criteria regarding who gets to control access to opportunities and resources are more tightly drawn, and in urban Africa these criteria have often been drawn along generational lines. Older members of a community attempt to maintain their privileges in face of a growing youthful population. Across Africa there were always many different circumstances that compelled various age groups to operate as "youth." All tried to find ways to negotiate new urban settings, acquire reputations and self-esteem, contest entrenched powers, and set specific parameters in their relationships with elders and other authorities.[2] In some cities youth styled themselves in ways that attempted to convey that they were beyond the reach of prevailing norms; from the Cowboys of Nigeria to the Leopards and Billyists of Central Africa, who, largely influenced by Hollywood bad guy Westerns, presented themselves as outlaws showing no respect for prevailing rules and conventions.

During the 1980s, networks of gangs, known as the *gloglo*, used their total disrespect of authority of any kind and the fear it generated as a way to be mobile across the city. This was a way of moving through different neighborhoods without paying attention to local power structures or cultural specificities. Here, lawlessness is used as a platform of articulation, a way of being in the city as a whole, even though it emerged from the specific situations of very poor settlements.

The dispersal of power is not simply the result of a weakening of big institutions such as the state or various forms of customary authority in traditional forms of government such as chieftaincies. It also reflects the particular complexion of a city where claims to be able to participate in national or municipal governance are made on the basis of being able to demonstrate that there are certain visible interests that operate in the city and with which the claimant has specific affiliation or knowledge. While certain localities and actors attempt to remain off the radar at all costs, the key for many residents is to make themselves known in a way that forces someone to take them into consideration.

For example, the *guatta* is quite literally a kind of platform, created by placing a circle of benches behind a group of upturned benches, in an alley or by a market, at night as an improvised place of prostitution. Several girls will be recruited to do the sex work, while the male youth run the operation, taking a cut of the proceeds, shaking down certain customers, and dealing with the police, who also inevitably will take a cut, often from an entrapped customer. A portion of these proceeds is then pooled with those from scores of other *guatta* in the neighborhood and deployed as "seed money" for buying influence or investing in other economic schemes from which further income might be generated. Of course, the *guatta* is a way for these youth to make an income, but, equally important, it is perceived as a platform for dealing with the larger city—for operating at a level they themselves have no direct knowledge of or capacity to play with.

Aspiring politicians could well mobilize to shut this prostitution down and clean up their districts. But this kind of activity just moves on to other areas, and so it is more likely that these politicians find a way of connecting these activities to other economies in the district. The youth involved in the *guatta* are already connecting amongst themselves, as well as offering underpaid police a consistent income stream. The viability of the politicians then rests on just how they are able to articulate different economies, legal and illegal, within their district.

In a similar way, what Sarah Newell describes as a moral economy of theft becomes a platform for forging social relationships across different urban spaces. Here, the purported obligation to steal from those with whom you are in a close relationship not only constitutes a particular circuit of exchange of goods and favors, but also elaborates a network of connections. It forges a working sense of just who one is related to and with what obligations. As such, it provides individuals a series of "stepping stones" across different neighborhoods, as well as providing a large number of channels of information through which individuals can be kept informed about what is going on. This is evidenced in Newell's case by the remarkable acuity on the part of some individuals to know just where in the city a particular stolen good has ended up.[3]

More recently, renewed religious affiliation is re-establishing frameworks of support, as well as platforms for accessing information and opportunity, especially as they relate to employment. In some parts of the city, ethnic cultural practices are reaffirmed by youth, particularly in those neighborhoods which claim to be the home of the original inhabitants of the city. The popularity of *nouchi* rap (based on the hybridized French dialect that is increasingly the city's common language) and the prolific spread of inter-linking music crews has also become a major platform through which claims have been made on the city.

Any politician who attempts to contribute their part to "running the city" must cross all kinds of lines—among different moral orders, actors, territories, and kinds of activities. Because as these lines make themselves visible, as events and processes that demand to take "their space," the ability to erase, contain, or even develop them cannot be a "police action." Rather, it is a matter of limiting what they can do in their own terms by bringing them into the orbit of several other different kinds of claims, activities, jurisdictions, or activities. In order to do this, politicians must be well versed in these different terms.

Some politicians will cling to the defense of a narrow range of interests. But then there will be those who enter the vacuum as interlocutors. They will try to demonstrate an ability to merge apparently discrepant ways of life to show that they have the ability to extend what many of these discrete activities have sought all along, which is the ability to operate in the city in ways that go beyond their own local spheres of influence.

No matter how fractured Abidjan may be, then, there are still certain spillovers that combine the residues of a once somewhat cosmopolitan culture with the exigencies of localities and actors that simply cannot exist within the fractures. For example, the district of Adjame certainly has not been immune to the contestations taking place across the city. But for much of the past years of civil conflict it has remained a place where Lebanese Shi'a merchants play table tennis with the local Christian gendarme in the basements of Pentecostal churches, where seemingly illiterate Mauritanian stall owners are entrusted to sell low-priced stock options for major Ivoirian companies, where Muslim and Christian bankers gather in makeshift bars set up in the parking lots of local municipal offices, and where the most important human rights organization has taken over the largest baby supplies shop in the area. This is not an assemblage of discrepancies, but rather the concretization of the intersection of elements that retain their very different properties and logics in a larger environment where actors seem to be "fighting it out" about everything.

BEYOND THE FAMILIAR DISTRICT—EXPERIMENTING IN THE LARGER CITY

What I am talking about here is something more than the defense of place or a particular walk of life. Let's return briefly to the example of Kali Baru. Districts like Kali Baru—as is the case for all different kinds of residential and commercial districts in cities across Africa and Asia—do have a discernible set of livelihoods, customs, sensibilities, and social arrangements that can be predictably identified with the district. But what is important is not the reproduction of the specific content of those social features *per se*. Rather, what is important are the skills and capacities that have been at work to ensure that those features associated with the distinctiveness and viability of the district can be sustained. For if these features are to be engaged and consumed—not as a stable series of unchanging elements—but more as a series of possibilities with widely drawn parameters—then what is important is the strategic practices through which the district demonstrates that its existence can be relevant to a wide range of different needs, styles, realities, actors, and situations.

On the business side, processes like digital reproduction in

Kali Baru can be made relevant and affordable to a wide range of small organizations; or traditional printing values and mechanics could be marketed so as to have an appeal to large corporations. On the social side, successful owners and managers, tempted to escape to wealthy outlying districts in face of local environmental inconvenience—traffic, flooding, disrupted services—remain in the district because of its proximity to a wide range of low-end services that reduce the costs and strains entailed in the domestic management of the household. Given the proliferation of consumer choices, the district must convey to a larger world that it is still worth maintaining some kind of affiliation with this district. In part, this is done by displaying the capacity to reconstitute itself in various ways while retaining a stable identity.

If these strategies increase the room for maneuver in the larger world, the specific tactics used to manage the intersections of the differences that operate within the district are largely applicable to the district itself and cannot be readily generalized to other places in the city. Kali Baru is information rich in that it enables different kinds of residents to be smart and flexible. Yet it is the ability of many of its residents to operate in larger spaces outside the district that provides the experiences that will enable the district to intensify and extend its connections to the city at large. In other words, wheeling and dealing among different economic activities, interests, and actors within Kali Baru provide an important platform for effectively managing local dynamics. But it is the ability to find out about, engage, and operate in the larger city that is necessary to ensure the ongoing viability of the district as the embodiment of a particular way of life.

The question then becomes, where do people from the district go if they want to experiment with engaging places in the larger city? On the business end, there are networks, associations, and commercial structures through which such exteriority can be exercised. But even here, supplemental efforts are necessary to find out particular pieces of information that are often the purview of highly personal and localized relationships. What our work in Kali Baru shows us is that residents, from the owners of print-shops, to the tea makers, to the motorcycle repairpersons, find small ways to insert themselves in various fissures and openings in districts across the city. This may take the form of a collective investment in a trading place in or near a particular market, or the construction of a small informal house in an available backyard in a district that is seen as "up and coming." It may entail taking over a food-selling operation near the parking lot of a new shopping mall, appropriating abandoned space for storage, inserting small trades in the fringes along busy thoroughfares.

Sometimes small social conflicts or divergences in residential conditions among neighboring micro-territories create an underutilized "no man's land." Outsiders take advantage of them as platforms from which to offer repair or protection services, or to set up gambling games. These small incursions may serve as a platform on which it is possible to gain a broader overview of what is taking place in this external district. Information is relayed back to residents in the district that may be better resourced or positioned to anticipate and cultivate larger opportunities over the long run.

These initial insertions—these "trial balloons"—put together active peripheries within economies and social relationships in other districts. Let's for a moment assume that the ongoing viability of individual districts depends to large degree on what happens to this region of Jakarta as a whole— where the futures of different districts are tied together. If this is the case, then, the viability of individual districts would also seem to stem from their actively making themselves peripheries for the outside operations of residents from other districts whose behavior and activity can markedly diverge from that to which they are accustomed in their own residential districts.

In other words, if the sustenance of districts requires residents to anticipate different ways of being in the city, and concretely experiment with them in places outside the district to which they are most linked and familiar, then there must be places across the city where this experimentation can be done. These places cannot be those that are well developed, thoroughly claimed, or whose futures are clear. Otherwise, they are just not accessible or are subject to contestations that go nowhere. This ability to "go out into the larger world" is situated in the messiness of built environments, the seemingly haphazard, incomplete, and strewn-out arrangements of buildings, infrastructure, and activity that continue to persist in many cities. For this environment forces residents to crisscross and side-step the markings and traces of many different movements, constituting a place always available to deals, small initiatives, and grand designs.

So when we take up the interrelationships of work and home, market and play, open spaces and private zones along which pass people, things, waste, resources, services, talk, civilities and tensions, shifting pockets of particular affective intensities and quiet—in a messy environment all of this entails people and things "stepping" through and around each other; and this is an environment available to being "messed with," open to different kinds of engagement.

Residents in these districts undertake hundreds of small efforts to become involved in places away from home. They bring these experiences back home, where they face the "imported experiences" of neighbors, co-workers, and other associates, as well as those of outsiders who have come to carry out their own experiments. All of this propels residents back into the larger world in still different ways, and it constitutes a wide range of propositions for how different districts might deal with each other over the long run, how they might put together a different kind of city.

In Kali Baru, the owners and managers of the 600 printing businesses must preserve the coherence of a territorially based and articulated economic sector through practices that don't undercut the viability of any individual business. This is done through price regulation, solidifying local networks for information exchange, problem solving and dispute resolution—as has been evident in commercial guilds and associations for a very long time. At the same time, the viability of any specific business is rooted in its ability to offer both generic and highly singular services. The latter is reflected not so much in the proficiency of the product but in a wide range of ancillary sensitivities, engagements, and accommodations related to the idiosyncrasies of specific customers.

Given the nature of competition, shrinking labor markets in specific sectors, the mobility of labor, and the overcrowding of informal work, workers of all kinds must become more flexible. The performance of that flexibility generates its own volatility that must be flexibly addressed through largely locally negotiated accommodations in order for all actors that are perceived as legitimate to have "their space," opportunities, and livelihood.

The result of these accommodations is that any particular sector, activity, and domain within the district will embody the nature of that accommodation. In other words, it will take on a complexity that reflects the concerns and ways of doing things of others. Thus owners of printing shops, technicians, domestic workers, informal hawkers, local youth gangs, clergy, street sweepers, and local power brokers don't simply have their own rules, sectors, domains, and spaces. To a large extent, they also come to take on the realities of everyone else as part and parcel of their ability to do their job and stay in place. They are all prepared to do something else when the time comes because of the volatility their capacities for adaptation have brought about. Their sheer ability to "roll with the punches" seems to guarantee that "more punches will be thrown."

On the one hand, this kind of "mutual citation" or bringing others into one's own fold can better synchronize the different things that take place in a district. At the same time, however, different residents, feeling like they now have what they need from others, are more inclined to go their own way, not really taking into consideration what others in the district are doing. As such, they may be more prepared to "cut their own deals" outside the district.

Again, these are not intersections among clearly defined entities but rather intersections between people trying to be more flexible, trying to insert their "stories" into the stories of others and making them somehow relevant to them. The ability to dispense with such "maps" of how to get by is important when these actors try and operate in other districts and situations outside "their own." Thus, life outside the district becomes a matter of learning how to play a lot of different games. It is a matter of reading situations and engaging others through the specific tactics of accommodation that likely differ from the ones individual residents, workers, and managers had negotiated within their "home" district.

BEING PREPARED TO DO MANY DIFFERENT THINGS AT ONCE— THE KEY TO STAYING IN PLACE AND MOVING AROUND

One can see this playing of different games in the career of one of North Jakarta's largest trash operators, a formerly poor man living in one of Jakarta's most overcrowded and destitute districts. These operations are not those of the big waste-collection companies, but of small entrepreneurs who find various ways to gain access to reusable waste. While major commercial enterprises rely upon large waste-collection companies, there are thousands of small enterprises that cannot access or afford such services.

Yusuf began his career in Tanjung Priok collecting plastic containers from the shipyards and parlaying them out to small industrial plants in the area. In several years he became the informal manager of many trash-recycling operations across North Jakarta. In part, this happened because he came to understand the diversity of logics and applications of waste collection and didn't impose a singular model across his expanding operation. In some contexts, local waste collectors focus on working out complementary relationships by specializing in specific sectors—such as plastics, glass, wood, clothing, metals, and so forth. Here pickers keep to their sector and do not infringe upon others—i.e. glass pickers won't simply decide to collect a cache of plastic trash just because they happened upon it. In other situations, businesses are territorially based, with specific businesses gaining dominance over all collectibles within a specific geographical territory.

In other instances, the trash business is based on contractual relationships between local operators and a network of particular small businesses that are dispersed across territories, with local operators gaining exclusive use of collectibles from certain vendors, whether it is owners of street stalls or small production or repair workshops. Additionally, in some areas waste retrieval is a collaborative project undertaken by specific communities in order to ensure a steady supply of critical inputs, such as wood for housing construction, metal for local workshops to make household items and security gates, or waste for composting for urban gardens. These operations are not necessarily run as a for-profit business.

Across North Jakarta many different logics of organization are at work. Yusuf's success was predicated on his ability to learn about the distinctive practices at work across different districts and then connect different specializations involving different kinds and scales of waste retrieval and re-circulation. Each specialization then acted as reciprocal resources and problem-solving mechanisms, especially as each operation confronted shifting markets, changing memberships, broken or new contractual relationships, or new opportunities at a scale which required collaborations among different kinds of waste collectors. In other words, waste pickers might work in different kinds of neighborhoods, with different kinds of trash and different systems of waste collection depending on local market and political conditions.

At the moment, this example is important not for the specificities of waste retrieval but rather to point out that even the poorer districts in the city emphasize finding ways of linking places to each other through the ability of individual residents to flexibly operate across different spaces in the city. As pointed out before, this ability is predicated on managing the heterogeneous characteristics of locality itself—i.e. the fact that livelihoods of a specific status or class of urban residents are becoming more diverse, with different ways of calculating what it is possible to do and how resources should be put to work.

What ensues is a nomadism like that invoked by Deleuze and Guattari. Their idea is that places are relays, always already left behind on arrival, always pointing to other opportunities beyond themselves, and always referring to movements yet to come.[4] Places then become staging areas for enabling a stability and continuity that depend upon the willingness of residents to find that very stability in many different ways.

On the other hand, cities certainly contain residents who are fixed to specific trajectories of accumulation and dispossession. When they are able, households certainly invest in education for their children as the most convincing way to ensure economic and personal success. Cities everywhere offer new opportunities for wealth creation and the use of consumerism to concretize particular lifestyles and advantages. On the other side, it is clear that many urban residents also get stuck and act as if they are trapped. In urban Nigeria and Pakistan, for example, it is resoundingly clear how fights over shrinking resources compel residents to act out of blind loyalty to particular religious and ethnic identifications, to the extent that they engage in sporadic episodes of self-destructive violence.

Urban districts across the South are replete with patrimonial, fraternal, and parochial organizations which keep themselves together largely by means of their opposition to someone else with whom they begrudgingly share a district or city. The experience of urban youth gang violence, and the predominance of drug economies in many urban districts, demonstrates incessant implosion where cycles of murderous revenge can take place without any clear understanding on anyone's part of how they began or where they will end. Social networks in many areas are tightly bounded in terms of place of origin, religious and ethnic identification, gender, and age status. Even when conditions would seem to demand cooperation, boundaries remain firmly fixed.

But the persistence of these affiliations goes beyond simply the need for belonging and anchorage, or the need to deal with growing uncertainties through the professed clarity of religion or social ascription. Economic and cultural precariousness are on the rise for many urban residents. Thus intensifying participation in religious and ethnic associations becomes a readily available "map" for navigating these uncertainties and organizing residential spaces according to "indigene" and "outsider," "believer" and "non-believer." What is offered, particularly in religious associations, goes beyond a stable interpretive framework and a belief system organized around particular certainties. Instead, a "shortcut" is held out for the difficult work of adapting to the heterogeneity that I have been talking about here.

HOW TO DEAL WITH UNCERTAIN URBAN FUTURES— MAXIMIZING RISK AND SECURITY

Intersecting different activities in order to make residents more flexible and mobile in their dealings with the city is hard work. Those associations that compel the most intense loyalties and numbers of followers tend to be those that embody a millenarian attitude that promises not just salvation in an afterlife, but greater abilities and riches in the present. Additionally, associations based on region of common origin, guild, or ethnicity increasingly take on millenarian connotations while invoking specific destinies and entitlements.

Jane Guyer raises the question of whether a sense of the "near future" has disappeared.[5] She defines this near future as the anticipation of what is to come in the short term, and this anticipation is an outgrowth of the rational planning and deliberations that take place in the present. In her discussions on the foundations of neoliberalism and conservative Christianity she finds evidence of a vagueness of definition in how temporal links are made between the now and the long run. This temporal bridge is cemented not so much through structured anticipation, planning, discipline, or savings, but by faith, submission to market forces, or speculation. Time is experienced less as an evolving process and more as a rupture. Intensified affiliations on the part of many urban residents with religious associations would seem to connote investment in deliverance across different divides, both spatial and temporal.

Instead of the risky and even arduous trial and error task of experimenting with different ways of being in the city and relating to others, adherents to these associations place their bets on the ability of the affiliation to radically transform them. This is particularly the case when they understand that what is needed is a rupture within themselves and where they believe that everything they know in the present just isn't enough to make this happen. Many complex motivations and incentives are certainly involved in any account of how these affiliations are taking shape. But in an important way they testify to the challenges faced by many urban residents to be more flexible in face of the increased heterogeneity of contemporary urban life.

Additionally, larger numbers of urban residents know that they can only really deal with the growing uncertainty of urban life by acquiring assets. For many, the acquisition of property is beyond their reach, as are stocks and bonds, vehicles, equipment, or bulk supplies of valuable provisions. Sometimes, households will acquire property and rent it out for their primary income, while residing in more provisional, frequently poorer conditions. Often the kinds of assets available—such as workshops, vehicles, storerooms, individual residences, small-scale capital equipment—do not contain sufficient value either as collateral, insurance, objects of resale, or as instruments for smoothing over rough times when income is in short supply. In such circumstances, individuals and households often look for acquisitions at a scale where potential values are greater. Such scaled acquisition is often only available when groups of individuals pool their resources.

Here, commercial properties or apartment buildings might be purchased, or people go in together to purchase one or more containers of goods that are imported and resold. In cities across the South, residents pool money to buy essential commodities in bulk, purchase larger commercial and residential properties, invest in small factories producing for niche markets, or purchase shares in businesses such as restaurants, stores, and sometimes even larger companies. These investments usually depend on the specific economic interests and capacities of residents—whether they are directly involved in certain types of retailing and trade, the extent to which they can mobilize low-cost labor for the operations of workshops, small factories, and businesses, or whether they simply want to diversify available income streams.

Because these collaborations are not usually among established and formally constituted commercial actors and because the nature of their collaboration is not amenable to existing frameworks of contractual regulation (or simply because those who are cooperating cannot afford to initiate legally binding agreements), agreements are largely based on trust. Here, residents are sufficiently connected to each other through history, kinship, shared residential location, or institutional participation to be confident in their dealings with each other. There are also times when potential collaborators are brought together not so much on the basis of a shared history, but on the basis of the potential complementarities of their distinctive positions in various markets, professions, geographical locations, or specializations.

Instead of a pool of people who share the same area of residence and similar kinds of jobs, experiences, incomes, and access to savings and resources, collaboration develops among people who know each other, but usually not for long. They also envision the possibilities that could emerge from pooling their different networks, experiences, and skills. In contexts where shared history and complementarities among residents are important, religious, fraternal, and other kinds of voluntary associations can take on the role of guaranteeing these deals. In other words, participation in these associations becomes a concrete way of expanding the field of possible collaborations beyond extended family and neighborhood networks. Instead of being simply co-congregants, members, or co-affiliates, participants in these associations sometimes use them as a framework to back up and provide a kind of moral security to a wide range of experimental economic ventures.

These ventures are risked as potentially important ways of attaining assets that existing levels of household income and savings could not otherwise access. Here, more conventional instruments of investment either do not generate sufficient earnings in the short term or are not readily accessible. Likewise, available institutional relationships—the workplace, neighborhood, trade union, family network—may only offer limited schemes for savings and investment. As these arrangements are largely informal, and have the capacities they do largely because they are informal and flexible, participants must find ways to ensure some form of security. The growing influence of religious associations, and the particular moral universe that common membership enforces, becomes an important entrepreneurial instrument for urban residents. This is the case regardless of how strong their individual religious convictions may be or of the extent to which they apply their religious beliefs in daily life.

Even if residents do not physically operate with great mobility across the city or beyond, their actions in circumscribed places increasingly take on a sense of greater circulation—of ideas, aspirations, experiences, and references. They "bring" to their performed activities a sense of openness and expansiveness that would seem to indicate a broader range of experiences than may have been actually experienced. As a result, assumptions about their interests, capacities, and objectives cannot be easily summarized or represented in conventional political terms.

On the other hand, if one arbitrarily picks a sample of residents in poorer districts to follow as they conduct their daily lives, these residents do seem to operate across many different segments of the city. This remains the case even as transportation costs rise, urban spaces become more privatized, and reliance grows upon local social networks to provide work opportunities. Thus there seems to be some reciprocity between actual circuits of movement and practices of movement that are concretized in otherwise highly circumscribed places. While familiar trappings of solidarity, social capital, and reciprocity may appear to be put at risk, the ability of some residents to move while others don't does not seem to intensify any major gap of advantages between the movers and non-movers.

USING THE NOTION OF THE STREET TO THINK ABOUT HOW RESIDENTS SHIFT GEAR

Another way to think about these capacities to move across and around cities is to think about the notion of the "street." For streets are the concrete instruments for moving people around and for dividing things up. But the question is what city dwellers actually do with these streets. Simply go from one place to another? Or, do streets make possible specific ways of living "in-between" the defined places of home, work, school, or leisure. Here it is important to remember that cities encompass not only multiple spaces but multiple temporalities as well. The rhythms of work and leisure, and the pace at which domesticity, publicity, and solitude are folded into particular individual and collective action, are differentiated in cities that at least must take into statistical account the diversity of their own residents. The terrain of the city, its enclosures and publicities, its variously configured channels of movement, its organization of different venues where people are assembled in different densities and forms of association, and its applications of work and attention, emerge as specific compositions of agitation, stillness, and receptivity.

Let me take the example of Audrey Estrougo's film *Regarde-moi*. In the film, the action takes place almost entirely in the courtyards of a large residential housing complex in the Parisian suburbs, and then mostly focuses on the youth who hang out in these spaces. Everyone is seemingly on his or her way somewhere but never really goes anywhere. Yet the youth appear to bounce off each other like balls in a pinball game; each encounter propels them into the next in various permutations of stories and combinations—full of camaraderie, rivalry, play, and conflict. Time seems to both quicken and slow down as these permutations generate hundreds of small events, fights, negotiations, and intimacies. But they all remain in a confined space, and do not break out into the stories of the larger city.

So if such complexities of time can take place in a highly constrained arena, then one can imagine what takes place at the level of the larger city, as reflected in its streets and by the overall notion of "the street." Imagine the frenzy of market trading grounds next to recessed interiors where there are quiet conversations over tea next to the receptions of official delegations next to the openings for the inflows and outflows of people and goods. All generate a productive volatility that continuously reopens the relationships that everything has with everything else. It reworks the forms of stability and interchange. The contiguities and relations of residences, offices, warehouses, roads, factories, entertainment halls, plazas, parks, stations, and ports make up a "combinatorial richness" capable of generating effects that go beyond the imposition of any particular form of organization.[6]

The street here is much less a space than it is a conversion and a switch. It is a moment of passage that makes its way through the noise and the muddle, through deals and compromises, evasions and embraces, concessions and impetuousness. It is a thoroughfare that always becomes something other than it was at its inception. As a tea seller in Khartoum who sat in the same spot on the same street for fifty years once told me, she always felt relief that another day was finished and excited for another one to begin. Perhaps not in the same way that young girls in Tembisa, South Africa, faced with the omnipresent threat of sexual violence, feel enormous relief when they make it to their homes safely each day after school; nor the same as what young Nigerian girls trafficked for the sex trade feel when the police finally stop and check their papers after months of roaming the Barcelona Ramblas uninterrupted. For the street to work, in the sense of work as invention, there can be no definitive content to it, no sense that the street is the culmination of human conviviality. Rather, the time of the street is an incessant process of being tripped up, re-routed, and side-tracked.

The street is what is left over after social life has been sutured or folded into different civil settings—from households, workplaces, associations, to educational institutions.[7] It is thus the promised fate for those whose lack of motivation and social skills makes them marginal everywhere else, and, as such, the incentive for them to adapt in ways that they may not really desire—as when parents and teachers tell their kids that if they don't succeed in school or work, then they will be out on the street.[8] The street here is not only something "outdoors," and thus not contained by rules and conventions of membership, but something outside normative social life. It is a final destination that seemingly renders those who find themselves out on the street ineligible to be taken seriously.

Yet, because the street is a place where survival cannot depend upon appeals to the principles and conventions of institutional life, it supposedly amplifies a certain raw intelligence that "sees through" pretences of all kinds.[9] It has historically taken on a visceral and intuitive character—a physicality that goes beyond words and thus promises something definitive.[10] As such, the street is very much "inside" the everyday dynamics of family, corporate, and social institutional life, since it points to the practices where things "really get done."[11] It is a highly regarded supplement to those careers that have now "made it." For example, take the frequent reference to persons who came from the street and who used their life on the street as a way to make it good in one of the professions.[12]

Just because the street may be outside an over-coded regime of civility doesn't mean that it doesn't have rules and norms. A person may become habituated to life "inside" other institutional spheres in ways that they need only pay minimal attention to all that is going on around them or, more precisely, can be selective about the events and information to which they must stay attuned. But one always has to be highly attentive on the street.[13] This might not always seem to be the case given the ways in which people can feel anonymous on the street, and the way the crossing of spaces is engineered for those who use the street to get from here to there. Yet, in a space of potentially innumerable interruptions and interference, it is important to maintain gaze and gait in ways that do not signal undue interest in the lives and intentions of others

passing on the street. We know that we must compose ourselves in such a way as to minimize the extent to which our
performance on the street constitutes some kind of gravi-
tational field for the unwanted or not easily manageable attentions of others. From the work of Erving Goffman, we are
familiar with the complexity of these micro-politics and practices aimed at reducing degrees of freedom so as to minimize
uncertainty.[14]

The navigation of the street also opens up possibilities for
desires that are constrained in other institutional spheres.
Here, it is not so much a matter of rationality being suspended
or the street being the place of a demiurge. Rather, the street is
a dense mesh of emotions, inclinations, objectives, styles of
bodily enactment, and perceptions in motion. It thus generates collisions, attractions, and repulsions in the sensory fields
that bodies have to navigate—all the cues, vibes, and intensities we have to at least implicitly pay attention to in order to
figure out what is going on—even as their physical comportments may keep a proper distance.[15] This is what is meant
when people talk about reading the "mood" of the street.
Whatever an individual understands about what they have to
do at any given moment in a particular location is propelled,
maintained, and undone by this sense of the street always
being on the verge of generating many different scenarios and
possibilities (what might be called its "virtuality").[16]

The street as a place of both potentiality and refuse—where
people end up when they have nowhere else to go—possibly
comes together in the notion of the "virtuality" of the urban
poor. Here, vituality points to a condition of the poor being
otherwise than what they are at the given moment. This is not
meant as a complicated way of saying that they are rich or
could be rich. Rather, it means that something exists within
the conditions of impoverishment that is not fully actualized

within the terms and implications associated with the conditions we refer to in understanding what it means to be poor.[17] In this formulation, the street is dense with the simultaneous presence of many different times, many different ways of existing—including a focus on past ways of doing things whose traces are not always evident in the landscape.[18]

Conventionally, people claim the use of specific places in the city in order to secure projects and institutional interests. Some of these people deal with each other in the same local spaces, some circulate around much more global arenas, and others deal at the level of nations or regions. These claims are concretized in various ways—through making things, connecting different things, tearing things down, as well as shaping actions, attitudes, and affects. As a result of concretizing these claims, particular ways of doing things become possible, while others remain off the radar. The leftovers of these claims provide inclinations, memories, and endowments for future reshaping. But there is always something more that is possible; something else can always be done, and, as such, the street embodies this articulation of potential and constraint.[19]

It is clear that urban life is more precarious for the poor, as their worlds are reduced to a "bare life." We conventionally understand this bareness as the narrowing of everyday life conditions to a minimal domain of safety or efficacy. In physical or social environments that are highly disordered, unhealthy, or dangerous, it is usually assumed that individuals constitute small islands of security or order from which they can better deal with the unhealthy or insecure conditions that surround them. For example, walk into any one of the tens of thousands of one-room cardboard shacks in Cape Town's massive settlement, Khayelitsha, and you will likely find it meticulously maintained in the midst of overflowing refuse at the exterior. But in circumstances where effective mediations

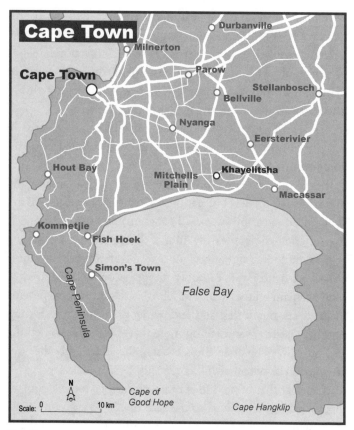

Map 6
Khayelitsha in Cape Town

capable of connecting urban residents to predictable sources of provisioning, meaning, and collaborations disappear, the "bareness" of what remains for residents is the city in its cityness. Here, people "let go" of any prospects for consolidating a sense of stability, and rather disperse themselves across discrepant urban spaces. They become scavengers of any small opportunity.[20]

Some years ago I was living in Dakar and spent a lot of time on *cars rapides*, the highly rusted remains of old delivery trucks converted into the primary vehicle of public transportation. I noticed that certain young girls seemed to be always in motion. After a time of making some inquiries, I found out that many of these girls were domestics working long hours for mostly middle-class households in the center city. Almost all stayed in barracks—rough wood constructions—in the most peripheral areas of the city, and usually had an arduous trip for girls already working twelve-hour days. The trips on the *cars rapides*, however, were not simply the routines of daily commutes. Instead, the girls would often take routes that they knew little about in spontaneous decisions to put themselves in other areas of the city where they had few if any connections.

Sometimes the girls would spend several hours doing this every day. Avoiding the responsibilities of childcare, cooking, water and firewood retrieval that fell to them at home, they risked being kicked out of home. Despite the arguments and threats that would meet them upon their late return, the girls persisted in these "explorations," taking the chance that something might happen. They took the chance that they would stumble upon other people, stories, and possibilities that, if they did not quite change their life, they could use at some point in the future. They believed that such excursions, and the opportunity they provided to know a wider space of the city, gave them some advantage in the conversations and transactions they performed when going to the market to buy supplies for their employers or taking the children in their care to school. They believed that some advantage would accrue to them.

ORDINARY STREETS

That said, the street is also a prosaic space. Here the street is no more than a necessary evil, the thing that has to be traversed on the way to the important sites. It says nothing about who happens to be there; it simply connects and is empty of significance on its own. So when people "take to the streets," as in strikes, demonstrations, and revolts, it is not because the street offers something that fortifies transformation. Rather, dissociated from classrooms, factories, and offices left empty, the intricate social architectures of institutional differentiation collapse into the crowd. Here, the calculation of crowd numbers indicates the likelihood of some rupturing event. Like billboards that advertise the particular identities and powers of commodities, streets end up hosting peculiar assemblages of national, ethnic, and religious distinction—as long as the proper permits have been secured.

Even walks on sunny days and under moonlit nights—where the street is a place of congeniality, familial togetherness, or romance—derive their magic from a certain domesticity projected on to the street, just as the kernels of incivility, with teargas, projectiles, and gunshots, are brought to the street from elsewhere. This prosaic character does not make the street any less powerful, or any less virtual. Rather, it relegates the possibility of catharsis—of letting loose, letting off steam—to a place where it is seen as having nowhere else to go. "Takin' it to the streets," far from generalizing revolutionary sentiments across the social landscape, usually means staying put in areas where sentiments for "big change" have been assigned.

In a process where either too much or too little is asked of the street, much of what the street does or brings to life remains barely visible. This is the case even as the street is supposed to contain the purported advantage of people being really able to see what is going on, "the real deal." In recent work on urban social economies and entrepreneurship, the street is a critical arena for livelihood and efficacy. For in many cities of the world the operations of markets, commerce, and entrepreneurship depend more on the management of social relationships than they do on the specificities of goods and services. The transactions of goods and services, then, become the occasions through which these relationships become concrete and recognizable.

The management of these relationships is something that goes beyond classification. When social life is divided into sectors, addresses, identities, classifications, and territories, these are instruments supposedly capable of summing up what people are, who they deal with, and what they are capable of doing and likely to do with others. The usual assumption is that you know a person and what it is possible to do with them if you can place them within an overarching explanatory framework.[21]

Yet such frameworks have only recently been critical to urban economies in many cities of Latin America, Africa, or Asia. Rather, traders and entrepreneurs would calculate the possibilities of what they could do based on the observations of the social life around them. They paid attention to others, not so much to get a definitive sense of their identity, but to position other people in terms of their participation in many different kinds of networks—e.g. as members of political parties, residents in a particular neighborhood, and partners in various economic activities. Such observation activated this multiplicity as a potential resource for the observer's own activities. In other words, economic actors observe each other pursue different trades, markets, deals, uses of the built environment, tactics to deal with authorities of various kinds, and financial schemes. All these become different ways for them to connect their own activities to the different conditions and events happening all around them.[22]

While life requires us to insert ourselves into each other's lives and stories, the practice, nevertheless, generates ambivalence. It is hard work, and you never know where it is going to take you. And there is the question of who exactly you are getting involved with in the first place. People tend to know that the definitions they use to make things familiar and predictable can be shaken up and realigned in terms of the many different other scenarios that simultaneously take place "in front of" and all around them.[23] No matter what a person does or how they conduct their affairs, these actions and conduct can be construed as aspects of other scenarios and stories whether the person has intended to be part of them or not. You may think you know where a person is "coming from"—but it is hard to tell all of the motivations and influences at work, especially since even those who claim to be simply acting as "their own individual selves" may be unwittingly or unconsciously doing the work of others. So when people try to deal with each other, get to know something about each other, they see not only specific histories and characters but also possibilities to manipulate and be manipulated, often in just a playful manner. But at the same time, the uncertainties raised by all of these different ways of interpreting people and their affairs are the source of fear and anxiety. This is then one reason why the street is used to try and trace the different ways in which people are hooked up to others.

In a film about Bamako by Manthia Diawarra, a group of storeowners sit in front of their shops in Bamako, Mali, next to an illegal market that has just been torn down by the police. They are relieved because the market was taking away their customers, attracting thieves, and making the area congested and dirty. But at the same time, their ability to watch what is taking place gives them a better sense of what people are buying, what is on their minds, as a more diverse crowd of customers from the city come to the area. The intensity of their relief soon gives way to a gnawing concern that somehow the real action is now taking place elsewhere. Even though they have re-established their former customer base, they feel that a substantial part of the "real commerce" they once observed only as tangential participants has escaped them. Once safe in their status as "official" and "real" *commerçants*—something reiterated by the proximity of the illegal market despite the drain on their income—they worry about the solidity of this status now that the market had been cleared out.

STREETS AS SWITCHES

In response to this fear, the street is a place of not only interchange but evacuation. It channels out excessive flows and possibilities to their proper locations through ordered conduits. Similar to Virilio's notions of broad avenues as a means for invasions to pass through cities while minimizing the disruptions to urban life, the street is something that passes danger along. It is something that doesn't let the intersection of histories, capacity, and affect settle into varying hybrids that would demand something different from the built and social environments around them.[24] In significant ways, the street assumes its potential as a site of remaking and provocation only when it disappears—only when densities of bodies, practices, inclinations, and ways of living are so great that there is no available architecture to immediately disentangle them and discharge the subsequent energies generated by their collisions.[25]

According to Vyjayanthi Rao, density brings about a sense of time in suspension and the sensation of constant anticipation.[26] The potentiality of this density can be reflected in the nature of a built environment increasingly operating outside of planning, regulation, and functionality. Here affect, prior knowledge, authoritarian discourse, and diffuse popular insight are intersected. Instead of the street offering itself as the key mode of channeling excess energies, tensions, and a city's worries about the future, the entire built environment acts as an amalgam of advertising, design, and prophecy. The built environment thus concretizes the temporariness of things. And so the city always points to the immanence of something more virtual or global.[27] In other words, there is something about the entirety of the city which appears more ephemeral. It exists more as a sign of something spectacular to come than as a mechanism for bringing together what exists in the present—what is valued and considered important.

Under these circumstances, the street is less a specific content or assemblage than it is a switching mechanism. Even more, the street is not really a street—i.e. not identifiable as a concrete infrastructure laid over a geophysical terrain assuming particular functions in an overall built environment. It has no specific location, yet still can be located; and it is neither inherently material nor immaterial—it rather entails elements of both. Inside and outside, physical and ephemeral, the street is more about relays of intensity and the conversion of one thing into another.

In his work on spatial analysis, Stephen Read talks about the vertical ecology of cities. Here, any neighborhood or district of the city is made up of different "tracks" or "depths." Some are localized and domesticated within the neighborhood space, and some primarily operate at a larger city-wide level but within that same space. Put simply, some people, places, businesses, and activities are more about events and processes that can be identified as "neighborly," even if they have wider connections and impacts. Others appear to deal with much larger circuits while still being situated within a particular place. As such, cities, Read says, are less about the laying out of discernible and categorized functions and attributes and more about shifting all kinds of different materials around, at different speeds and trajectories. Places are never static, but always on their way somewhere and along various networks. What they are at any given moment is continuously transformed by the passing (of bodies, materials, and communications) through them.[28]

Highly localized communications and exchanges take place in proximity with those of great reach and complexity. They interact with each other, shape each other, and sometimes are folded into the other and re-differentiated. Take a new boutique restaurant in an "up and coming" neighborhood. The highly localized livelihoods for migrant workers in the restaurant kitchen constitute an insular shell significantly removed from other transactions around them, yet are still intensely articulated to diaspora networks in other cities. At the same time, the cosmopolitan array of customers in the dining area may bring together entertainment, business, finance, and personal services sectors in concrete collaboration. Some of the food is flown in from all across the world and it "meets" other foods that come from dedicated gardens at the outskirts of the city. A single trucking company may handle the final delivery of both. And, of course, the restaurant is next to something else—a residence, a grocery, or another restaurant.

A person always exists in the city in multiple ways, wherever they happen to be. Here, the street—not as the concrete street we conventionally think of it—is the switching mechanism pointing a person's perception, thinking, and performances to more or less one dimension of this multiplicity or another. In other words, city residents are always in several places at once, heading in many different directions at the same time. Of course, it is impossible to be aware of all of these places and directions; there is simply too much already to pay attention to. It is difficult enough to perform everyday routines and fulfill everyday tasks. Yet anyone can be potentially "switched" into another gear, become aware of "new" surroundings, with the possibility of seeing something around them that many others probably do not yet see.

One way to envision this metaphorically is to take any aerial photograph of a large metropolitan system, such as Bangkok for example, and remove all of the grids, streets, and buildings. This leaves only the constellation of road junctions—traffic circles, carrefours, u-turns, fly-overs, exit and entrance ramps —that operate as relays and switches in what the French architect Pierre Bélanger has called "knot city." This is an infrastructure for redirecting, speeding up, or slowing flows down, for modulating the intensities and rhythms of movement, for translating multiple directions and flows in terms of each other. Whereas these actual constellations of road junctions have specific shapes and locations contingent upon the areas in which they are embedded, using them as a metaphor for the street here requires thinking about them as omnipresent. They are something that is located everywhere given that all places entail switching and translation mechanisms. The street disappears from the version of how we have come to know it, and reappears across the city and, in significant ways, is the city. This is why it is possible for residents in Kali Baru, for example, to so readily seem to "know" what to do when new tasks are "asked" of them.

WATCHING THEM WATCHING THEM: BRINGING THE STREET INSIDE AND THE INSIDE TO THE STREET

Let's take a particular example of how this sense of the street works. The Protea Gardens Hotel, once one of the Johannesburg inner city's premier hotels, is largely cordoned off, its last function being as a long-term rooming house for a primarily Malawian and Nigerian clientele. Located at the corner of Tudhope and O'Reilly roads in the Berea district, the hotel fronted one of the city's main drug trafficking thorough-fares—a veritable carnival of commerce as the trade supported scores of food stalls and other services to both dealers and passers-by. Two hotels, the Mark and the Sands, had been appropriated in the early 1990s by mostly Nigerian dealers as nerve centers for the trade. They spawned other commercial activities and housed hundreds of foreign migrants who, if not directly involved in the drug business, provided services from money laundering and real estate to working in the cosmetic and beautician outlets that were often used as fronts for the trade. O'Reilly Road was an impenetrable bastion yet at the same time there was little effort to disguise this local economy.

Subject to many unsuccessful crackdowns, the lucrative trade provided too many opportunities for corruption until units within the elite Scorpion police task force deployed advanced surveillance technologies. They not only monitored the comings and goings of the trade on the street but more importantly conducted infrared scanning of the interior of the Mark and Sands Hotels in order to facilitate fast-track pro-secutions in the criminal courts. The prosecutors brought U.S. RICO (Racketeer Influenced and Corrupt Organizations Act)-like laws to bear on the interlocking syndicates that controlled local and international distribution.

Surveillance units were set up on the 17th floor of the Protea Gardens using infrared scanning devices and clandestine CCTV units installed within the hotels. As the documentation produced with this technology had been legally authorized, the aim was to accumulate enough evidence not only to elim-inate the "runners" but to establish links to the top managers of the trade, who rarely were visible in Berea. Even though dispersed across a wider network of hotels, apartment build-ings, and businesses across Johannesburg, the effort was successful in closing down much of the drug trade on O'Reilly Road. However, this was not without several interruptions.

I had many conversations with the hotel manager, Bernadette, which focused on the conflicts between different national groupings within the hotel and the problems keeping the hotel financially viable. One day she showed me the remnants of an operation on the 18th floor. Here, one floor above the Scorpion surveillance teams, Nigerian "technicians" had torn down the walls separating several adjoining hotel rooms and had set up surveillance devices of their own. The intent was to interfere with the equipment below—distorting images, inserting static in the video feeds, and even attempting to interpose remixed images of the same sites being surveyed but in different time and action sequences.

The question is, if the dealers on O'Reilly Road knew they were being watched from the 17th floor, why did they not simply change their operations on the street or, alternately, gradually disperse them long before they did? As this surveillance operation was staffed twenty-four hours a day, there was really no way for the technicians on the 18th floor to verify whether their interference was successful or not. On the other hand, given these layers of observation—Nigerian technicians watching Scorpions watch the street as it was enfolded into the two hotels—the street itself becomes the test of two competing efforts at engineering specific visual evidence.

While more transactions were taken off the street, the reluctance of many customers to enter the hotels necessitated keeping a portion of the trade on the street. If the drug operations, or at least a particular sector of them, knew they were under surveillance, then the street functioned as the "great set-up." Perhaps the dealers tried to lead the Scorpion watchers on, getting them to look at particular scenarios and scenes and follow them to their various "destinations" inside. Here the play on the street might have been meant to orchestrate the subsequent movement of vision as it attempted to track the petty trades on the street to the big decisions and transactions inside. Clearly, everything taking place inside couldn't be scrutinized, could not be immediately transparent or meaningful, and so the surveillance team had to take "leads," had to take the "bait." And so, again, the street becomes a switching mechanism. It is nothing in itself but a system of relays and switches, just as the Nigerian technicians tried to switch the tables on the Scorpions by messing with the switches on the machines.

ONCE UPON MANY DIFFERENT TIMES IN INNER CITY JOHANNESBURG

Movement, whether it is circulations through a familiar and limited terrain or moving out into a larger world, requires putting together particular vantage points. In the discussion below, I want to use the case of the inner city of Johannesburg to demonstrate the importance of such vantage points to the process of movement. For if movement is an important factor in sustaining heterogeneous urban districts, and this sustenance is key to the viability of cities—their promise and capacities—then it is important to understand what vantage points are and what they do.

The inner city of Johannesburg is part of an urban system that has experienced substantial changes over the past twenty years. Johannesburg is moving away from a city centered on the management of mining economies within its borders. It now provides quality info-tech and financial services required for expanding and introducing new efficiencies into mining, agriculture, and oil production, while linking gold, oil, diamonds, platinum, agricultural, and various financial products. Given the character of the former apartheid South Africa, with

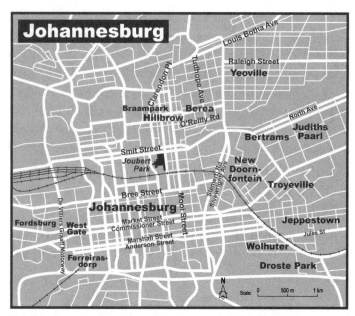

Map 7
Inner City Johannesburg

its mix of economic advantages and distortions, the insulation of the manufacturing sector, and a captured labor force, many changes have taken place in the past two decades.

Interactions between multinationals, domestic actors, and production processes have changed the spatial character of the city.[29] The central business district has been mostly relocated to the north of the former central city, near new, often heavily fortified, residential areas. As industrial manufacturing continues to decline, and thus also the need for miners and factory workers, Johannesburg is physically reshaped to cultivate new connections among finance, telecommunications, energy, engineering, construction, informatics, and tourism.

Large numbers of migrants, businesspersons, academics, sojourners, and NGOs from other parts of Africa have been a potent force in remaking the city, as the South African presence in the rest of the region has also expanded.[30] Additionally, the speed with which a major South African commercial and political role in Africa has been consolidated also points to the substantial capital flight which occurred in the years preceding the political transition, as well as the networks through which this capital flight was organized. Operating outside official regulations, money and goods have circulated through sophisticated conduits across territories whose varying banking and trade regimes would otherwise impede such flows.[31]

Through a combination of centralizing regional services, dominating regional inward investment, and elaborating unconventional circuits of resource flows, South Africa maintains a strong comparative advantage in terms of the costs of moving money, goods, and people across enlarged spaces of operation.[32] This makes Johannesburg a center not only for a formal regional economy, but also for a variety of other "real" economies at different scales and degrees of legality. A more sophisticated formal trading, service, and financial infrastructure has its counterpart in a more invisible, "informalized" one. The latter is composed of diverse economic activities and actors operating at different scales and with different capacities. It often draws upon illegal goods and the illicit exchange of conventional goods or services.

Residential and occupational segregation based on race began to break down in the mid-1980s. For the forty years prior to this point, Johannesburg retained a clear geographical separation of black working-class communities in the south of the city and a white middle-class in the northern suburbs. Deindustrialization in the areas immediately south of the central business district combined with the reorganizing of manufacturing that remained shifted investment and jobs to the north. The preference for more secure, campus-style, and automobile accessible office developments, as well as emphasis on sub-contracting work to informal enterprises, severely affected the central business district.[33] This re-location of the economy has also led to a shift of commercial and residential investment to suburban-type shopping malls and gated communities.

While an emerging black, educated middle class has been able to follow this economic shift, the vast majority of black urban residents face escalating unemployment and impoverishment. While the largest black community, Soweto, is the site for new shopping malls and middle-class developments, it has not captured other major economic investments. The gaps in the relationship between the skill levels of the black majority, the skill requirements of available employment, the location of job opportunities, and the location of affordable residential opportunities skews the housing market. Here, there are few transitional opportunities where residents can incrementally graduate to improved livelihoods. In light of this situation, the use of the inner city as a transitional space only intensifies.

Perhaps only 10 percent of the inner city's current residents were living here ten years ago.[34] Foreign African and Asian immigrants and black South Africans coming from across the country are all vying to establish some foothold.[35] All attempt this without much institutional support and with an urban infrastructure in severe decline.[36] It also appears that most residents live in ways that are different to the way they have been accustomed to in the past.[37] Elaborate relationships are pieced together among hawkers, individuals with some form of formal employment, social networks organized around a set of individuals' patronage of specific bars and hotels, taxi drivers and passengers, railway workers, and the clients of the large number of hotels in the area.[38] There are many who simply wait for something to happen. Otherwise, they aggressively pursue an opportunity to steal, work in someone else's scheme, or live off of someone else's income.

The hundreds of mostly handwritten notices advertising and requesting accommodation hung across the outside walls of the Hillbrow Post Office embody the arbitrary arrangements of vantage points strewn across the inner city of Johannesburg. In other words, the inner city often feels like a sea of disconnected fragments that momentarily float into each other, make a quick life with each other, and then float away. While spatial analyses tend to emphasize fragmentations and disjunctions in the urban fabric, this topography of patchworks must be augmented by the criss-crossing sensibilities of residents who have to maneuver across the city from sometimes highly peculiar configurations of security and risk. In other words, residents "read" the specific kind of buildings and blocks they pass, and the routes they attempt to stabilize, as some kind of a "shell" or "capsule" that takes them from home to work to family and friends, to shopping and services. Residents need specific "vantage points"—not only ways of seeing the city, but of stabilizing a way of moving through it, paying attention to it, and, as a result, stabilizing their own presence within it.

The inner city "suburbs" (as they are known), such as Hillbrow, Joubert Park, and Berea, with their large stock of medium- and high-rise residential buildings, and Yeoville, Jeppestown, Bertrams, and Troyeville, with their smaller apartment blocks and single-family dwellings, house perhaps 400,000 people within high-density conditions. In general, the physical conditions of these buildings have deteriorated over the past two decades. But this overall impression of the depreciation and overcrowding of housing stock and the shrinkage of formal commercial activity must be qualified by the fact that many buildings in these areas have been continuously maintained in a stable condition and that some buildings and blocks have "turned over many futures." As a result, it is hard to determine any consistent pattern of ascendancy or decline.

As the histories of buildings and blocks are scattered across a landscape of an apparent decline of the central city, and within neighborhoods that are highly compact, residents frequently talk about how easy it is for the inner city to "switch up" on them. So assessing just how safe or dangerous it may be to do something or go to a specific place can be a matter of complicated calculations about how to manage different situations and territories that seem to be randomly arranged. It is true that entire blocks acquire reputations in terms of the kind of people who are most visibly present. There are areas that are to be avoided at particular times of day. But when inner-city residents are interviewed about their specific itineraries there are often few common patterns of movement. There is only provisional consensus as to what specific routes, blocks, and neighborhoods may have in store.

These diverging impressions are not a matter of individualized approaches to navigation or the absence of more broadly social ways of generating common knowledge about the inner city. Indeed, these matters of what particular places mean and the risks and possibilities they entail are constantly being talked about. For example, foreign-born African residents are always assessing just where it is most viable for people of particular nationalities to situate themselves. Is it safer to concentrate in specific areas, gradually building a certain ethnic or national solidarity within a given building, block, or neighborhood? To what extent do the benefits of such concentration give way to risks entailed by greater visibility and, depending on the legal status of these residents, open them up to greater scrutiny and police control? At what point does co-residence with common nationals reach a certain saturation point, limiting economic opportunities, and motivating individuals to spread out into other areas? Sometimes specific "archipelagos" are created—i.e. small enclaves of consolidation (for example specific Congolese blocks) that anchor movements across the different districts. Of course, migrants from, say, Senegal, Congo, Nigeria, and Ethiopia are not homogenous groupings. They come from specific cities, ethnicities, and professions that equip them with specific capacities and affiliations. Individual histories of settlement in the inner city are highly dependent upon many different other histories and decisions.

In Johannesburg, Eritrean migrants, who manage most of the clothing stalls in the crowded Jeppe-Troye-Bree Street part of the inner city Fashion District, would seem to be extending the activated memory of their country's long history of being scattered around the world—something compensated by strong communal ties. Even though many men and women migrants are quite young, they come from families where older generations were refugees who moved among different countries in the Horn, the Gulf, Europe, and North America. From the beginning, the trajectories of this older generation were less individuated, as movement and money were based more in the collective operations of particular clans and towns back home, of which they become, in a very loose way, representatives.

Some Eritrean Muslims attend a mosque on Moii Street that serves the largely South Asian merchants who formerly owned and operated the shops in the areas. As a result, some of these Eritreans began to work in and eventually manage these stores for the South Asians as they became nervous about the lack of security. As the immigration status of many of these migrants remains uncertain, thus foreclosing opportunities to buy businesses and buildings in the area outright, they have entered into sub-contractual relationships with the original owners. These provide the Eritreans unlimited use rights, but usually only for a period of time, which the owners keep vague.

Additionally, even though Ethiopians and Eritreans have much in common culturally and religiously, the political relationships between the two countries have been antagonistic ever since Eritrea won its independence from Ethiopia. Nevertheless, migrants turn the fact that they are usually lumped together by others into an advantage, opening up circuits of trade and commerce otherwise not readily available to either Ethiopians or Eritreans acting on their own. They operate in a part of the city where the differences between day and night are pronounced. Because the area is located in what is known as a "community improvement district," a business consortium pays for security during the day but not at night. Streets full of shoppers during the day are replaced by nefarious activities at night. As a result, Ethiopian and Eritrean merchants have put together a tight security operation across an eight square block radius. As these merchants revitalize the area and establish a viable niche for their families and fellow nationals in the city, they become a more visible target for the police. More important, they leave themselves vulnerable to either the re-appropriation of "their" businesses by the "real owners" or the speculative actions of new developers. As was the case for the Malian, Senegalese, Nigerian, and Congolese artisans and merchants who came before them, they are forced to establish new ventures in more precarious parts of the inner city.

As networks of fellow nationals, family, friends, and collaborators become more dispersed, cell phones become important instruments. They meld different locations and vantage points into an experience of proximity. Migrants in the inner city are always inquiring where people are and informing them of their own location, reporting events and situations on the street and in buildings, seizing opportunities when they come up, such as finding good prices or meeting someone from their original home who has brought news or important things. Finally, it is an instrument that attempts to minimize danger by having people watch out for certain places or people, and by publicizing one's own journeys and intended schedules of moving from here to there. This practice makes relations dense, and this can in turn "thicken" a particular vantage point or way of doing things as it tries to function across what appears to be a chaotic city where every agenda and journey could be potentially interrupted in adverse ways.

In some instances residential opportunities are contingent upon simultaneously ruining and developing property. Because of the raids on illegal immigrants during the past few years, some Malians, kicked out from their long-term homes in Berea and relocating in smaller apartment blocks in Jeppestown, would intentionally gut the front sections of small apartment blocks, making it appear as if they were just squatting, while developing and reinforcing the back flats. Even in some of the larger apartment towers in Hillbrow and Berea, migrants have remade and fortified large parts of the interior—into workshops, residential compounds, and businesses—while intentionally maintaining the most visible parts of the building in a functional state of disrepair. For it is important that the building not appear to be totally run-down in order to avoid foreclosures or the turning off of services. In a very few instances, consortia of residents have been able to buy buildings behind the name of a co-national that has legal status. In most instances, they have had to rely upon costly arrangements with various management companies.

The forces of "slummification" have been clear. First the Sectional Title Act of 1986 made it possible for units within an apartment complex to be individually owned. This was a move which placed the onus of servicing buildings onto management companies retained by a corporate body to be organized by the individual owners of the apartments. These companies had to ensure the collection of fees from a diverse profile of multiple owners, some of whom lived in the premises and others of whom rented them out for income. Thus the management of buildings grew more complicated. This was something that worked under relatively stable markets and social conditions, but became problematic in a rapidly changing urban environment.

White flight during the late 1980s and early 1990s, when the inner city became a *de facto* place of black residency, was also accompanied by black professional flight as their incomes increased and they had access to new residential opportunities opened up by the end of apartheid. Many property owners wrote off their holdings, or ended up being dependent upon management companies who failed to pay bills or provide adequate maintenance. For some years after the political transition, the newly constituted municipal government, inheriting a highly outdated cadastral account of existent properties, did not have a full account of arrears. As a result, some management companies pocketed rents and avoided taxes without facing services being cut off. Because of the provisional nature of much employment, tenants would often pay the first and last month's rent upfront as required and then not pay anything else, just waiting for the eviction process to take its course.

While many buildings required prospective tenants to remit proof of employment, bank accounts, and South African identity cards, many of these tenants would quickly move on to better neighborhoods, subleasing flats to tenants who would sublease them again. In some situations, renting to foreign migrants in precarious legal situations could generate much more income than renting to South Africans. Still, the demand on inner-city housing has been intense. With limited incomes, transportation from the outlying black townships is too costly and time consuming given where work opportunities are located. Thus, a huge rental market has continued to exist.

As such, the extraction of rents from tenants has continued—where buildings are not maintained and municipal taxes are not paid. It is difficult to read through the opaque web of ownership structures. For example, companies with various permutations on nautical names—Green Wave, Ocean Blue, Dolphin's Crest, to name a few—acquire buildings, extract rents for several months, and then disappear, only for a "new company" to acquire the property for an even cheaper price, pay a discount on the past debt, and repeat the cycle all over again.

This practice is combined with a kind of "Russian doll" subletting of spaces within individual flats. And thus the handwritten signs on the wall of the Hillbrow Post Office. Here, the tenant of a flat will subdivide the premises and then rent out particular rooms and spaces to others, usually not only covering their own costs, but making a profit as well. Thus, the overarching management company has no idea who is actually living in the building. As these arrangements are often transitory, there is a great turn-over of occupants within a given building, with no one knowing really who "belongs" or doesn't. As these subtenants usually have no contractual basis for their tenancy, they are subject to the arbitrary inclinations of those who hold some kind of lease. At the same time, as the tenant with the lease has often coerced it from a prior tenant, of whom he or she was a subtenant, there are often struggles on the part of tenants to win control over a flat—given its capacity to generate income. Sometimes these fights turn violent.

Whether or not the antagonism among co-tenants gets out of hand, the basic conditions of such arrangements require incessant negotiations about the working out of financial and domestic responsibilities among what are for the most part strangers. There is often a limited basis or "language" in which this can be done. Sometimes tenants try to avoid each other altogether and minimize any kind of social relationship so as not to be caught in burdensome obligations. At other times, a semblance of functional households emerges, but this is rare. Still, in some circumstances, co-tenancy is arranged on the basis of attempting to forge limited complementarities among very different kinds of actors that serve some kind of mutual interest. For example, foreign migrants looking for some way to better integrate themselves in local South African networks may share a flat with South Africans looking to get involved in the entrepreneurial activities popularly associated with foreign Africans. At other times, common church membership becomes the basis of co-tenancy, just as that church membership is a domain through which certain kinds of mutual collaboration can be attained and practiced.

Some buildings have been able to sustain effective resident management committees that have attempted to maintain the properties and have linked up with various municipal programs and non-governmental agencies specializing in housing development in order to access financing for regeneration and secure management. In some buildings, these efforts have been difficult in face of transitory populations and political conflicts.

If the buildings on any given block can convey radically different residential and management histories, as well as be subject to the constant uncertainty generated by unaccounted subtenant arrangements, the vantage points from which any individual resident proceeds to navigate their everyday lives across the inner city are fraught with complexity. By definition the consolidation of vantage points into fairly well-established points of view shared by a sufficient density of residents proves difficult. As a result, these neighborhoods become, in an important sense, the intersection of a plurality of different vantage points that implicitly must come up with ways of dealing with and accommodating each other. But since these intersections are not stable, there is the resounding sense of places within these neighborhoods switching up on each other.

While residents may come to know that a particular corner is the hang-out of "bad guys" or a particular building has a long history of being in pretty good shape, what cannot be anticipated in a consistent way are the results of the contiguities of all these different claims on places or the histories of decline, stability, or regeneration of specific buildings or blocks. Does the existence of a couple of "good" buildings on a block do something to those that are considered "bad"? Is this existence a deterrent to further decline, an incentive to rejuvenation? Do the more resourceful stock and activities in a given space become an object of parasitism by others? Is the existence of the "bad" an incentive for greater efforts at consolidation by those associated with the "good"? Even though there is much in the social-psychological literature which offers clear knowledge about these dynamics, its application to the dynamics of an inner city with such a multiplicity of enclaves and temporalities remains tentative.

This inherent difficulty in confidently predicting the outcome of such proximities—of the good, bad, and ugly—is important in terms of what municipal policy can do. For example, the Johannesburg Development Agency, the implementing arm of the municipal government for infrastructure operations in the inner city, is rebuilding the major public spaces and streetscapes of Hillbrow, Berea, and Yeoville. Sidewalks and drains are being torn up and re-laid. While there is a clear engineering need for such rehabilitation, the idea behind the project is also that well-made thoroughfares themselves will act as a disciplinary incentive, promoting more ordered uses of the public space that could be transferred into a more positive overall attitude about the neighborhood. In other words, the idea is that these limited interventions will generate a more widespread multiplier effect. When the streets and public spaces look "good," residents will be motivated to approach the general urban environment with a sense of the "good"—in terms of their relationship to each other, to waste, and to more private spaces. Of course, the relationship between these interventions and the broader hoped-for outcomes is mediated by the quality of policing, the regulatory capacities of both public and commercial actors regarding the management and transfer of property, and a wide range of both macro and local economic factors. There are no overarching reasons why such a multiplier effect either can or cannot occur.

In part, it is important that residents perceive that the municipal government is capable of intervening, of doing something. By focusing on the very visible remaking of streetscapes and public places the government shows that it is making its mark. It shows that it is at least symbolically capable of exerting some kind of control in face of an urban terrain where often those with the most muscle and impunity, those able to best mobilize disposable and unaccounted cash from illicit economies, come to dominate specific buildings and blocks and force other residents into a state of constant worry.

It remains to be seen whether this symbolism forcefully provokes the disposition intended. But it does add another factor, another piece to an already complex patchwork of vantage points.

These vantage points are also those of policy. For example, there are differences between the vantage points of maintaining the right to residence as opposed to maintaining the health and viability of either a specific group of residents or an area. For example, the San Jose is a fifteen-story apartment block in Berea that has been abandoned by its owners for several years. There are some 369 residents in the building living without water and electricity, in highly unsanitary conditions despite the efforts of a residential management committee that enforces tight rules and attempts weekly clean-ups to ensure a modicum of order—including collecting small fees for maintenance and the disposal of night buckets. The building is situated in a part of Berea which is considered a key transitional zone in the efforts by municipal agencies, NGOs, and private developers to regenerate this area. The municipality's efforts to close the building were blocked in court, which ruled that the evictions of residents could not be undertaken unless adequate provisions were made to relocate these residents within affordable and suitable housing.

After protracted negotiations with the residents and their legal advisors, a site was identified in nearby Hillbrow. In the long period necessary to establish the identities of residents of San Jose so as to know who exactly was eligible to move to the new building, the resident committee provided the city with a specific list where the names of who was eligible changed many times over the course of the year. While it was to be expected that some residents would have moved away or died, what is also evident is the fact that many residents do not see it as in their interests to opt for the new building. For the new residential situation will require them to use fingerprint identification to enter the building and assume a contractual obligation to pay rent and services, even though subsidies will be available. So while a great demand certainly does exist for tight and secure management structures, there are large numbers of inner-city residents who prefer to operate under different kinds of radars.

Still, it is difficult for key urban policymakers in Johannesburg to imagine an approach different from the one that attempts to "take back" these districts and regenerate them one building or block at a time. While the demand for safe and secure housing has been intensely felt by residents having to navigate precarious conditions with constant agility, it is not clear what the medium-term effects will be of the seemingly draconian measures that are applied in order to provide such security. For example, the Metropolitan is one of Berea's largest apartment complexes. With 400 studio and one-bedroom units it was one of the best-run complexes of its size until it rapidly deteriorated several years ago. Acquired by Paul Miller, along with ten other properties in Berea, it has been completely refurbished and has 1000 tenants. Each unit is allowed no more than three residents, and entrance is regulated by a series of gates and fingerprint systems. No parties are allowed and visitors are strictly regulated—even more so than in your usual prison. The tenancy agreements are strict and permit no leniency when rules are violated, and the internal security system is run by former members of the South African Defense Force—who are commonly referred to as the "bad boys" and whose reputation around the city nearly equates them to the worst gangs. Yet when residents are interviewed they relate to these measures as if a trauma was being relinquished. They are readily receptive to the harshness of the security measures, even if the inconveniences cited far outnumber those that residents enumerate in much more chaotic buildings.

These efforts, however, would probably not have been possible without the track record of the Johannesburg Housing Company (JHC), which owns and operates twenty-four mixed-income apartment complexes in the central city. Fifty percent of the units are designated for households earning less than US$500 a month, who are thus entitled to government subsidies. Because of its emphasis on social housing and the fact that it ventured into areas of the city where no one else was able to go, JHC leveraged highly favorable prices and was able to keep costs low while generating sufficient profit to cover its costs. But prices have been going up fast. A frequently cited example is that of the Landdrost Hotel, which was bought for $400,000, with the upgrade and conversion into 240 units costing $2 million, and each unit costing $7,500. An equivalent building bought eight years later went for $2.5 million, costing nearly $3 million for upgrading, and with units going for $12,000.[39]

As prices have escalated with the high demand for low-to middle-income housing and the more visible success of regeneration efforts, more complex maneuvers from both public authorities and property developers are required in order to maintain affordability. The municipality sponsors a Better Buildings Program which enables investors to acquire buildings at market value even when the arrears for rates and service charges exceed the market value, and thus the debt owed to the city is written down. However, administrative procedures require these exemptions to be made on a time-consuming building-by-building basis. In some instances there has been an extension of sectional title where conversions are opened up to individual investors in a way that enables banks to lend almost the complete purchase price and with developers also guaranteeing a base rent for a two-year period to investors in order to minimize their income risk.

Even as the provision of low- to middle-income housing takes, the problem remains of what to do with residents with very provisional incomes. These residents provide a vast market for syndicates that barely maintain the buildings they hold and that subdivide them incessantly so that it is possible to rent a part of a room for $25 a month. There is a substantial inner-city population which live in such circumstances, earning their meager incomes at the lowest end of an informal service economy—a situation which absolutely requires them to live in the inner city. When more of the inner city regenerates, they simply move into the interstices, raising the possibilities of new kinds of social collisions.

The Ekhaya Neighborhood Association, anchored on Petersen Street in southern Hillbrow, has worked with twenty-two buildings over the past seven years. The idea was to mobilize residents in a series of relatively small events, from a safe New Year's, with celebrations that avoid gunfire and the dumping of furniture from apartment windows, to community festivals which emphasize different ways of getting residents acquainted with each other. This moved to working with a coalition of building owners to repaint and refurbish properties, conjointly supporting a coordinated network of building managers to whom tenants could report complaints and service problems. While these efforts have been largely successful in stabilizing this street, it remains situated in a very volatile district of the city. Two blocks down toward the central city begin streets largely controlled by Zimbabwean gangs with a reputation for ruthlessness, and much ruthlessness will be required to dislodge them. As drug trafficking was largely cleared out of southern Berea, it moved further toward the central city and along much more publicly traversed corridors in order to blend in. While interventions like those of Ekhaya are crucial to the city, they become another point of divergence in the overall landscape, setting up points of contact, bringing about new frontiers that face a protracted "tug of war" in these interfaces.

While residents across the inner city are persuaded that substantial change is possible, new spatial competitions occur in the pockets where this change takes place. Residents who make a viable life by their ability to operate in both legal and illegal activities have to come up with new tactics to ensure the survival of the weakly controlled spaces they depend on for their ability to maneuver between these legal and illegal worlds. Regeneration inevitably displaces particular kinds of residents and economic activities in favor of the overall interest of the majority of residents in safe and affordable housing opportunities. An important dimension of this process is the displacement of thousands of petty jobs—from hawking, running errands, running interference, providing informal security, and working across the "low-end" service sectors of cell phone shops, beauty parlors, prepared food, pawn shops, and cheap clothing outlets, as well as various street trades, such as repairing cars and shoes. To what extent will this undermine a local economy on which residents of all walks of life depend?

Even as inner-city residency becomes more stable, there is the ambiguity of uncertain costs, particularly as both licit and illicit economies find new ways of surviving and remaking themselves. Although the government supports the employment of small local firms to conduct much of the upgrading work—from cleaning up parks, repaving streets, constructing new public facilities—the stringent requirements for receiving publicly subsidized employment and tenders rule out many local artisans. Artisans must bring identity documents, proof of residence, qualification certificates, and references. Small-, medium-, and micro-enterprise contractors must bring a company profile, company registration papers, tax clearance certificate, bank statements, and proof of payment of their rates and taxes. Bureaucracies here are tedious and costly.

Additionally, it is not clear where development is going. This is particularly evident in the central commercial districts of the city that in recent years have been replete with new initiatives of all kinds. During the past two decades most of the business in the center city moved north to the "new downtown" of Sandton, which today houses the bulk of corporate headquarters and is the geographic center of the South African economy. Yet, the central city continues to anchor the large headquarters complex of the mining conglomerate Anglo-American, First National and Standard Banks, and six years ago a new corporate headquarters was built for Absa Bank in the eastern section of the central city. The regional provincial government has reconstituted a sizeable portion of the central city as its administrative precinct, also ensuring that large numbers of employees continue to fill the central city. It has proposed the building of enormous public squares and networks of underpasses that would require the demolition of many buildings seen as important heritage sites. While these plans have been blocked, the provincial government sits on sizeable holdings that they have yet to do anything with.

Large numbers of vacated commercial and administrative properties have been acquired; many initiatives have been proposed. While scores have come to fruition—i.e. mostly centered on the development of both luxury and middle-end housing—scores of projects have also stalled. One major developer, Ocean Blue, with some 25 projects in the central city, sold units for 10 percent down payments, with the balance due on completion, but has only finished a handful, and questions have been raised about its prospects of finishing more. The formerly largest and best known hotel in the inner city, the Carlton, abandoned a decade ago, has recently been resold several times in quick succession, at one point reportedly ending up in the hands of the Russian Mafia. But in one of the most run-down parts of the central city, the conversion of 120 End Street from offices to residences is billed as the world's largest such project, and will provide 924 flats, a $6000m^2$ shopping centre, a $500m^2$ gym and a 400m jogging track.[40] These residential complexes tend to emphasize a large degree of self-containment since there remains a dearth of surrounding amenities, such as restaurants and food stores that remain open past 6 p.m. Thus these projects remain highly enclaved and not, for the most part, integrated into the surrounding area—which accounts for the city's emphasis on constructing cultural, service, and leisure corridors in the city.

In a central city where many new initiatives have taken off and many have stalled and gone nowhere, the intricate proximities of a stalwart corporate economy, the reinsertion, if only partial, of a dynamic governmental precinct, prolific regeneration, and a thriving low-end retail and service economy interact in multiple and uncertain ways. Combined with efforts to build new corridors, to construct new public and cultural spaces, and to rationalize transport systems now dominated by the daily commutes of scores of thousands of minibus taxis, future trajectories cannot be easily subsumed under the tags of gentrification, regeneration, or slummification.

Compact territories, often within one square block, may contain a heritage site converted into a new cultural center, a Chinese textile wholesaler, a Congolese cell phone shop, several Ethiopian car retailers, Mozambican car repairers operating informally from the curb, a corner where young Zimbabwean teens are solicited to help carry bundles of goods to the sprawling taxi ranks, an office building converted into Manhattan-style lofts, a building completely abandoned and used as an informal drinking place and brothel at night. Eventually specific blocks and territories will become specific and homogenous. But when a lot of the inner city is characterized by these diversities and multiple vantage points, it is not easily evident how to characterize it as a whole. This is particularly the case given all the apparent and underlying complicities that exist in these relationships. For example, foreign immigrants who run medium-sized retail businesses provide low-cost goods for low-salaried civil servants, for small traders coming into the city from all over Southern Africa, and for a new generation of young professionals looking for a more urban vibe.

WAITING FOR THE RIGHT TIME AND THE RIGHT ANTICIPATION: HOW TO THINK ABOUT THE COLLECTIVE FORCE OF CITIES

The mixed-up worlds of central Johannesburg demonstrate that it is often not clear what facets of urban life have a better claim on being more viable, legitimate, or right for the city. The intersections such as those I have explored in inner-city Johannesburg make governing difficult and primarily a process of striking deals and making sure things don't get too far out of hand. While policymaking and governing are essential aspects to the survival of cities, there is also something at work that can't be really captured by policy or government. For many cities in the Global South, there is an important political dimension to these mixtures that has to do with their efforts to be "normal" and "modern" cities, but also expresses aspects of individual and collective life that were interrupted by the impositions of colonial rule and the ways in which the powerful determinants of local urban economies continue to come from the outside.

Pheng Cheah writes about the "spectral nationality" that hangs over and haunts peoples of the postcolony.[41] What he means is that the effort to build nations in the Global South often finds itself dissipated and fractured by war, indebtedness, exploitation, or stuck in highly disadvantageous relationships with global capital. Despite all this, a dream-image of a particular way of life—a way of life fought for in wars of liberation and struggles for independence—continues to exist, albeit in ways that have changed drastically over the years. According to Cheah, it is a dream where people go beyond the particularities of their local circumstances and relations; something concretized in and through the idea and form of "the nation." If the spectral is thought to exert real effects on what people do, then what are the "architectures" and conditions of existence for these effects? How do people in often dire circumstances keep the dream of "the nation" alive—especially if the nation in this instance is something more than a set of institutions, laws, and borders? Especially if the nation is a means of experiencing new kinds of connections among people with whom one shares a city; something more just; something with more space for the majority to not only improve their material conditions but to also make all of the years of living by their wits count for something else.

The spatial arrangements and social relations of the city that currently exist could not by themselves make up the incipient form of such a nation. Given the realities of urban life for the majority of the urban residents in the Global South, they would be hard pressed to see much signs of hope in what currently exists. Aspirations for new forms of collective life would seem "dead in the water" before they had any chance of suggesting any concrete visions. Neither would urban residents go out of their way and risk everything to insist on an all or nothing realization of dreams and ways of doing things that starkly announced themselves to be either antagonistic to the world's dominant models or an alternative to them. If they did so, they would likely experience a "second defeat." If independence and liberation never were able to fulfill the hopes which lay behind struggles for nationhood, then the all or nothing demands of a specific alternative would offer today's more powerful political and economic forces an easy target.

Likewise, signs of the spectral—this dream of the nation—which show themselves in the daily practices and arrangements of the "not-yet-citizens" of the "real nation" could not simply be placeholders for what is to come. In other words, all of the creative efforts urban residents make to survive in cities and to keep open the possibilities for a better life are not just compensations for the lack of jobs, services, and livelihoods. They are not the kernels of a new way of being in the city that simply needs more time, political support, and money in order to be realized. Rather, as Cheah implies, something must be set in motion that addresses the turbulent and uncertain experiences of the present; something that constitutes a reminder of a way of life and being together that could have taken place but did not. Something set in motion that brings about a continuously renovated, flexible, and improvised series of tactics that "look everywhere" for opportunities to take "things forward." In other words, there has to be a way to lead people's thoughts, actions, and commitments into versions of themselves for which there are not any clear terms of recognition or clear links to the hopes and dreams to which people aspire.

Therefore, for those who aspire to be something more than they are in the present, the objective is not to tie themselves down to prevailing notions about what can be taken into account, what makes sense, or what is logically possible. The idea is to keep things open, keep things from becoming too settled or fixed. The messed-up city, then, is not simply a mess. In the very lack of things seeming settled, people keep open the possibility that something more palatable to their sense of themselves might actually be possible.

An urban politics that focuses exclusively on defining who is included and who is excluded, who has rights and who doesn't, and who belongs and who doesn't—all in the effort at proficiently calculating the balances between the needs of different kinds of urban actors—will always produce a situation that doesn't fit that calculation.[42] Although no individual or group can find a place outside of the prevailing logics of urban accumulation, power, and governance, there remain processes and figures not fully understood or captured in terms of those logics. There is something that remains aside, if not outside. In part this may be, in Cheah's terms, a kind of possession—i.e. where images and ways of doing things that people feel are connected to the struggles of the past take hold of people's efforts, even as they go about their daily business. In such possession, routines and common practices may persist, but there is something always a little off, as if thoughts and actions are on the verge of breaking away. The "dams may not burst," but something seeps into everyday conditions, steering them off into unforeseen directions. The kinds of intersections of actors, practices, and locales pointed to here in these reflections on Jakarta, Abidjan, and Johannesburg suggest that, despite all the difficulties of everyday survival, some new anticipated life, perhaps waited for a long time, is already being lived.

Whether such a way of life is ever recognized or concretely experienced, it remains a haunting presence. It is something that hangs over many cities—keeping life from being worse than it reasonably should be and, at the same time, seemingly keeping residents from giving their full attention and every effort to making their cities simply copies of those in Europe and North America, even when it seems that all cities are heading in this direction. In Chapter 6, I want to explore some of these notions of haunting. I do this by offering some provisional formulations about how cities from Dakar to Jakarta may be connected in ways that exist outside of the comparisons usually made by geography, sociology, and demography.

Six

Along the various lines that could run from Dakar to Jakarta, there are many different cities. Some are ancient, others relatively new. Some are located in areas criss-crossed many times by various armies, migrants, sojourners; others are somewhat isolated from the major circuits of trade and geopolitical maneuvering. Many different histories, positions, social compositions, and forms of articulation to the world are at work. What I am interested in here is not so much a comparison but finding ways to take the differences into consideration or temporarily hold any random collection of them in view all at the same time.[1] This is not a matter of finding out what they have in common; this is not an effort to find deep structural correlations. Instead it is to imagine a situation where Dakar, Lagos, Nairobi, Dubai, Karachi, Bangkok, and Jakarta—just to take a few to make an example—are "neighbors" in a single metropolitan space, and what that experience might be like for people who would live within it.[2]

RE-IMAGINING CONNECTIONS WITH A LARGER WORLD

In an essay built around a series of photographs of a "disappearing" Harlem taken by Alice Attie, Gayatri Spivak raises the question that has run throughout this book: What can we do together, be together? In an ever-changing culture —where ways of living that exist in the present disappear— the act of taking note, of singling out, of invoking something is inevitably the "opening act" of memorializing, of slowing things down. This is an attempt to refuse to disappear, as Spivak calls it. This refusal to disappear can only "succeed" if it jumps headlong into the distance, imagining new affiliations, new ways of "touching distant others," building up new legacies. It does not have a chance if it tries to hold on to or claim some kind of overarching identity or authenticity. Here the facts of connection do not matter; neither does empirical evidence, as the connections do not have to be verified. In her meditation on Harlem, Spivak cautions that it is not possible to look back or to see in the traces of what is being ruined a clear picture of collective life that now is no longer. Rather, the residual and always incomplete signs of a collectivity steer us to the "hope of resonance" with possible ways of being together that the disappearance compels us to imagine. It is this possibility that refuses to disappear.[3]

The past has been replete with imaginings of connections among cities from Africa to Asia—political, religious, and economic imaginations that have brought various connections to life, that then fade away or are actively dismantled. As matters of urban policy such efforts are rather thin on the ground. Cities are pulled into being exemplars of national aspirations, embodiments of particularized identities and histories, and constrained by wide-ranging anxieties of over-crowding and excess diversity. As Ananya Roy points out, cities must find authoritative ways of recognizing each other, seeing in each other not only certain possibilities of collective strength but also built, social, administrative, and economic environments that clearly have something to offer each other.[4]

Sometimes, certain shortcuts are taken to fast-forward these connections. These usually entail cities opening up special spaces for investments and businesses coming from other cities. While these spaces sometimes attract considerable investment, they are often poorly imagined and barely integrated with what goes on in the rest of a city. It is true that if money, factories, and services coming from different regions across the Global South are to be connected in a given place specific spaces must be put together to facilitate those connections. The connections also produce spatial effects in that they provide new possibilities of access to people, experiences, and information. When different flows of capital, factories, services, communication systems enter a city, provisions must be made to use these inputs in ways that multiply potentially positive effects on national and local economies, accommodate the specific conditions and aspirations associated with those inputs, and get rid of impediments to the potential productivity of those inputs.

Therefore, to put it simply, these investments and activities originating from elsewhere are accorded their space. These spaces attempt to mediate divergent and potentially conflictual trajectories of accumulation, sectoral interests, as well as attempts to integrate investments into an overall economy. At the same time, the reasons that people and companies are investing in this space often have a lot to do with the autonomy they have negotiated with governments to pay certain wages, bring materials into the country without having to pay duty, and send profits back home—i.e. through a wide range of exceptions and exemptions related to law and regulatory regimes. Often the development of these spaces is characterized by different rules for acquiring property, for developing infrastructure and providing water and electricity, or for accounting for how money, land, and labor are used. Sometimes different rules apply to different investors, and so it is difficult for anyone trying to regulate the situation to get a handle on what is going on.

In theory, the presence of different firms and ways of doing business from different parts of the world would seem to benefit those who operate within these spaces—opening up a wider world of contacts, experiences, and expertise to everyone involved. The question concerns not only the extent to which any agglomeration effects are attained, but also whether there are real collaborative arrangements among the key actors involved aimed at maximizing connections among the different financial streams and entrepreneurial networks. Or do these spaces simply house an increasingly large number of discrete firms that have little to do with each other? Can local actors progressively use these spaces as a vehicle through which they exert an impact over a larger domain of economic activity? Are these spaces full of different transnational networks and circuitries, or are they more intensely and extensively transnational spaces themselves, capable of acting as platforms that facilitate the consolidation and extension of cross-regional trade and communication? Granted, much of what facilitates cross-regional trade and other economic flows has to do with macroeconomic policies, the management of national economies, regional coordinating mechanisms and frameworks.

While experiences across cities are varied, it appears that spaces as development corridors, growth triangles, incubation and export zones do not really experience a substantial cross-fertilization or even cross-referencing of activities or contacts.[5] In part, this is because many of these corridors have been designed as abstract entities, with little thought as to how they are to connect to the histories and complexions of the cities. Since they had international credibility as the modality for capturing and managing foreign direct investment, national and metropolitan governments simply set them up. But now that various kinds of finance, actors, networks, interests, commodities, and production plants are being actually situated in these corridors, the kinds of relationships and effects actually emerging are quite limited and demonstrate a paucity of imagination.

WHEN THOSE WHO HAD DISAPPEARED COME BACK INTO VIEW

In light of these experiences, what I want to do here is to stretch the imagination and push the ways in which connections between cities across Asia and Africa could be envisioned. Of course there are many ways to elaborate such an imaginary situation—this contiguity of cities that somehow are brought into a more direct relationship with each other than is usually the case. So what I want to do here is to take one particular analytical instrument in order to move around in such an imaginary space. For this, I want to draw upon something very real, which is the long history of movements undertaken by people of African descent into a larger urban world, both in Africa and beyond. Part of the reason for choosing this particular approach has been my own work with African entrepreneurs in Southeast Asia. It also entails many years of looking at the many different ways Africans move from city to city, country to country, and how their personal trajectories, taken individually and together, make important connections between their places of origin and the different cities in which they come to live, temporarily and for long periods of time. Much of the effort on the part of Africans to move around the world has been made peripheral in discussions about urban development or seen as a problem that needs to be solved. As such, bringing these experiences back from the periphery may be important as a tool for envisioning new ways to think about relations between urban Africa and Asia.

So, the task is to imagine the proximity of cities from Dakar to Jakarta, in order to try to more intensely experience the possible intersections among them and the kinds of things that they could offer each other. A good place to start may indeed be a form of analysis based on the concrete experiences of those who both willingly and unwillingly have acted to make discrepant, often wildly diverse cities close to each other. This is largely an imaginary exercise taken to make visible the possible ways in which major urban areas from Africa, the Middle East, South Asia, to Southeast Asia might have more to do with each other either than has been thought in the past or than is realizable in the present. Accordingly, I will use an "inventive method" for making this exploration; something which I will call "black urbanism" as a means of tying together the various situations and tactics that have been at work in the long history of African people moving out into and around a larger urban world.

First, let me cite two small stories and one longer one that I think capture the kinds of connections I am trying to make. It is February 24, 2008 on Street 37 in the old commercial district of Deira in Dubai. We are in one of hundreds of nondescript housing blocks in this area that now houses thousands of economic migrants who work in various sectors of Dubai's burgeoning service economy: secretaries, media technicians, engineers, drivers, electricians, restaurant managers, store clerks, accountants, and ICT specialists. Ferdinand is chief concierge at Le Meridien Hotel. He has been receiving news from Douala, his home, about the popular revolt that filled the streets of the city following a transport strike. People are fed up with the escalating costs of basic necessities and the attempt by the ruling regime to amend the constitution to overturn the term limits faced by the long-ruling and highly unpopular president. Ferdinand has been on the phone and on-line keeping up with the news while also keeping one eye on a CNN documentary on James Brown being replayed for the fifth time.

Even in the specificities of the Arab work week which make Sunday a work day, laundry night remains on Sunday for the majority of residents in the building. Ferdinand is restless, hyped up with the sentiments conveyed from home. He takes to the hall with his basket of clothes and at the top of his voice begins to alternate the James Brown tune "I Am Black and Proud" with "Sex Machine" all the way down to the basement. Within thirty minutes, seemingly half the building is mingling through the halls dancing and cavorting around, and no less than ten different flats produce tape cassettes of these very same James Brown songs. With this synchronized sound the building cathartically comes out of its usual shell of polite avoidance. Many residents speak to each other for the first time, invite each other into their flats to meet roommates and friends, fetch tea and soft drinks. Living space is very difficult to find in Dubai. Most foreigners move constantly among different arrangements as prices escalate and landlords make deals with tenants whom they consider to be of a "better status." As such, residents in these buildings usually keep their head down; keep whatever they're doing under the radar.

But tonight, kicked off with its frivolous invocations of black pride, a different kind of visibility takes place, as residents have the opportunity to more explicitly visualize just how people are living with each other in various and sundry combinations. People cannot afford these flats on an individual basis. As the majority of tenants are living in Dubai without their families, they have to share apartments and different configurations of individuals have to be put together. Since Emirati landlords for the most part insist upon renting only to conventional households, these arrangements must either pretend to be made up of relatives or remain off the radar. Tonight the architectures of the clandestine become more apparent to neighbors. And it is the relishing of this diverse complexity which seems to keep the "party" going deep into the night, long after the catalytic powers of Ferdinand's incitement with blackness had worn off.

On March 6, 2008, Concrete Stilettos sponsors a party called Amsterdam 2012 at the Gallery Bar in New York. Concrete Stilettos describes itself as an "innovative media, fashion, guerilla marketing, journalism, and training-consultancy/ movement." Its members are all black and most have either grown up in or now reside in Amsterdam. The party is one of those networking affairs, no real program, no announcements or speakers, just cocktails and a video that is looped every ten minutes. Watch the video and there is nothing obviously "black" about the presentation. There are pictures of the main Amsterdam tourist sites, pictures of cheese, sex districts, canals, Central Station, the new gentrified areas of Zuid Amsterdam, cafés, and squares. But inserted in these visuals are the domains of an "other" Amsterdam—but just slightly hinted at—a glittering new office block overlooking a graffiti-covered wall, some empty grounds at the largely African populated housing project Bijlmer, Surinamese families leaving a wedding reception at a fancy hotel. All of it understated, even slight, but enough to make the point that "blackness" is somehow normal in Amsterdam. It does not demand extraordinary attention, it is just something that is there in as mundane a way as anything else. But at the same time what is signaled is that it doesn't take much—no grand statements or images, no invocations of long-term struggles and autonomies—to alter the stability of the "larger scheme of things."

MAKING INFRASTRUCTURES FOR CROSSING THE WORLD

Next to the Bangrak Police Station on Naret Road is a large run-down rooming house formerly known as the Welcome Palace. It is a massive structure of 450 rooms which in its heyday accommodated mainly Chinese sojourners at a reasonable cost. Today, from the outside, it looks like the classic image of a dilapidated public housing project in the *Neuf-trois* suburbs of north-east Paris. In fact, the building now houses the largest African population in the city. Laundry hangs to dry from each inevitably broken window; the plumbing in many of the rooms only sporadically functions; and exposed wiring hangs from many of the hallway ceilings. The cavernous lobby contains a few pieces of broken furniture and the trappings of security are non-existent.

Given the popular reputation of Bangkok's Africans as crooks and drug dealers, there is rarely any effort by one of the

Map 8
Central Bangkok

city's largest police posts, located directly across the street, to monitor what is going on in the building. In fact, there is greater scrutiny of African merchants in the café and bar at the New Trocadero Hotel on Suriwongse, which provides far more upmarket accommodation for a primarily African clientele. It is not clear whether the rumors that have circulated over the past few years about the building's imminent destruction have convinced the police that there is little need to spend too much effort keeping things in line, or whether it is just indifference to residents who look as if they are not into too much of anything significant anyway.

Granted, the surrounding area is dense with people and activities which soften this concentration of foreignness and its movements to and fro; perhaps with the exception of the hundred or so men one can see at midday on a Friday, making their way back from a mosque some 10 blocks away. Men make up 80 percent of the residents in the building. They are, in one way or another, linked to the gem and jewelry business, which is the primary commercial activity of this district.

This does not mean that everyone is necessarily a gem trader. Many wait for either money or orders from home; others do odd errands for their patrons, and still others scout out various opportunities to invest proceeds from gem sales. In addition, much of the gem business acts like an unofficial banking system. Instead of trying to move cash around through bank or wire transfers, particularly risky or unconventional deals are financed by using "gem deposits" as guarantees or collateral. This is an improvisation on the *halwa* system, where cash can be distributed nearly anywhere based on a paying-in—either in equivalent denominations or, as in this case, a valuable commodity—somewhere else. In the Suriwongse gem business, many of the "bankers" also take a part of the proceeds of any deal which is financed.

Many of the residents of Welcome Palace congregate cross-town on the lower-numbered *sois* (alleys) of Sukhumvit. Massive gentrification has pushed out cheap accommodation. But the cosmopolitan atmosphere provides an important opportunity for small-scale entrepreneurs to observe each other pursue different trades, markets, deals, uses of the built environment, and tactics to deal with authorities of various kinds and financial schemes. On the basis of such observations, it is then possible for these actors to identify different ways of trying to connect their activities to the multiply situated and enacted identities of others.[6]

At times, large deals and investments are linked to smaller-scale commercial exchanges; at other times, legal and more illicit transactions are intertwined, then pulled apart. Some activities are clearly illicit or illegal, others are not. Some are simply unconventional in terms of what a given city is used to. Some involve an intricate mesh of various national and sectoral actors.[7] Some are rash and impulsive, others are highly systematic and sophisticated, and still others combine these tendencies. Some of these activities find their niche and are protected over time, while others are incessantly mutating in terms of the goods, territories, and players they are dealing with. The materials involved vary, from items like rice, radios, toothpaste, to bartered goods, currency, visas, and tickets.

The Welcome Palace, as a mobile version of the Parisian *banlieue*, goes beyond simply being a sociological image derived from a history of African migration to France, while at the same time drawing upon it. This is a history that saw men from Senegal, Mali, and Guinea, in particular, take up military jobs during the First World War and in the automobile factories in the aftermath of the Second World War. This labor became a significant platform for the emigration of individuals and families from across Francophone Africa in the subsequent decades, all attempting to access various economic activities and consolidate an African presence across French cities.[8] As many of the important more centrally located African neighborhoods in Paris were cleared out, both immigrants and the French-born became isolated in high-rise residential wastelands. New forms of solidarity, resistance, and livelihood had to be pieced together.[9]

While significant networks of shops, markets, restaurants, and businesses servicing diverse African populations remain, many have also been priced out of central Paris and have limited opportunities to install themselves in the suburbs. Lines of connection, then, in terms of the exchange of goods, information, and services, have to be established much more informally within the residential complexes themselves. They operate out of apartments and in the enclaves and hollows of garages, underpasses, storage rooms, lobbies, and recreational centers. Associational life was built on the networks of dynamic individuals and a plurality of initiatives. These initiatives sought various umbrellas of interconnection and rarely embodied ties to specific groups or categories of work or identity.[10] Flexible categories of belonging were emphasized that exceeded the compensations offered by religious communities or political ideology and instead aimed for a greater autonomy of individual and collective public action.[11]

Whereas the street once provided the organized space where concrete connections among various nodes of commerce and service were navigated, the streets of the *banlieue* are either more circuitous, filled with cul-de-sacs, or take on a foreboding character. As such, commerce and networking are enfolded into residential spaces. Commerce is brought into the hallways, garages, kitchens, and laundry rooms. This is a process that makes what anyone does more available to the intense scrutiny, interference, or collaboration of others. It thus brings both new capacities and problems to residents living in these circumstances.[12]

Until recently, Bangkok has been a relatively easy city for foreigners to move around in, to come and go in, to move things in and out of, and to purchase commodities covering the full spectrum in terms of kind and price. Africans are not new to the city, having first established roots in the textile and rice trade some three decades ago. Recently, Africans (primarily West Africans) have also been using the city as a base to extend their acquisition base into China, Vietnam, and Indonesia, which provide cheaper goods but which are somewhat more difficult logistically to operate within. Culturally and economically, there is little basis for them to enter the labor market as the professional sector only relies upon expatriate participation in very specific domains and lower-end service work can draw upon a vast reserve of Burmese, Cambodian, and Laotian labor. Various forms of trade, then, are the key economic activity that grounds the African population in the city.

For most merchants, it is important to keep overhead and transaction costs as low as possible and, more importantly, to be able to flexibly move money around from one opportunity to another. Such transaction costs entail not only those related to providing for food and shelter, but also assisting others in the event that you may need their assistance in the future. Merchants need a little extra to explore unforeseen opportunities, or to take a chance on some deal where there are few guarantees of success.

Here, circuitries of information are important. It is critical to know who others know; what kinds of collaboration are presently being put into motion; what seems to work and what doesn't. Streets have typically been the occasion and context through which such witnessing could take place, and where different configurations of actors could talk, both in perfunctory and intense exchanges. While the lobby of the Welcome Palace is exceedingly bare, a different story emerges in the upper stories. In the hallways, both men and women prepare food using gas canisters and Styrofoam containers. Fax machines are rigged up on card tables; the walls are covered with announcements of various things for sale, or requests for things like tickets, or opportunities to share cargo containers. Some of the rooms are rented just to store goods; there are prayer rooms and small chapels; the fourth floor has two adjoining rooms where the wall has been torn down and a large television installed connected to a satellite service.

The hundred or so women in the building—some *cormorants* (merchants), some partners, some providing various domestic services to the resident population—even organize *tontines* and *sousou* (savings associations). The building houses a transient population, staying at most several months, although increasingly there are those who operate as the Bangkok "representatives" of syndicates or trading groups cobbled together with varying degrees of formality.

Even though residents complain about the conditions in the building, and the ways that their autonomy of operation is predicated upon the management not taking these conditions and the need for repairs very seriously, the cost remains cheap, less than $10 per day. More importantly, the street can be brought inside, or at least a version of a street. Here, existent and possible relations can be viewed, and there is the possibility of different kinds of intersections—among stories, scenarios, backgrounds, trades, and experiences. In some areas of central Bangkok, streets remain important venues of commerce and social relations—particularly in parts of Sukhumvit, Charoenkrung, Banglamphu, and Phra Khanong.

Yet for a long time, the spaces of commerce have been

ensconced in large shopping malls and dedicated business and wholesale districts. While not completely invisible, the performance of transactions is privatized. Folding the street into the Welcome Palace then creates, for many of its residents, a welcome and necessary supplement to their residence. It is a way of better preparing for the conduct of their often provisional forays into complicated worlds of enterprise. Those worlds are now sectored and specialized. Yet, largely relying on their wits and initiative, most African entrepreneurs have always to keep in mind the connections between trades and retain the flexibility to convert one opportunity into another, even if, on the surface, they may appear to have little to do with one another.

ON BLACK URBANISM

Blackness is not exactly a term that has been applied to cities. In the U.S. the media business employs a long-term practice of avoiding the term by referring to black markets as the "urban" market. Across many issues and sectors, blackness as a concept for anything is to be avoided—in part because no one has any really clear idea about what it points to, and its continued use seems to keep alive bad memories of social divisions that seem more accurately accounted for by references to social class or culture. The substantial inequities imposed upon black people could have potentially challenged the fundamental views whites had of themselves as moral people. But this possibility was kept at the periphery of Western self-perception. Here, blackness became something concrete, something psychologically and culturally specific about being black that precluded a fuller participation in the mainstream of U.S. and European societies. In response, blackness itself has become a term pushed to the periphery.

Since the term has been pushed to the periphery, much of

its "baggage" may also have been unloaded, making it available to new uses. In other words, as a peripheral concept it didn't have to have precise meanings or uses. It is clear that more African Americans have lived in cities since the end of the First World War; that more black people presently live in European, Australian, Brazilian, and Canadian cities than ever before; and that Africa is now officially an urban continent (if one counts all of the small towns and cities). But these phenomena have nothing to do with blackness *per se*. At all levels, any possible spin on a notion of blackness would have nothing to do with these historical and sociological facts. There is nothing within any concept of blackness that could draw any sensible explanatory lines between these occurrences. There is no sense of equivalence or commonality.

Yet, is there something about the particular situations and spaces where people operate that has something important to say about the dynamics of urban life? Is there something important in the fact that the people referred to here in some important domain of their lives are recognized as different because they are institutionally, culturally, or personally considered as "black"? Is there something significant to be noticed about the diminishing black populations of particular parts of the city? Does this go beyond the simple equations which indicate that because of specific histories of slavery and colonialism there is a greater tendency for black urban residents to be poorer? And as such, do they have fewer assets in cities and are they thus more vulnerable to being pushed further from city centers as they are remade for the upper end of capital and residential markets? We assume that to a large extent urban life goes beyond keeping specific ethnicities, classes, and ways of life locked into specific places of residence, jobs, and spaces of operation. If this is the case, what does the persistence of spatial segregation that sometimes looks as if it is based on racial identity indicate about the power of the city to transform identity?

While blackness has a history of keeping real power relations peripheral to thought, what I want to consider here are the potential ways in which reusing the term can bring certain dimensions of urban life from the periphery into a clearer view. As such, the use of blackness here is a tactical maneuver and not a means of sociological explanation. Blackness does not constitute a particular kind of urbanism, but rather tries to bring into consideration certain dimensions of urban life that are too often not given their due.

The key dimension of black urbanism is to put blackness to work as a device for affirming and engaging forms of articulation amongst different cities and urban experiences that otherwise would have no readily available means of conceptualization. It is thus an "inventive methodology" in that it relies on the rhetorical force of a constellation of historical and political experiences inherent in black urban experiences to bring into existence a transurban domain that both includes and goes beyond the prevalent notions of the Black Diaspora.[13] Yet it also attempts to account for the intensified urbanization and spreading out of that Diaspora as an important event in and of itself and as a means of elaborating new forms of urban livelihood.

Just like everyone else, black people from all national contexts are moving around the world in greater numbers—as students, workers, artists, and professionals. But black people are also moving through and across urban spaces that are at least nominally considered "black." For example, Africans have established clearly recognizable residential and commercial zones in Guangzhou and Bangkok; African American tourists visit the slavery sites of the Ghana coast in large numbers; the Parisian *banlieues* become intersection points for long-term residents and migrants coming from Africa and the Antilles; Nigerians have come to dominate the African American working- and lower-middle-class districts of Houston. Through these multiple and discrete sojourns and implantations, blackness takes on an active cosmopolitan dimension. This is not a new "global identity" or a concretization of commonalities, but rather an arena of "convenience." Here, circumstances have thrown together individuals of different nationalities that happen to be black. As such, they find greater possibilities of access to particular places to stay, make a living, exchange information and favors, and conduct business.

But to keep black urbanism only about black people is to defeat the purpose of black urbanism as a means of saying something about the city as a whole. Where variegated black urban lives in different parts of the world may be the logistical entry point, the concept must use whatever specificities exist in their conditions and social practices to think about urban dimensions which go beyond these specificities. Thus, black urbanism is a means of addressing a situation where the theorization of global urban change has paid insufficient attention to practices and technologies that bring an increasing heterogeneity of calculations, livelihoods, and organizational logics into a relationship with each other. It is a way to make them appear more proximate and connected, even if it is difficult to talk substantially about what the connections actually are.

Increasingly, urban economies are focusing on how intersections are actually practiced and performed. This is done through comparing city credit ratings and the trade in municipal bonds, or analyzing express mail flows and the flows of property investment. There are also scores of small stories: The stock exchange in Lagos opens up an office in Shanghai. Rich Congolese businessmen buy auto parts distributors in Dubai. Businessmen from Nairobi buy into a Bangkok-based shipping company. But what analytical tools are there to navigate the intersections, to make them produce specific outcomes, or to direct them into being resources for specific projects or aspirations?[14] What happens to the traces and effects of these intersections after they occur?

Cities everywhere are a patchwork of increasingly dense infrastructures, including fiber optic cables, surveillance systems, bundled packages of diverse services, and highways dedicated to private use. As indicated earlier, there is little about the modern city that provides a common point of reference. There are often wildly different impressions about what is going on and how the city works or doesn't. There are often no clear sides or angles; no clear way to tell how things are intersecting with each other.

For these reasons, the multifaceted experiences of black urban residents—spread out across highly divergent sites— and their ongoing struggles to carve out spaces of operation within them can be a particularly salient means of understanding these urban intersections and what kinds of spaces they can produce. Because black urban residents have had to maneuver their residency across incessantly shifting lines of inclusion and exclusion, overregulation and autonomy, their experiences provide an incisive platform for coming to grips with the combination of possibility and precariousness that seems to be at the forefront of urban life.

While black residents in many parts of the world have historically had to play by the rules governing urban life, many did not have recourse to these same rules as a way of guaranteeing that they had the same chances in the city as others. While black residents in different historical and regional circumstances may have experienced strong internal borders that kept them out of different parts of the city and kept them within racially defined places of residence, often little attention was paid to what black residents actually did in their districts. Everyday life became an ironic mixture of both tight controls and autonomy.

Additionally, there is a constitutive paradox to black urbanism in that in many parts of the world blackness informs what it means to be "urban" in a cultural sense but still struggles for recognition as a critical factor in the production of urban space and the built environment.[15] While black people have had enormous influence on the music, lingo, fashion, and styles of urban life everywhere, there is little recognition of how various collections of black residents have actually organized their environments. Too often, they are simply seen as inheriting old, dilapidated neighborhoods, or hastily and badly constructed social housing complexes. In all of this, it may be important to remember that, as C.L.R. James pointed out, black life since slavery was in essence a modern life.[16]

DISENTANGLING BLACKNESS AND RACE

Key black social theorists have clearly established the limitations of solidarities based on the assertion of common blackness. They have talked about how such an assertion reiterates the debilitating logics of racialism.[17] Even claims of subjection to a common racism are fraught with ambiguities. For it is difficult for economically disadvantaged black urban residents to accurately attribute their conditions to the persistence of institutional racism, the impact of past racial injustices, the lack of personal initiative, neoliberal globalization policies, or some combination of these factors.[18] Yet the pragmatics of black urban organization, as perhaps best exemplified in the work of Tommie Shelby, while eminently reasonable, come off as somewhat lame in face of the persistent ubiquity of racial materials in cities. Shelby insists that what he calls "black interests" can only be associated with the pursuit of racial justice and nothing more. While the heterogeneity of black urban life certainly does rule out collective action based on any notions of shared cultural, economic, historical, or physiognomic identity, it doesn't necessarily rule out the use of blackness as a means of articulating a wide variety of political demands.[19] It doesn't obviate the troublesome and volatile efforts on the part of blacks to work out complicated stories of how lives and situations may be intertwined within a city and beyond—a process that risks being made increasingly peripheral in urban life.[20]

These efforts to work out forms of articulation can be critical platforms for a more egalitarian urban politics. For example, in Mary Patillo's work on the black gentrification of the historically black neighborhoods of North Kenwood and Oakland in Chicago, poor and middle-class blacks continue to try and work out a viable sense of black cohesion. This takes place despite the continuous efforts on the part of a black middle class to distinguish themselves and their sensibilities from their poorer neighbors. Even as black middle-class tastes gain legitimacy from financial investors and backing from the state, this legitimacy is reinvested as a tool in efforts to ensure greater economic participation for the poor with whom they nominally share the neighborhood.[21] Middle-class blacks move back into historically poor African American neighborhoods hoping to live a conventional middle-class lifestyle. Still, they have used whatever social and political power they gain through their investments in these areas to try and make sure that many of the economic practices that poorer residents have relied upon to make ends meet still find legitimate places of operation.

All of the work that has been done in deconstructing race over the past decades may have dismantled its conceptual architecture, discursive economy, and forced its retreat as an explicit instrument of urban organization and politics. But it is likely that this work has simply "scattered the remains" of race across the urban landscape as something that is more invisible and pernicious. As Michael Taussig has pointed out, race is "a very different apperceptive mode, the type of filtering and barely conscious peripheral vision perception unleashed with great vigor by modern life."[22] As John L. Jackson, Jr. put it, it is difficult to really get rid of race since it combines a submolecular answer to social inequalities with a sense of taken-for-grantedness and thus feels applicable despite whatever sense of critical analysis is brought to bear on an event or situation. Jackson calls race the "walking dead," whose sightings are everywhere, and which becomes the very embodiment of the commodified form of death that had been at the heart of the production of surplus value which the exploitation of blacks provided.[23]

Retaining a notion of blackness is thus important as a vehicle for circulating through the scattered remains and temporary resurrections of new forms of racial feeling and action. It is perhaps the most readily available means for creatively re-imagining the "restlessness" of racial materials. In other words, if racial identity is maintained by finding ways to detract attention from it, to do the work of race without relying on it, then blackness becomes a tool that potentially draws lines of connection between these scattered instances and maneuvers. At the same time, it is also not bound to stay among these instances and maneuvers. It can also draw lines outside of these orbits in which race has been displaced and open up new uses for them. It is the notion of blackness, according to Jackson, that "recognizes the dangers of playing with racial fire in the first place—its burns that never vanish, its quick-paced volatilities and spontaneous conflagrations, its cannibalistic propensity to consume everything in its path."[24]

The usefulness of blackness is not because it produces conceptual clarity, but because it is such a volatile term that it forces those who use it to try and be as creative and responsible as possible. It exists not only to "break the rules" for how people and things are to be associated, but also to generate new ideas about what associations are concretely possible.

DEVICE AS A WAY OF RAISING QUESTIONS AND PAYING ATTENTION

Although blackness concerns so many things, entangled with contradictory connotations and histories of use, the concern here is the use of blackness as a device; in other words, a way of formulating questions, concepts, practices of engagement, and methods of investigation.[25] To employ a device does not presume the right way to do something. Nor does it presume particular subjects, causes, or standardized relationships between time and space.[26] Blackness as a device embodies a conceptual solidarity grounded in its continuous and shifting political use rather than in any empirical basis in fact. Its use as a device of course acknowledges all the ways in which blackness is used as both a problematic political instrument of solidarity and a purported scientific and sociological object.

But this acknowledgment takes a particular form: It sees these past uses of blackness not only as having produced realities where individuals have been excluded from certain norms and rights to the city. Instead, this exclusion also implies the existence of undocumented worlds of limited visibility thought to haunt the city's modernity or posit radically different ways of being in the city. In other words, exclusion does not point to an intrinsic vacancy in black life —a life drained by oppression. Rather, it points to the possibility of something else that may or may not have been at work all along. There is a possibility that something is at work which continues to motivate people's determination not to adhere to urban norms as they exist but rather to create a different kind of city. Again, this is not to ascertain an empirical fact, but a possibility for investigation. As a result, it is important to consider the extent to which the actual bodies of black urban residents live in the interstices of this problematic—of a life of simultaneous inclusion and exclusion that blackness points to. For the resilience of blackness as a device rests precisely in the fact, as pointed out by Gooding-Williams, that there are "manifold forms of race-conscious [black] political solidarity characterized by diverse purposes and by diverse understandings of the significance of being black."[27]

In the classic example of race consciousness cited by Fanon, the white gaze upon blackness fixes the observer in a fear and shock that force the black person who is observed to think of themselves more as an object rather than a thinking and feeling subject. When blackness is used as a device, however, it attempts to work out a way of seeing that takes blackness seriously without taking it at face value. In other words, this is a way of seeing that is constantly aware of playing with fire. Always dealing with something that makes no easy sense, but seems to be a ubiquitous consideration of urban life, forces the investigator to bring other considerations into view. The device functions as a kind of relay. It is a way of passing certain assumptions and feelings along to new "neighborhoods" of consideration, of switching attention, or relaying materials to unexpected sites and relationships. Like the previous discussions about the street, a device redirects, speeds up, or slows down particular intersections of events, thoughts, and observations. It modulates the intensities and rhythms of movement. It translates different ways of analyzing things in each other's terms—for example, it may look at social fields as if they were individuals and individuals as if they were social fields. It forces us to say, "Wait a minute, we can get past this way of thinking about this and move on to something else." Alternately, it is way of saying, "Let's slow things down in case we have missed certain connections."

Blackness as a device in a black urbanism attempts to navigate through the entanglement of possibility and precariousness in urban life. Here, the very conditions thought to point to the collapse of urban civility and justice can also be considered as the conditions under which new forms of urban life are generated. Many black urban residents were excluded from full participation in urban life and their residency was considered significant only as something to be controlled and disciplined. Accordingly, much of what blacks did in cities then, albeit under often dire conditions, could veer off into directions and forms that did not need to be useable or understood by the prevailing urban norms.

CONCEPTUAL THICKETS AND POSSIBILITIES IN USING BLACK URBANISM AS A DEVICE

Blackness is of course a volatile device. For there is no avoiding that it is partly based on the ubiquity of race as an available instrument for orderings of all kinds. These are orderings which shift in terms of their legitimacy and salience but yet demonstrate a persistent mobility across the urban landscape. As Michael Keith points out, the histories of insertion of black people in the city and how they adapted to particular conditions had a major impact on how the city was spatially organized. These spatial organizations, in turn, created conditions which made particular forms of solidarity, collectivity, and particularity visible. Sometimes the emphasis is on national origin; at other times, ethnicity, religion, or class.[28]

Race in the city was endowed with a particular kind of clarity. The demographics of settlement patterns, the spatial economies of livelihood and service provision in the U.S., pointed to the systematic construction of segregation as a fundamental urban reality.[29] As Lefebvre indicated, colonization did not refer simply to a specific historical era of territorial expansion. Rather, it was a process of arranging relations of production and control based on organizing spatial arrangements in terms of core and periphery. This is a distinction that requires the use of arbitrary divides and distinctions. For the very notion of what it means to be "urban" is something that cannot be easily divided into terms where something is definitively "core" or "peripheral." As I indicated earlier in the book, the "urbanization" of relationships amongst things entails a speed and intensity of diverse positions and practices of inhabitation that can't be stably represented in clear categories about how space and resources are used, or how social relationships are conducted.[30]

At the heart of city life is the capacity for its different people, spaces, activities, and things to interact in ways that exceed any attempt to subsume them into cemented trajectories of social, symbolic, or semiotic relationship, and thus regulate them. Despite the many sociological studies that divide the rich from the poor, the core from the periphery, the residential from the commercial, or even the night from the day, these divides are never fixed in city life. They are, at most, a temporary snapshot of what exists at a given moment. Therefore, if keeping the poor impoverished is going to be a way of adding profit to the rich, of ensuring the availability of cheap labor and making many urban dwellers feel so vulnerable that it keeps them politically passive, then these divides between rich and poor cannot depend upon any clear-cut categories that would seem to give precise definitions to what it means to be "poor" or "well off" which are applicable to all situations and times. Instead, they require more arbitrary determinations about which residents can engage in specific kinds of activities and life possibilities, where, and under what circumstances.

Race has been the instrument through which such arbitrary determinations attain some internal coherence—i.e. some way of accounting for who gets excluded or who does not. At the same time, the use of race circumvents the possibility that the excluded or marginalized would have recourse to demonstrating their capacities to assume the same responsibilities, rights, and possibilities as those who are not excluded. No matter how the excluded may demonstrate that there isn't any rational basis for their exclusion, the use of race goes a long way to cancel out the impact of such effort. If an arbitrary decision prevails as to whose life is to be accorded value and possibility, then blackness has been associated with the absence of appeal. In other words, no matter how smart or capable a person is, there is nothing they can say or demonstrate to alter their emplacement in a particular set of circumstances and political relations.[31] Because a person is born black, no matter how smart or capable they may be, the fact that they are black would place an absolute limit on what they could legitimately claim to do or be. As such, blacks would occupy a specific space in relationship to others.

This logic of spatial organization can operate at multiple scales and becomes the vehicle to draw connections amongst various histories and modalities of territorial division.[32] Importantly, it enables us to connect late colonization in Africa and Asia, particularly, to the remaking of cities in the Western metropolis. This remaking draws upon the distinctions between citizen and subject that were enforced in the colonies. But it also refers to the many ways that cities of the North and South are connected and operate through various financial infrastructures, migration, and economic circulations at all scales. The continued efforts Africans make to access opportunities in European cities and the efforts made by Europeans to keep them out can be reasonably seen as a by-product of colonial administration and its impact on white European citizens. As mentioned earlier, the seeds of this "game"—where Europeans need African labor but also need to strictly dictate the terms of what that labor will mean—were implanted long before contemporary Africans started coming to Europe in larger numbers, aspiring to better economic opportunity, education, and everyday conditions.

Working through Fanon's notions of decolonization, Kipfer points out how important it is to transform the objectifying and alienating spatial arrangements that racialized encounters produce in urban life. The day-in-and-day-out banalities of these encounters are condensations of social, political, and historical geographies of colonial and neocolonial domination.[33] These everyday events are the raw materials that demonstrate the persistence of segregation and skewed opportunities. When residents deal with each other through race—through the arbitrary calculations of who counts and who does not— a vast number of actual or potential complementarities get minimized and put out of view.

At the same time, such arbitrary divides must also apply to the very logic from which they originate. As notions of development, modernity, progress, and selfhood have largely been predicated on both their distinction from and applicability to the cultural and political practices of colonial subjects, the failure to universalize these notions is attributed to the lack of capacity or readiness on the part of the colonial subject or citizen of the "under-developed world." But this culpability cannot be permanent. Some colonial subjects must "make it." They must demonstrate the efficacy of the "civilizing mission," or, more currently, show they are capable of taking the path toward development and democracy.[34]

At the same time, exposure to training is no guarantee. Think about how many capacity-building exercises have taken place in former colonies to promote good governance, human and social development—often to little effect. While the list may be long as to what went wrong, the question of who accedes to modernity and who becomes modern or developed is as much a matter of chance as anything else. As Harry Chang put it, race "does not aim at an air-tight predictable outcome when it comes to the question of who shall be in what class; the rule has to work itself out actuarially as an elaborate system of gambling-house odds." "What is a gambling-house mentality if there are no winners occasionally? Nonetheless, the abstract need of class relations (e.g., there shall be slaves) demands some concrete demographic solution (e.g., Blacks as 'candidates' for slaves)."[35]

Urban segregation remains a powerful dynamic even if it is not always centered on racial divides. But it is difficult to make precise determinations about the extent to which racial thinking hides behind notions of social class. The gradual ascendance of a black middle class in the U.S. is cited as evidence of the breaking down of racial logics and the emergence of new urban cosmopolitanisms. But what urban life also demonstrates, as indicated previously, is how distinctions, fractures, and marked disparities no longer need territorially based markers of distinction. Different walks of life can be maintained in close proximity to each other while not having to take the other into consideration. As individuals have become increasingly responsible for governing themselves— for making sure that they make the right decisions—more extensive intersections among diverse residents and walks of life do exist, but usually in a highly superficial way, without people really having an impact on each other.

The capacities for dismissal are more extensive and arbitrary

—there is simply not enough time to go into any depth in any particular story of things. There is too much to pay attention to, too much that could be legitimately seen to be an important factor in one's life, and so there is an acute need to not pay attention to everything around you. Individuals do take into consideration an expanding world of people, events, and situations. But often this expanding world is taken into consideration only for it to be dismissed—either because it is not relevant or because it threatens to overwhelm the individual's ability to find some kind of limited stability. If too many things could have some kind of relevance to how individuals live their lives, then at some point they are likely to decide just not to pay attention to a lot of different experiences and people. These decisions may have no discernible or reasonable basis. Thus, the arbitrary essence of racial distinction remains a key historical underpinning of this practice of dismissal even if race itself is not cited as the instrument at work. But it does mean that race is diffused across more tricky versions of itself.

Additionally, the more recent obsessions about urban security, regulation, and the containment of various, and very often diffuse, threats is also predicated on changing the ways we visualize the city. These changed forms of visualization add new relevance to this notion of the arbitrary as a form of transaction which eliminates the need for social negotiations and for developing stories about how people are related to each other. As Brian Massumi notes:

> Containment has more to do with the patterning of exits and entries across thresholds than with the impermeabilities of boundaries. This is as true for the regulation of codified event spaces as for spaces characterized by coding. What is pertinent about an event space is what elements it lets pass, according to what criteria, at what rate and to what effect.[36]

This patterning across entries and exits as a form of control operates in many dimensions. Traffic management, for instance, is based on patterns inferred from a range of data that turn the seeming chaos of traffic into a series of temporally and spatially coordinated flows. Lights are programmed differently in peak hours so as to keep the patterns of traffic smooth and predictable. Bar coding contains the flows of products by matching the lines on the bar codes. Patterning is something quite different from representation. Scanning is a very different "look" to that of the camera. The "look" Massumi talks about here is for verification and not representation.

The look here does not signify anything. Nevertheless, it reveals a crucial connection between the bio-cultural operations of how we interpret things and those of bodies. If there is no match, between patterns, eligibility, and entitlement—if the biometrics do not line up, if the credit rating is not pegged to a particular score, if the right credentials are not presented—there is nothing much individuals can do about being kept out.

There is nothing necessarily new in the diffusion of racial materials into the deep musculature of urban societies. Fanon repeatedly talked about the circulation of images that cut across the various affective and psychological channels of society, showing up in dreams, symptoms, neuroses, and taking root in various ways of talking, thinking, and problem solving without necessarily being, as Derek Hook says, reducible to the psychic level of realization.[37] As cultural considerations have often replaced race as an explicit form of critical deliberation on the dynamics of cities, race remains in play through reifying the notion of culture at work in these considerations. For example, judgments are made all the time about whether certain people are nice, friendly, honest, or hard working. These judgments may make no explicit reference to race but it is often clear that people who possess certain qualities just happen to have a specific racial make-up.[38]

DEVICES OF BLACKNESS AS A MEANS OF SELF-ORGANIZATION

In large U.S. urban centers, popular public discourse on the street sometimes makes easy reference to something being a "black thing" or a "white thing," for example a way of negotiating space, of looking, of responding to things, or of carrying one's body. These attributions can be applied to a wide range of micro-level behaviors and politics, without anyone quite knowing what the composition of the particular "thing" is; what makes it black or white. When people are asked to explain what they are talking about, the narrative tends to weave an unsteady course through various examples and qualifications. Yet such referencing acts as a kind of "common sense" because it is open to anyone to add supplemental commentary and criteria. These circulations of racial materials and references, and the way they mutate into a wide range of forms and citations, may correspond to what Nigel Thrift has identified as the increasingly important role of affect in cities.

According to Thrift, affect becomes the vehicle for a kind of practical knowing in the course of everyday interactions. It concerns what can be paid attention to and with what degree of readiness and openness. Affect is about what possibilities might emerge from being attuned to the detailed performances of everyday interactions and observations. Affect is a vehicle of modulation that heightens receptiveness to information and experiences, stimulates involvement in a particular setting or event, facilitates the cognitive processing of what is taking place, and enables the individual to evaluate what to take seriously.[39] The insertion of racial materials into affective domains is more than a matter of how individuals orient themselves to uncertain events and territories. It is more than the management of anxieties about other urban residents, or the embodiment of felt distinctions between self and others. Rather, it entails the spaces and times for making decisions. It is about where I should place my body and attention in competing and often "flooded" fields of calculation and consideration when a decision is needed immediately.

In cities where there is a great deal of ambiguity as to who makes it and who doesn't, where people circulate through part-time jobs and flexible labor, where supportive services are available, but on mostly a privatized basis, and where dispersed networks of acquaintances, strangers, colleagues, and friends can sometimes be counted to open up new possibilities, but also are seldom reliable, the surface connotations of a black solidarity seem increasingly irrelevant. This is even more so as racial materials mutate into increasingly ephemeral forms.

This does not mean that people's collective efforts have to rely upon the seemingly clear-cut categories of race, class, gender, ethnicity, ideology, religion, and so forth. After all, the struggle for social justice can only be predicated on a form of self-reliance, self-organization, and initiative that can't rely upon making reference to any sense of destiny, any certainty that a "right way" will always win out. The city is always something yet to be made. This remaking goes beyond the equitable apportionment of services and opportunities. It is something more than simply a matter of making the right calculations, providing the best security, or performing the most precise risk analysis.

Blackness, then, is the commitment to make something without clear maps or certainties. Cities experience forms of control that are more fragmented and dispersed—there is not one overarching form of authority in charge. The powers that regulate the city are increasingly ephemeral, having once perhaps had a more visible face. So that which had the most recognizable of faces, blackness, instead becomes a device for thinking about how to create the most opportunities in cities that often seem to have no face.

This process of self-organization takes on a particular form. As blackness points to the assemblage of materials whose connection has no stable historical antecedents or empirical grounding, the assertion of blackness cannot be voiced as a corporate entity or clearly defined political subject. As da Silva points out, "the black subject is neither an actualization nor an expression of an African essence but a modern political figure, an existing thing, which can be re/assembled with the tools of knowledge that carved its place of emergence."[40] This subject cannot speak as a coherent entity which sees evidence of its coherence all around it. As the well-rehearsed philosophical foundations of postcolonial thought have made clear, the black subject came into being not as "consciousness for itself," not as a transparent thing capable of recognizing that all that exists outside of itself is always already a manifestation of its efforts and being.

Rather, the black subject emerges as an external and spatial entity, a product of global relations that was brought into consideration as an effect of universal reason and the relationships between things that race and culture regulate.[41] If self-organization is the only vehicle for a black consciousness to articulate itself, then blackness cannot act as if those who have been excluded can now be included in terms of a transparent and self-contained self. Rather, a notion of black urbanism as a way of thinking about cities is brought into representation through weaving together the disparate experiences of the black experience and its struggles against oppression in its different guises across different historical periods and locations. This weaving becomes a shared material condition. Here there is no reference to any culturally authentic source of origins. Rather, what is required is to look upon a wide canvass of struggles undertaken by peoples of African ancestry and put them together as an invented universe of operation. Inside this universe, the practice of self-organization in the present can contextualize "its world" and reason for being.

Again, what is meant by self-organization is the use of blackness as a tool for materializing connections among all the disparate things black people across the world have experienced. It is a way of holding the experiences of living in New Orleans, Lagos, Salvador Bahia, and Casablanca in a moment of mutual reflection. Whatever we know about slavery and Diaspora, whatever we know about the mechanisms that brought black people to these cities, the weight of historical analysis tends to separate their experiences, making them distant from each other. And common sense tells us that these experiences are distant, but that distance shouldn't distract us from using whatever is available to draw lines among them, see them as cities somehow coming into their own through a relationship they have to various other cities.

These efforts at self-organization may have particular salience for the prevailing conditions of urban life.[42] Cities are increasingly the critical locus of technological developments, embedding residents across diverse geographical spaces and scales into complex networks of exchange and interdependency. Cities embody virtual or immanent forces provisionally concretized in diverse associational networks of varying duration, reach, and function. These networks are open-ended sites of circulation that mediate, re-direct, and translate flows of information and matrices of connectivity.

A conceptual language based on metaphors of territoriality

and place, capable of privileging the actions of discrete urban citizens—whose behaviors are accountable through their placement in specific local dynamics—is now less applicable to urban life. The interweaving of individuals with technology and virtual knowledge systems produces a very different kind of urban social subject than those of autonomous, self-contained human agents. How these agents get along and do things with each other no longer has clear political or sociological categories to draw from.

The key factor in governing cities is the political management of complex and incessant trade-offs that must be made by all cities in the context of being more exposed to a larger global world. How much should a city emphasize economic growth as opposed to equitable opportunities for residents; how much should democratic participation be emphasized at the expense of making quick and needed decisions? While these facets of governing are not by definition opposed, they often are difficult to bring together in the same policy or practice. Here the key is how different forms of participation, negotiation, contestation, and partnership can be combined, related, and balanced to ensure a vibrant politics and constructive collaboration to solve real problems. This will entail re-imagining and activating ways for urban residents to feel like they all share the city in a period where the contradictions of expanding global capitalism are more extensively interwoven in local urban life. The important question is how this sense of togetherness is re-imagined in a context where formerly valued practices of social cohesion fade away, as do the territorial parameters through which cohesion has been conventionally recognized and performed.

POINTING TO UNKNOWN CAPACITIES AND POTENTIALS IS THE WORK THAT BLACK URBANISM DOES

From the time of W.E.B. Dubois' classic sociological investigation of the Philadelphia Negro at the end of the nineteenth century, black residents have haunted analyses of urban life. In his relentless detailing of how black residents were the objects of discrimination and diminished value, what is not really talked about are the ways in which blacks were able to acquire substantial capacities to operate in cities in the first place. The basis for exclusion was not because black residents were not educated, trained, entrepreneurial, diligent, and creative. Rather, it was because of the fact that they indeed brought many different kinds of capacities to the city that their exclusion was able to represent the success of a particular kind of power based on racial difference. This was a power where the *cityness* of cities—their thick permutations of relationships of all kinds—could be arbitrarily curtailed and ordered.

Despite the implications that such exclusion would have for what blacks could do across the United States, Europe, South America, and Africa, a question remains as to just precisely how black residents were able to continue to use the city to maximize their intellectual, affective, spiritual, and economic resources. Such enhancement would undoubtedly require a wide range of reciprocities, transactions, and collaboration. So what haunts the modern urban experience may be these more invisible modalities of sociality that circumvent the normative mechanisms of social exchange. As such, black urbanism accounts for not only the specificities of racial oppression, but also the more shadow-like dimensions of urban life.

The notion of shadows, particularly as discussed by Filip De Boeck,[43] derives initially from colonial efforts to define and maintain a captive population—one that had no rights over the territory it occupied. Achille Mbembe cites the example of slavery and the plantation economy.[44] Here, the shadow is not a form of self-possession but a reflection able to draw upon any object, instrument, or gesture, incorporate it into a performance, and stylize it. The maintenance of a slave population meant the making of slave quarters. While these quarters were regulated and surveyed, the gaze of masters did have a limit given that the slave quarters were places where whites did not belong and which they were compelled to avoid. As such, a limited zone of autonomy was conceded that was protected by slaves always crafting an acceptable image to be consumed by the white gaze. As long as they showed the outward signs of their subservience and dependency, they could experiment with other forms of living behind this façade. Such shadows have of course extended across quarters of all kinds, from slums and war zones, to refugee and work camps.

TODAY'S SHADOW WORLDS

Much sensationalism is attributed to the seemingly unimpeded and "flagrant" sojourning of Africans. While Africans certainly have no special claim to dominance in the world's vast range of illicit business, they are often singled out for special interdiction and controls. The reputation of Nigerians, Congolese, and Cameroonians in particular is that of some of the world's master crooks, and many countries require nationals from these countries to go through especially arduous bureaucratic hoops in order to secure visas. Given the long existent stereotypes regarding Africa's supposed preoccupation with mystical forces, the often innovative means through which African entrepreneurs gain access to markets and generate viable trades with little capitalization tend to reinforce general impressions about chicanery and fraud. Of course, part of the ability of some entrepreneurs to extend their circuits of movement and opportunity do center on trades such as counterfeiting, black money, drug trafficking, credit card fraud, and theft.

The demeanor and strategic practices through which African entrepreneurs operate in places long marked by either racial prejudice or cultural unfamiliarity also vary. There are those who keep a low profile and diligently ensure that everything about them and their activities is in order. And there are those who seem to flaunt indifference to how they are perceived, and who seemingly cultivate an intimidating image that is to be feared. Many young men on the streets of Guangzhou, Bangkok, São Paolo, Madrid, and Jakarta are hardly entrepreneurs, and rather could be considered "chancers" or foot-soldiers for mafia-like syndicates whose national origins and line of business are often opaque.

Given the importance of trade as the key way for Africans to make a living, the search for cheap inputs is incessant and extensive. Africans have long plied diverse networks and circuits of movement and exchange. Forced to keep costs down, they circumvent often draconian customs controls back home and cultivate extensive relations of credit and trust across large territories. This work has elaborated a history that then becomes available for others to use, and the drug, sex trafficking, fraud, and counterfeit goods businesses have certainly benefited from this history.

Given the weakness of many national regulatory structures, the proliferation of conflict, and the continuous scramble for primary resources, Africa has been the site for the imposition of nefarious business practices from the outside. Networks of resource extraction, gun running, pharmaceutical dumping, and humanitarian assistance have sometimes been easily articulated with various other illicit economies. Quid pro quo relationships are common, whereby powerful political actors accord privileges to external businesses—such as customs waivers, cheap property, exclusive rights to specific resources or trades, or cut-rate prices for critical economic assets—in exchange for African access to visas, contacts, airline tickets, accommodation, and business licenses in Europe, South America, the Middle East, and Asia. These can be parlayed into strengthening the infrastructure of illicit trade and business.

Cities across the world are replete with the manifestations of largely cash economies, both licit and illicit. Entertainment is a particularly vast economic area that includes a wide range of activities that at one level are clearly delineated into specific customer bases, niches, and degrees of legality. But sometimes the distinctions between gambling, accommodation, dining, karaoke, sex, dancing, nightlife, movies, theater, shows, cabaret, family leisure, and sports are not so clear. The key factor in many illicit business activities is the capacity to intersect these domains in ways that enable distinct cash streams to subsidize each other or provide legal covers for what in a particular context would be considered illegal activity.

Within these worlds many different kinds of actors intersect and, as such, they become important contexts for making deals of all kinds. For example, the opening of a bar in an upscale neighborhood in Jakarta entails the intersection of publicity agents, politicians, models, fashion designers, alcohol distributors, advertisers, journalists, magazine editors, bloggers, media agents, drug dealers, security specialists, photographers, gossip columnists, high-class sex workers, moneylenders, bankers, and investors. All do something for each other—to which the bar serves as a kind of catalyst and occasion. The licit and illicit are then by no means clearly or consistently discernible or distinguishable domains. There are certainly activities and places that are illegal, and the object of control. But the extent to which they are implicated within and across a broad band of regular businesses and conventional economic actors is never clear in any specific context.

So the so-called shadow world here is not so much a specific world, with clear-cut boundaries, but an ever shifting hybrid across which certain Africans, Armenians, Russians, Chinese, Pakistanis, Brazilians, Moroccans, Japanese, Greeks, Lebanese, and Columbians—according to their popular reputations—now move. Within the various games of different illegalities, Africans, in particular, are considered the most adept at switching gears. They move from one trade to another and cross the lines between more institutionalized syndicates and mafias. In some ways, they then become those that ply the shadows of the shadows.

EVERYDAY SHADOWS THAT FEATURE IN ALL CITIES

Seemingly outside the ordering processes, capacities, and networks of late modernity, these contemporary shadows accommodate what Nigel Thrift in another context labels the "fugitive materials" that increasingly find their way into all cities. By "fugitive materials" he means traditions, codes, linguistic bits, jettisoned and patchwork economies, pirated technologies, bits and pieces of symbols floating around detached from the original places they may have come from. The city attracts not only human migrants from elsewhere, but also all the bits and pieces of ways of doing things, long dissociated from their original uses, that "wash up" on the shores of the city. These materials become part and parcel of the ways certain urban residents will evade rules or surveillance, trespass on places they don't belong, and pretend to be something that they are not. They reflect the determination of those without secure urban positions to maintain viable lives within the city.[45]

All those who must wheel and deal in the midst of urban

uncertainties with few apparent resources at hand need to ensure some form of inclusion that would get rid of divides —especially racial ones—and, at the same time, continue to find a way of valuing what they managed to accomplish in the "shadows." In other words, certain kinds of urban residents were excluded from the benefits of adhering to practices and norms that would reasonably seem to ensure that they could thrive in the city. They then had to make do by relying on their own inventiveness, but without any guarantee that this inventiveness would work. As the basis for exclusion changes, and individuals formally have the same chances and opportunities as anyone else, the excluded do not necessarily jump at or completely commit to this opportunity.

This is a matter of the modulations through which residents switch between two strategies. The first entails an apparent adherence to conventional narratives of efficacy, propriety, and citizenship—often implicitly recognized as having little use but still kept alive as residual forms of social anchorage and coherence. The second involves the complicated elaboration of relations of all kinds that are too prolific and transitory to organize into stable institutional forms. Or they are enacted without the necessary resources of time, money, and political support to gain widespread credence as a series of "new norms."

The liberal idea of social integration in Europe and the United States, where black urbanites could be brought into the mainstream of normative urban development, was to assume that what the city had excluded could be easily integrated. It was to assume that whatever debt was to be paid for this exclusion could be paid off by ushering the excluded inside. As Hortense Spillers has said, this idea that blacks could be fully incorporated in mainstream society denies that certain aspirations and desires will have no home in language. There is no definitive way to tell when certain aspirations have been fulfilled, no possibility of a pay-off or compensation. These aspirations might be the black desires for freedom, for not having to struggle, for recouping a loss that cannot be recouped, for not having to account for and measure whether they truly have been integrated into the city, for making space for themselves in circumstances that did not provide any, and for putting all of these issues to rest.[46]

Ironically, the ways in which the proponents of what has conventionally passed as normative and planned urban development often exclude themselves from the *cityness* of the city coincides with this notion of an exclusion of that which cannot be included. Here, a parasitic relationship to the city—where resources, spaces, and bodies have been seized without replenishment or held in fixed models—has enabled certain residents to buy themselves out of the *cityness* of city life referred to earlier. They can opt out of its thickening and unpredictable intersections of things of all kinds. They can exclude themselves from the tos and fros of the street and live in exclusive, highly privatized worlds.

Again, black urbanism does not point to a specific experience or repressed dimension of urban life now made available to scrutiny and use. Rather, it is a device for engaging the heterogeneous flows of cultural materials, money, ideas, and apparatuses across specific materializations of the urban in Europe, the U.S., Africa, Asia, the Caribbean, and Latin America. In all of these places, the social and economic infrastructure has been significantly derived on the basis of racialist logics. By following the various dispersions, displacements, and Diasporas of black people, architectures of urbanity emerge which connect disparate cities and regions to each other. At the same time, the situation where blacks of varying backgrounds and orientations are thrown together in many cities regardless of their affinity for each other is a by-product of the racial territorializing of urban space and possibility. A "common blackness" may have no empirical or political existence outside its sheer invocation. Nevertheless, it has been repeatedly used as a cover by African Americans, Africans, Caribbeans, Black Hispanics, and Black Europeans to elaborate both competitive and complementary uses of urban space that don't fit such racial logics.

CONFINEMENT, SOVEREIGNTY, AND MOBILITY

What Achille Mbembe describes as the operational modalities of mobile forms of sovereignty can also be applied to the localized politics of many urban systems. He considers sovereignty to be a situation where "a patchwork of overlapping and incomplete rights to rule emerges, inextricably superimposed and tangled, in which different de facto juridical instances are geographically interwoven and plural allegiances, asymmetrical suzerainties, and enclaves abound."[47] Many cities experience an intertwining of various agendas, extractions, interventions, infrastructure, individual calculations, and livelihood practices. If this is the case, how are such meshworks—forms of intertwining—perceived and navigated by those who find themselves entrapped there? But who, at the same time, is also able to use the neighborhoods and districts where they live as platforms for their own mobility, however constrained it might be? If the multiplication of divides, borders, jurisdictions, and enclaves is a feature of late modern colonial occupation, then how are they lived through by those subjects of "occupation"—e.g. the urban poor—in ways that the imposed architectures of control cannot fully specify or predict?

The emphasis on control and sovereignty, on the appropriation of the law to erode the law, on the reinvigoration of the colonial present through new forms of militarization, is a critical feature of the present era. Yet insufficient attention is being paid to the ways in which massive numbers of urban residents do something more than participate in their condemnation to bare life. This is not to overestimate the capacities and resilience of the poor, but to open up large, previously under-examined aspects of urban life to "proper" consideration. These are complicated stories that require non-linear lines of investigation. They require creating platforms of connection—previously mentioned as the foundation for the self-organizing practices of black consciousness. This is not the valorization of heroic struggles or the incantations of "we shall overcome." The situations and stories are messy, full of mixed tendencies and emotions.

THE STORIES OF AN URBAN POPULAR CULTURE

Yes, many of these stories center on people in search of a better life. There are also those about people pushing the limits, trying to make use of anything around them. There are stories about those who tempt fate and try to push the limits too far while aiming for some cathartic transformation. There are stories that try to prove that the real change can never come. For many urban Africans particularly, the story lines have been full of curves, unexpected twists and turns where it is almost impossible to predict what will happen next. These stories abound in what we understand as an urban popular culture. In other words, in addition to the language and musical styles of the urban streets, the fashions and slang, the visual styles and diffuse collective practices of making something from little, I want to talk about a notion of urban popular culture that deals more explicitly with these curvy stories and non-linear lines of everyday investigation. In this way I want to demonstrate a way to think about black urbanism as it draws lines between different places and different ways of doing things; and the potential and problems of these lines.

When I first came to Douala ten years ago, I stayed in a compound in New Deido, a district in the central area of the city. One evening while entering the compound I noticed an acquaintance of mine, Clara, remind a rude boy, sweating and more than a little bit anxious, to watch his manners. It certainly was not an uncommon request. After all, even though only thirty-eight, she would be considered an elder, deserving some respect. The interiors of the thousands of small shops providing a household's basic link to the larger world were also the spaces in which social solidarity was to be displayed and reinforced. Clara was in the middle of handing over the small coins for a purchase of rice. The shopkeeper had hesitated a moment in her count in the dancing rays of a kerosene lamp.

Demanding matches, the boy had pushed her aside, perhaps more in a rush to complete whatever mission he had started than out of arrogance. Clara had never become used to being pushed around—even as being pushed around is unavoidable in the daily overcrowded taxi rides to and from the office, in queues to pay for her daughter's schooling, which absorbed the bulk of her salary, and in the demands of a husband whose real place of residence she preferred to remain unknown. With more a symbolic gesture than anything, she had rebounded with fingertips on the rude boy's shoulder and a glare, and left it at that. She did not particularly want the fifteen or so people in the shop to use the boy's infraction as an occasion to parade old wounds.

In most every minor commotion, the easy rise of passions inevitably results in picked pockets or, in general, things missing from the immediate vicinity. The shopkeeper would select someone to blame for starting the incident. Most often, this would be the person obviously aggrieved. They would then be

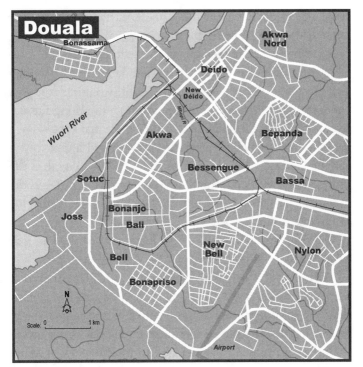

Map 9
Central Douala

refused credit just before the end of the month when it was most needed. Leaving the store, Clara stepped through the circle the boy had made with his small posse in order to decide on a final destination. She pretended to whisper something in the boy's ear, but she said nothing intelligible. After all, it was a weekday night. Nothing stands out except the threat of danger around every corner, and she felt somewhat bored with feeling afraid.

She did decide to pass on the quick schnapps she often took with two friends after their husbands had passed out early after a bout of heavy drinking. Clara enjoyed the camaraderie. But the discussion usually gravitated toward their relief at once again being freed from their nocturnal marital obligations. One of the reasons she had chosen a life of relative poverty in favor of investing in her daughter's schooling was that she hoped the daughter, Nzumi, would end up as a chemist, spending her days in laboratories researching alternatives to the tired complicities and attractions that kept women orbiting male planets. For herself, Clara wanted little except a certain kind of oblivion. She would be content with a life centered on deep philosophical conversations with the street touts and beggars. She would do the chores of everyday life in complete silence, or laugh constantly at the empty boasts of drunken uncles instead of being forced to pity the way the city had worn them down.

What I would later learn was that when Clara arrived at her small room in the compound, the boy had somehow slipped behind her. The distant relatives, who charged her an exorbitant price for the meager accommodation, probably did notice. They were always prepared to think the worst about her idiosyncrasies. As she turned the lock, the boy turned a knife in her back, ripped the slight silver crucifix from her neck and, stuffing it into the front of his pants, ran off. She managed to crawl to the courtyard where the men were drinking, who, in turn, beckoned the women to manage the situation. They covered the wound, placed her on a sisal mat, and carried her out in search of a taxi; in search of a hospital that might be convinced to wait weeks before receiving all of the necessary fees.

The story continues some eight years later on a rooftop overlooking Phnom Penh's O'Russey market on the sliver of a veranda between the building's edge and where the makeshift two-room dwelling begins. There Nzumi sits with a young Khmer woman, Dara, and her boyfriend, Sann. Dara runs a crew of young women who move through the recessed spaces of the major markets, braiding hair, doing body piercing, and supplying stalls with smuggled cosmetics. These crews also insert themselves at key junctures in the ebbs and flows of secondary school traffic, peddling Japanese accessories and make-up, and at night running a variety of just-expired pharmaceuticals to bar girls and sex workers, as well as doing a brisk trade in selling music cassettes of Khmer singers who were popular in the 1970s, who have made a big comeback in the city. The crew of girls is drawn primarily from the rooftop population, an intricately woven circuitry of wooden shacks, cardboard shelters, and even sophisticated masonry that run across the tightly packed interiors of the central city.

Phnom Penh was a small but vibrant city before the Khmer Rouge emptied it out in 1975, forcing everyone they didn't kill to labor in the countryside. During the first years of Phnom Penh's resettlement beginning in 1979, residents bargained to occupy the higher stories of buildings as a way of warding off frequent incursions by the authorities looking for hoarded and banned goods and seeking to curtail illegal trading. As commerce was liberalized, residents with higher incomes or with trading connections and commercial skills bought or bartered their way to the ground and second floors, where shops were opened. These were usually residents of Chinese and Vietnamese origin who plied their historic connections to Diasporas elsewhere as a way of rebuilding the urban economy of the city. In the process, darker-skinned Khmer residents were pushed to the upper floors and then the rooftops of these areas, where entire informal settlements have been constructed.

These spatial arrangements give rise to a particular social dynamic. While those with greater economic power often attempt to impose their interests and ways of using spaces supposedly held in common—particularly stairwells and street-fronts to buildings—such imposition is often contested by those of the upper floors and roofs. This is particularly the case when these spaces become important ways of linking upper-storey settlements across the neighborhood divided by streets and other gaps between buildings. While rooftop constructions are officially consigned to some legal twilight zone and could be torn down by the authorities at any moment, residents on the lower levels have been known to "run interference" between these settlements and the authorities. In part, this is because these settlements are relied upon for various kinds of labor, from porters, security guards, housekeepers, and even local "spies."

Some of Dara's crew are or have been domestics for households living in the apartments below. Some have worked in the garment factories and don't feel like going back to their rural homes once the contract is finished. They are simply small facets of a massive machine of young, single, female laborers, often living on their own, who in important ways drive the urban economy of Phnom Penh. Their services consist not only of sewing pieces of fabric, but in articulating disparate parts and actors in the city through the sexual use of their hands. And then some find small schemes and hustles like the ones that Dara puts together.

Her boyfriend, Sann, works for an NGO dealing with migration. He leaves early in the morning for IT classes, puts in a long day at his organization, and is attempting to start a master's degree and finish English courses at night. He is lucky to have found this rooftop spot through a woman who made tea at his office. She took him under her wing, and then made him responsible for tending to her house when she took a sick husband back to his village some months ago. Sann's family lived in the massive inner city squatter settlement, Sambok

Chap, before the police moved everyone out to a distant part of the city. His family is one of the several hundred families still living in plastic far outside the city in Andoung Thmei, waiting for a plot that was supposed to have been allotted by the government.

It was in the course of his work that he met Nzumi, when he was doing an inventory of different voluntary associations in the Khan Chamkarmorn district. She was helping with various errands for the pastor of a small apostolic church that attended to various dilemmas faced by the African congregants, who were mostly Nigerian. After her mother's death, as I would learn during several conversations with Nzumi, relatives did not know quite what to do with her. They gathered up money for a ticket and sent her off to visit a cousin working with English property developers in Bangkok. The cousin had told her she would find work helping manage the accounts of some older West African aunties who had bought up old buildings in the small lanes near the Nana Skytrain stop and were turning them into rooming houses for scores of young Africans buying and selling all kinds of things. The cousin turned out to be a real jerk, constantly running dangerous errands for his handlers, who were involved in fraudulent real estate deals that also served as a cover for narcotics transactions.

A quick trip with him to Phnom Penh was to be a last favor, and then there was to be a ticket to Milan, to another cousin, another possibility. The details of her story about first arriving in Phnom Penh were sketchy. There was a night drugged in a penthouse suite decorated with the typical garishness of quickly built luxury Chinese hotels, lines of white powder on an emerald encrusted mirror, a guy named Min Yah yelling on a phone in broken French, a dash down back stairwells, refuge in the flat of a Jean-Pierre from Douala, whom I had met on the upper balcony of the former Butterfly Lounge on October 17, 2004. This is how I came to have re-met Nzumi, who only had vague memories of a strange light-skinned guy who had moved around her neighborhood a few years back.

The three gathered on this sliver of a veranda on this rooftop are an unlikely trio. But these are the lines the city draws; the disparate stories the city makes intersect and the topologies it calculates. Who people are in the city—their roles, identities, functions—is not important in itself. Rather, they are devices that steer contact in particular directions. They are the nodes of absorption and deflection that push and pull people and things into specific openings, corners, and streams. From the rooftop there appears to be an intense compaction of bodies, dreams and delusions, and sediments of failed plans and improvisations wound so tight that nothing is able to escape. Everyone's lives are so implicated in everyone else's that any gesture takes on too many meanings. Individuals or institutions have little control over any schema of interpretations necessary to make anything make sense. Here, cities not only collect the "fugitive materials" mentioned earlier but seem to produce them as well. They act as machines of fractures, scattering and circulating parts, gestures, bits and pieces of ritual, livelihood, and sensibility. Such circulation produces an incessant sense of incompleteness and haunting in whatever arrangements are momentarily put together by diverse residents trying to figure each other out and live together.

WHAT IS AFRICA IN THE LARGER URBAN SCHEME OF THINGS?

In all regions of the urban world, the present moment is one of intense conflict over how cities are to be used and by whom. The notion that urbanization is the key to social integration probably doesn't mean much anymore, even as a popular myth. The spaces and objects of urban life are increasingly used as ways of making highly particularistic claims and solidifying zones of disengagement. As a result, the ideals of interchange appear remote and abstract.

In contexts of intensified contestation, then, how things in the city can be used takes on a wider range of meanings even as a sense of crisis becomes more pervasive. Territorial and cultural proximities thus do not facilitate collaboration or negotiation—a point brutally exemplified by the contemporary Middle East. So other forms of "coexistence" and complicity will have to ensue. Proliferating urban conflict wrecks public institutions and commonly shared spaces. As such, those who are relied upon to mediate between different interests and aspirations often use this position as a way to accumulate advantage and resources. People take whatever they can without regard to any sense of its inherent significance. But in these situations of crisis, new forms of intersection may arise, where the impediments to previously unimaginable conjunctions of identities, objects, spaces, and bodies are removed. New information and possibilities are thus permitted perhaps only momentary glimmers of existence.

Yet these moments may be sufficient to keep open possibilities of urban living not yet thought, not yet having concrete material underpinnings, but nonetheless alive. This is what I mean by popular urban culture—i.e. a way of mapping such conjunctions between what exists and the glimmers of existence that are here in the present but whose full realization is yet to come.

I want to move from Phnom Penh back to Douala, where Nzumi's story started, and talk about how the tensions in Douala point to the emergence of a new urban sociality even under dire conditions. What I talked about as a critical feature of a black urbanism. Here popular culture does not so much specify a particular way people inhabit spaces when they feel vulnerable and the conditions seem uncertain. Instead, people experiment with various ways to engage with their surroundings and with each other, while making these "trial balloons" visible to each other. This availability of methods is not undertaken for comparison, or even the possibility that countervailing trends could be synergized. Rather, these methods of engagement perhaps simply establish a situation of "co-impossibility." In other words, no particular experiment, expression, or social practice can by itself represent a concrete possible future or course of action. Nothing can be seen as the key factor for a government, police, military, or other powerful institution to go after in order to bring a particular population under control. There is no such thing here as putting all of one's eggs into one basket, even if it may be necessary at some point to have a strong message and point of view so as to "rally the masses." Instead, the edges of a new world to be made are roughly outlined as a protected space of constant rehearsal that wards off any final effort to close it down.

Popular culture, instead of showing the new horizon or the pathway into the future, may simply be about buying time as productively as possible. It may provide elements—of speech, gesture, and materials—that can be worked and experimented with, and that provide a haven for people's passions to live differently. But it does not consolidate them into a definitive strategy or program that would make those passions an easy target for those who have the power to eliminate them.

THE MARKET, NOT ONLY FOR GOODS AND SERVICES, BUT FOR PROJECTS AS WELL

The market remains the center of gravity and grand spectacle in most African cities. It is an arena in which everything is performed and where everything becomes its own truth. Of course the market is the place where goods and services are bought and sold, despite the large volume of these which seem to appear endlessly static and immovable, and that people will never buy. From pharmaceuticals to tomatoes to hardware, certain inventories seem to always remain in place beyond the purchasing styles or capacities of consumers. This complements the rapid turnovers in used clothing or sudden swells of foodstuffs released from price-fixing during times of potential political unrest. Equally important, the market is the site for incessant performance, for feigned connections and insider deals, for dissimulation of all kinds, for launching impressions and information, rumors and advice. The resultant confusions as to what is really going on breed home-styled interpreters, those who profess themselves to have real skills at discernment, who can steer customers to the best price, quality, or hidden deal.

Because the incredulous attains such high levels of publicity, this state of affairs serves as a mask for increasingly bizarre and even hideous transactions, where there are few prohibitions as to what can be bought and sold. As the volumes of such transactions grow, from the sale of body parts to the commissioning of violence, the more normal domains of economic life are increasingly implicated as vehicles of laundering and diversion. Yet by far the bulk of navigators through the market are simply taking a chance to see what happens, to see what deals they can insert themselves into, to observe who is talking to whom, and who is buying from whom. They look for those who might be open or vulnerable to some form of a "helping hand," an empty promise of assistance, or, alternately, who actively recruit participants in any number of "projects." As most decisions are quickly taken, people must be prepared to be anything to anybody without prolonged deliberations or assessments as to whether one possesses the requisite skills or daring. There is little overview, little room for planning out strategy or best practices in advance.

The temporality entailed is one of seizing and being seized, of taking what one can quickly without undue calculations as to the relative values or risks involved. Even though African markets demonstrate increasingly complex capacities to bundle various goods and services, to pay for consumption over time in advance, and to carry out their own versions of futures trading, most actors seem to live constantly in the present, without much attention to a sense of the past or future. Their actions can generate wild fluctuations where different "scores" can provide enough money to live months down the line or simply until the next day—there is no predicting.[48]

PERFORMING THE MINIMUM

Residential neighborhoods abutting such central urban markets have largely sunk into a prolonged malaise that seems to be a by-product of this very proximity. For example, in the New Bell district—Douala's sprawling historic inner city neighborhood—which is near to the city's main Nkololoun market, the interface with the market appears sometimes reduced to the most petty of initiatives. The market is rife with the easy thefts of a few items in the early dawn hours as the market opens. These items are then resold for the purchase of a few beers and rice. In fact, for the youth who make up the majority of these quarters there are few apologies for the extent to which theft constitutes a daily living, and the way the market itself seems to concede to this thievery as a kind of excise tax.

As more players use the market, there are more participants who slip from any effective control. As more items are smuggled from loosely controlled borders and docks or are dumped in large volumes at neoliberalized ports of call, profits are reduced for many entrepreneurs, in turn reducing their ability to maintain adequate controls and storage. An indifference to theft escalates. But the more thieves there are, the smaller the takings, and the lower the expectations. It is not uncommon to see middle-aged men still residing in the house of their parents, even subletting their rooms for a little cash, while sleeping by the side of the house. In Cameroon, barely 2 percent of school graduates will find formal employment, but in most parts of the country parents still make a concerted effort to send their children to school. But in many parts of New Bell, school attendance is a rarity. Instead, youth adjust their lives to living off what can be attained through a minimum of effort.

When New Bell was first designated as the primary site for permanent African urban residence by the colonial regime, it was an intense laboratory of entrepreneurship. The convergence of peoples from different towns and villages of the exterior gave rise to new forms of collaborative effort that largely remained opaque to the scrutiny of the authorities. As Lynn Schler describes in her history of New Bell, artisans, traders, tailors, vulcaneers, and mechanics of all kinds helped secure an economic platform on which many households were able to access land, build homes, and invest in a so-called modern urban future for their children.[49] While New Bell today remains full of entrepreneurship and improvised making-do, there are simply too many people making too many demands on available resources. Physical, built, and social environments are progressively eroded by overuse, the lack of money for repair and rehabilitation, and the incessant shortcuts and improvised uses of objects, tools, and spaces. Little is replenished or renewed. The discarded remain in plain sight. In a market area with a protracted history of countless performances, and where so many have attempted to make their existence relevant to so many others, interference in lives and activities has become legendary.

For everything that is attempted, it is not clear just who the endeavor will implicate, and it is never certain just who has to be looked out for, who will demand a cut of the proceeds, or who will see it as their duty to remind the enterprising individual of his or her obligations. In economic sectors that have become vastly overcrowded, the need to come up with something new is incumbent upon anyone who wants to emerge from the crowd and eke out a little bit of profit. Improvisation thus stands out like an ambulance on a choked highway. Everyone tries to follow the path-breaking move. Again, under such conditions it is difficult to make plans, to project into the future, and to pace oneself with a series of advancing steps geared to some overarching objective. This is the case particularly when the state, at all levels, no longer cares what happens and when politicians are mostly parasites. Thus the challenge for popular culture is how to maintain spaces where diverse actors and ways of doing things can intersect, but in practices that enable the intersection to generate new imaginations rather than simply being another occasion where people "feed off" the resources and energies of others.

INITIATIVES FOR MAKING EVERYONE COUNT

On the surface, the residential quarters more removed from the central market seem to be more dynamic, such as New Deido, the birthplace of Nzumi, or Bepanda Casamondo. Here, the semblance of initiative must be maintained, whether it is the pursuit of education, trade, or a more long-term involvement in the income-generating schemes of others. It is also in these neighborhoods that the effort to get out and work elsewhere is the most intense. This getting out is a project which requires great levels of dissimulation, networking, and greased palms. So even in these neighborhoods, the market is not far behind.[50] The evidence is displayed even in the many initiatives youth undertake to motivate creativity and community development.

In many cities across Africa, youth have often undertaken efforts to upend social practices and local power regimes which they believe hold them back or contribute to the suffocation of change and progress. From Filip De Boeck's work on the appropriation of the dead and funerals in Kinshasa as a way to challenge local hierarchies to the efforts of the young to take over local government councils in Nigeria in an attempt to try and run local affairs in new ways,[51] the intensity of the desire to break with the past finds different forms. But while these initiatives may exude ominous undercurrents and ways of pushing notions of "creative initiatives" to an extreme limit, they usually pull back from the "brink," and stop short of bringing about a complete rupture. Given this, particular manifestations of popular culture may seek to get urban residents to think of new ways of operating together and of providing idioms through which they can collectively view their everyday life situations as somehow more interconnected than they would otherwise think. A possible extreme position of this process, then, would be getting rid of everything that stood in the way of people being fully exposed to each other's lives, capabilities, and limitations.

New Deido is a neighborhood just beyond New Bell. It is a kind of spill-over district, made up of households with a better standard of living and living conditions. Still, there is widespread concern about the future of youth on the part of most local residents, particularly as New Deido was seen as the source of roving youth gangs responsible for many of the armed robberies across the city. In 2005, a group of youth, some formerly associated with Doual'art, the preeminent arts association in Douala, and others coming from different Catholic youth organizations announced plans to hold a week-long culture exhibition at a local private school. The objective was to showcase local talent and to reiterate the notion that the district possessed a great deal of local resources of all kinds. By bringing together various examples of this resourcefulness, local residents might feel more confident about what it might be possible to do.

What was particularly interesting about this effort was the very broad and open-ended sense of so-called cultural materials that were to be included in the exhibition. In part, this openness stemmed from the group's recognition that many other cultural events across the city were fraught with debilitating conflicts about whose works were to be considered worthy of inclusion, and the frequent complaints about favoritism and patronage connections. The group in New Deido wanted to avoid being perceived as using this initiative as a way to consolidate local political power. But additionally, many in the group genuinely were committed to an idea of popular cultural materials as going beyond the arts and embracing various forms of creativity and achievement of all kinds.

Thus, the group attempted to include crafts, inventions, business plans, achievement certificates, art works, cartoons, writings, video productions, diplomas, photographs, fashion, fake visas, and travel documents generated by youth in the neighborhood. The showcase was intended as a veritable archiving of expression and documentation that in its momentary and centralized compilation was almost expected to act as a repository of dreams that could launch everyone's discrete initiatives into a different orbit. It was a collective talisman that could concretize the strivings of neighborhood youth. Here again is the market's dream of agglomeration at work, of putting diverse things and actors in connection with each other, where each can rub off onto the other some new found capacities or possibilities.

The New Deido group worked carefully to canvass the different associations, religious and business groups in the area. They did this not only in order to solicit donations but to make sure that they had a broad base of support and that they themselves might have maximum exposure to creative materials that they could exhibit.

THE NIGHT OF SEEING RED

Shortly before the scheduled opening of the exhibition in July 2005, two stalls in the main New Deido market began playing cassettes of the psychedelic pop of the renowned Khmer singers Sim Sasmouth and Ros Sereysothea from the period of the mid-1970s just before the Khmer Rouge took power. Although these cassettes were finding their way across markets in different parts of the world, it is likely that in New Deido they also spurred a wave of new graffiti that began appearing on walls throughout the neighborhood. The tags included various combinations of Cambodian references that were, for the most part, distorted—i.e. even though "Khmer Rouge" was sprayed in red across a few walls, most of the tags were composed of fragments such as "Ka-Mer Rouge," "K-Mart Rouge," "Château Rouge," "Cum-ma-mère Rouge," "Genocidaires Rouges," "Marché Rouge," "Ka-Ka Rouge."

Although the surfaces of New Deido walls were accustomed to tags of various references—political, scatological, millennial, and idiosyncratic—no one I spoke to knew quite what to make of this rash of "rouge" tags. While urban Africa often makes reference to the zones of war and destruction in other parts of the world as a source for the names of local places, gangs, or styles, it is seldom clear why one particular reference is chosen over any other. But something did become clearer on the opening night party for the exhibition, although, again, it was a momentary manifestation, a flash that quickly came and went.

The long opening night consisted of a talent show, where groups of kids donned a variety of different garb to show off their abilities to play a wide range of different roles and styles. Whether it was that of the devotee in full religious garb or the sports illustrated swimsuit model, rapper, businessman, or soldier for hire, the role itself did not matter. What was important was the versatility and the commitment to pursue any angle, all gathered in sight of the other.

At the peak of the night's attendance, shortly before one in the morning, a shower of flyers was dropped from the rooftop of the school by a small group of masked persons, who quickly disappeared along adjacent buildings. The flyers were printed in red ink and referred to the gathering in process as an "internment camp for the re-education of souls." Attendees were instructed that they were to remain in this camp, that all of their houses and possessions had been appropriated and put in a communal trust for some unspecified future use. Everyone was to "begin again," "from the start," with "no preconceptions and no memory." "You have now come naked into the new world," the flyer went on to read, and "there is nothing to stop you from being one of us." Perhaps most important was the fact that the flyer was signed "The Khmer Rouge."

The crowd was mostly bemused. Many had no idea who the Khmer Rouge had been, and little idea about what the content of the flyers meant. Most had been exposed to various exaggerations of religious sentiments pointing to rebirth, and this was simply an addition to a long line of such messages. But many in the crowd were also making connections to the rash of tags that had started appearing in the weeks before and didn't know the extent to which they should feel alarm. They didn't know whether the event was simply part of the show. In fact, the organizers were asking each other, during a hastily arranged meeting, whether someone had invited a theater group to make this manifestation. After the evening's event it was difficult to pursue any answers as no more manifestations took place.

It is perhaps ironic that in an exhibition devoted to assembling diverse manifestations of a community's talents and resourcefulness the opening night was disrupted by a "group" identifying itself with a signature related to one of the world's most despised political cliques. The Khmer Rouge had attempted to remake society from zero and ended up killing millions when they found they could not really do so. In this instance one can only speculate as to what this "group" had in mind. Was it that the organizers of the exhibition were not going far enough in terms of taking seriously the objective of getting residents to really value each other's contributions? Was it that the objective itself was flawed from the beginning since no amount of exhibition, representation, or exposure could ever be sufficient to the task of concretizing real collaboration? Rather than exhibiting the apparent "fullness" of community life through the accumulated talents of individual residents, is it perhaps more important to strip all of these things away? No matter how much a project may accord "equal value" to these talents, comparison and competition—and thus value judgments—are inevitable; and the more talents are shown, the more judgments are made, and thus the more the community is strewn with impediments.

These were just some of the questions the organizers asked themselves after the exhibition. Questions that, however abstract and removed from the process of trying to do things in a district like New Deido, nevertheless tend to haunt the proceedings. After all, for most residents of this city, everyday life approximates to emergency conditions. If one does not want to retreat to the minimal parasitism of many in New Bell's zones of facile theft, then one has to be prepared to consider almost anything outside of the order or logics in which they are presented. One has to keep all possibilities close at hand in some "democratic" relation with each other. And as for me, I would have loved to have claimed that all of this had happened because Nzumi had returned home, bringing with her some actual residues of Phnom Penh. I looked for her. She was nowhere to be found.

EXACTLY WHAT IS POPULAR?

Today, some African cities seem to be experiencing unprecedented efforts to define what they are—i.e. the social, economic, and cultural identities of those who reside and operate within them.[52] Some cities are literally hemorrhaging young men and women to distant locations or condemning other youth to a much more circumscribed existence. These urban situations are not just the product of spiraling impoverishment or the absence of sustainable development. It must be kept in mind that for generations Africans were prevented from using cities as a mechanism to give voice to their specific aspirations or give rise to new forms of social and political existence. So, in some fundamental sense, keeping alive the prospects for creating new societies means to a certain extent running inherited images of what a city should be into the ground.[53]

Individuals and households in many residential quarters of Africa are often stuck in highly redundant relations with neighbors and family members. This is because there are few institutions that can be used over the long run as platforms for exploring and negotiating new affiliations and domains of personal operation. Cognitive proficiency—the ability to assess information and to adapt to new conditions—requires differentiation, where information is to catapult individuals into new abilities. Even a highly circumscribed and narrowing social universe becomes punctuated with many dramas and conflicts, if only to ward off atrophy.[54]

So even though stability is retained in people dealing with a known set of others for much of their lives, this stability is incessantly put at risk—through disputes, jealousies, and provocations—to give the "social body" punctuation and texture. Family and neighborhood life often come to face incessant crisis, which requires a series of compensations. These compensations become particular economies because sickness, accidents, social fissions, and death have to be serviced. Communities often seem to be exposed to an incessant recycling of suffering and compensation—where there is a rhythm of movement and fluctuation, but one that doesn't seem to proceed in any developmental sense.

Still, the weight of remaking urban everyday life lies in the extremities of those gestures offered, for example, by both the organizers of the cultural exhibition and the "Khmer Rouge" in New Deido. The former allows almost everything produced in the neighborhood to seek some kind of affiliation with everything else, without pre-judgment as to how these affiliations might take place or what value they might have. The organizers might not have gone far enough. They may be faced with contradictions and limitations that will question any initiative they might undertake. Or they may simply inadvertently add to the existing impediments to the collaboration and community confidence that they are seeking to bring about. Still, they attempted to do something and tried to organize an assemblage of what New Deido is so that it might be something else.

At the same time, the "Khmer Rouge" signals, through stealth, the infiltration of voices from elsewhere, even if the group calling themselves by this name was indeed probably made up of local residents. But their manifestation, and the tagging of the walls that came before, is a reminder that communities like New Deido cannot, of course, go it alone. For, with everything a community does, there is an inevitable sense of uncertainty that can never be identified or put into local idioms and which must be lived with and engaged. The critical question is how to live through this uncertainty. For all assemblages that seek to bring diversities—of people, practices, inclinations, styles, backgrounds, and aspirations— to some "collective table," there is, in the end, no certain method of making an account, of fitting the pieces together, or of ensuring balance and viability.

In the first instance, then, urban popular culture entails the practice of a certain ethos of egalitarianism. No matter how preoccupied Africans may be with status and hierarchy in everyday transactions, no matter how much those lower in social status may get ordered around or disabused, the extension of the market across the city, as an arena of everyday transaction and performance, requires a sense of acknowledging all who are present. No matter how educated or rich one might be, the resounding conclusion of a large number of African urban residents is that, no matter the empirical realities of their livelihood, they believe their privileges could all disappear at a moment's notice, as very few are definitively protected.

Again, this is not to say that there are no differences between social classes in the city. Here, I am not so much talking about the structural conditions of urban economies. I am not talking about the fact that large numbers of the urban middle classes are skipping meals. Rather, I am talking about a set of attitudes and ways of talking about urban life. In these ways of talking about what is going on, potential complicities amongst different classes of urban residents cannot be ignored. Residents across the board have to pay attention to what is going on, to what everyone is doing. For while privileged positions remain and the gap between rich and poor continues to grow, there are few privileged points of view or vantage points from which a person can confidently consolidate a secure position within contemporary urban life.

But such egalitarianism is also a trap. It can quickly turn into an incessant preoccupation with undermining the capacities of others, with getting in their way, blocking the path, turning oneself into the satanic double. In such circumstances, the ability to survive is articulated in the ability to upend and to unsettle. We must keep in mind that, throughout the world, youth continue to constitute an enlarged pool of surplus and expendable labor available to do the menial, dirty, and violent jobs that enhance the power and wealth of various political and business elite, syndicates, and mafias. Their futures are only tentatively in their hands. This is because the high degree of unrestrained competition increasingly evident in a wide range of illegal businesses raises the stakes entailed in ground-level transactions involving narcotics, guns, and contraband and the concomitant use of violence as a form of advantage. Additionally, the complicity of police, judges, customs officers, and other officials induces a more arbitrary application of legal sanctions, of which youth bear the largest burden. Without recourse to predictable dispositions in terms of how courts, prisons, and social welfare agencies work, everyday actions of the street also become increasingly provisional.

On the other hand, this is not the situation whereby innumerable sufferings are acquired in anticipation of some messianic return that will redeem all that has been borne. Here, the popular rests somewhere in the middle, keeping open the possibilities of taking what has been past—the once fundamental connections with ancestors, anchorage in a lineage of connections with personages both here and there, alive and dead—with relations still to be built in the time ahead.

Related to this ethos of the egalitarian are the ways that many residential quarters make connections among the various facets of urban life to create new arenas of action. These arenas are not the church, not ethnic or business associations, extended family gatherings, or social clubs, but something else, something whose definitions may be constantly changing. In a city like Douala, there are scores of gatherings, consultations, reciprocal favors, improvised work crews and business ventures, group prayers, publicly shared meals, clandestine exchanges of goods, and hastily pieced together solutions to extended family or neighborhood crises, all of which take place in a wide range of settings across the urban terrain—from markets, abandoned hotel ballrooms, deserted factories, to crowded intersections.

These ways of acting are set off from the characteristics of participation prevalent in the household and other more formalized organizations, whether they are political parties, work places, or community-based organizations. They are also contexts which are themselves repeatedly rehearsed and revised. For the process of coming up with new modalities of associating and cooperating capable of dealing with rapidly changing realities is continuous.

The popular is then the shifting social architectures that residents put together—using their time, their bodies, inclinations, tools, and all the material stuff that exists around and within them—to reach and connect to public necessities, such as water, opportunities for income, for good times, or even to disappear, fade away, fan out into a larger world of operations. These architectures are not easily mapped out with their ever shifting topographies of openings, closures, circumventions, retreats, and dissimulation. They are both material and ephemeral, infused with shifting tactics but also a concrete shaping of bodies and places. They are conduits, connectors, spinning out unanticipated by-products and opportunities.

WHAT IS THE RIGHT TO THE CITY? WHO HAS IT? WHAT CAN BE DONE WITH IT?

In light of these practices of popular culture, the entire notion of municipality becomes complicated. It becomes especially complicated for cities where the "right to the city" was established along racial lines that, by default, made it clear exactly what the right to the city might mean. Now this very right, as it struggles for an application to cities thoroughly mixed up with widely diverging histories of residence, aspirations, livelihood, points of reference, stakes, and states of preparedness, can find no unequivocally clear expression. Instead of mitigating its importance, this confounding makes the notion of "right to the city" all the more important. Its connotations of hospitality, accommodation, and productivity would seem to compel different social groups to make the most out of each other rather than simply reproducing some essential integrity or coherence—be it those of national, racial, territorial, or ethnic identity. In other words, the right to the city may be the right to be messy and inconsistent, or to look disordered. This is not the right to be left alone, but to be engaged, to be the object of request, to be re-settled or re-aligned—to thrive in unanticipated ways.

Black urbanism thus concerns how such platforms of engagement can be built. It concerns how connections are built across cities in ways that circumvent the dominant histories, frameworks, and policies that largely determine how they are to be seen in relationship to each other. It concerns the inextricable experience of possibility and precariousness that seems to now locate the positions and operations of the world's urban majority. It concerns the ways in which urban residents live with their neighbors, participate in multiple networks of association, and calculate their chances. It concerns how residents tactically keep open multiple futures, maintain information-rich environments necessary to continuously adjust how they survive and accumulate resources, and how they contest specific constraints on their maneuverability. It concerns the willingness to leap forward into new affiliations, new versions of what had been familiar and comforting, and new ways of expressing the refusal to disappear in provisional new friendships and collaboration that could easily disappear.

The composition of racism has often been tricky to follow. It has never been easy to constitute social and political solidarities sufficient to the task of justly negotiating political resolutions of racist materials capable of insinuating themselves into the smallest recesses of the urban landscape. As such, blackness has had to assume an incessantly inventive practice of maintaining the creativity of black people and warding off all the impediments this creativity has faced. As such, blackness is a resource for better understanding the ups and downs and the possibilities of urban life everywhere.

Again, none of this is to underestimate the dire circumstances in which much of the world's urban population is forced to live. But we also must be clear about the choices we make in terms of how we think about what is going on. For the past three decades I have participated in scores of conferences, programs, and projects that have focused on urban poverty in the Global South. Much important work has been done, and there have been many lessons learned. Across the world, residents have struggled to make their lives better, and have patiently pursued modest agendas and interventions.

Still, access to essential services, security, and livelihood remains highly problematic. Many warnings have been issued about the social, political, and climatic catastrophes that could ensue from the continuation of an urbanization that does not significantly improve the basic conditions of life for the majority. But still everyday life does not significantly change for millions. In many cities, there are few prospects of employment, few signs of a viable life for the young growing up. In such circumstances, then, it seems crucial to find a way to valorize the many efforts that residents make to use the city as an arena in which to say something about what it means to be alive and to practice whatever form of aliveness they might eke out from the city. If we pay attention only to the misery and not to the often complex forms of deliberation, calculation, and engagement through which residents try to do more than simply register the factualness of a bare existence, do we not inevitably make these conditions worse? If we are not willing to find a way to live and discover within the worlds these residents have made, however insalubrious, violent, and banal they might often be, do we not undermine the very basis on which we would work to make cities more livable for all?

Endnotes

ONE

1. Matthew Gandy. 2005, Cyborg Urbanization: Complexity and Monstrosity in the Contemporary City. *International Journal of Urban and Regional Research* 29: 26–49.
2. Thomas Osborne and Nikolas Rose. 1999, Governing Cities: Notes on the Spatialisation of Virtue. *Environment and Planning D: Society and Space* 17: 737–760.
3. Paul Virilio. 1995, *The Art of the Motor*. Minneapolis, Minn.: University of Minnesota Press.
4. Ash Amin. 2002, Ethnicity and the Multicultural City: Living with Diversity. www.cwis.livjm.ac.uk/cities/Papers/ash_amin.pdf
5. Mike Crang and Steve Graham. 2007, Sentient Cities: Ambient Intelligence and the Politics of Urban Space. *Information, Communication and Society* 10: 813–814.
6. Sean Fox. 2007, Blue Cities: Encompassing Governance, Urban Integration, and Economic Reform. The World Bank Urban Research Symposium 2007. Washington, D.C.: The World Bank.
7. Jean-Paul Azam. 2002a, Looting and Conflict between Ethno-Regional Groups: Lessons for State Formation in Africa. *Journal of Conflict Resolution* 46: 131–153.
8. Patrick Chabal and Jean-Pascal Daloz. 2006, *Culture Troubles: Politics and the Interpretation of Meaning*. Chicago: University of Chicago Press.
9. Beatrice Hibou. 1999, The Social Capital of the State as an Agent of Deception. In Jean-François Bayart, Beatrice Hibou, and Stephen Ellis (eds.) *The Criminalization of the State in Africa*. London: James Currey; Bloomington, Ind.: Indiana University Press.
10. Jean-Paul Azam. 2002, Statecraft in the Shadow of Civil Conflict.

International Forum on African Perspectives. African Development Bank and OECD Development Centre, Paris, February 4–5, 2002.

11. Paul Collier and Jan Willem Gunning. 1998, Explaining African Performance. WPS/97-2.2, Working Paper Series of the Centre for the Study of African Economies, University of Oxford; International Labor Organization. 1998, *Jobs for Africa: A Policy Framework for an Employment-Intensive Growth Strategy.* Geneva: International Labor Organization; S.V. Sethuraman. 1997, *Africa's Informal Economy.* Geneva: International Labor Office.

12. Nazneen Kanji. 1995, Gender, Poverty, and Economic Adjustment in Harare, Zimbabwe. *Environment and Urbanization* 7: 37–55; Annelet Harts-Broekhuis. 1997, How to Sustain a Living: Urban Households and Poverty in a Sahelian Town of Mopti, Africa. *Africa* 67: 106–131; Claire Robertson. 1997, *Trouble Showed the Way: Women, Men and Trade in the Nairobi Area 1890–1990.* Bloomington, Ind.; Indianapolis: Indiana University Press.

13. Brian Van Arkadie. 1995, The State and Economic Change in Africa. In Ha-Joon Chang and Robert Rowthorn (eds.) *The Role of the State in Economic Change in Africa.* Oxford: Clarendon Press; Kenneth King. 1996, *Jua Kali Kenya: Change and Development in an Informal Economy 1970–95.* Nairobi: East African Educational Publishers.

14. Joe Lugalla. 1995, *Crisis, Urbanization and Urban Poverty in Tanzania: A Study of Urban Poverty and Survival Politics.* Lanham, Md.; London: University Presses of America; Kisangani Emizet. 1998, Confronting the Apex of the State: The Growth of the Unofficial Economy in Congo. *African Studies Review* 41: 99–137; Janet Roitman. 1998, The Garrison-Entrepôt. *Cahiers d'études africaines* 150–152: 297–329.

15. Peter Geschiere. 1997, *The Modernity of Witchcraft: Politics and the Occult in Postcolonial Africa.* Charlottesville, Virg.; London: University Press of Virginia.

16. There has been marked controversy over just exactly what constitutes "productive investment," see Richard Rogers. 1990, *Return Migration, Migrant's Savings and Sending Countries: Economic Development Lessons from Europe.* Washington, D.C.: Commission for the Study of International Migration and Cooperative Economic Development. No. 30, May.

17. Mike Davis. 2004, The Urbanization of Empire: Megacities and the Laws of Chaos. *Social Text* 22: 9–15; Mike Davis. 2006, *Planet of the Slums.* London: Verso.

18. Laura Berlant. 2007, Nearly Utopian, Nearly Normal: Post-Fordist Affect in *La Promesse* and *Rosetta*. *Public Culture* 19: 273–301.

19. Karim Rahem. 2005, Maladie, anomie et monothéisme à Khartoum: Le Cas de Mayo Farm. Dossier Khartoum: Lettre de l'oucc no. 6–7. Centre d'Etudes et de Documentation Economiques, Juridiques et Sociales.

20. Ibid.

21. A popular designation of Sudanese for individuals having a West African ancestry.

22. Tshikala Kayembe Biaya. 2001, Parallel Society in the Democratic Republic of Congo. In Simon Bekker, Martine Dodds, and Meshack Khosa (eds.) *Shifting African Identities*. Pretoria: Human Sciences Research Council, 43–60; Filip De Boeck. 2003, Kinshasa: Tales of the "Invisible City" and the Second World. In Okwui Enwezor, Carlos Basualdo, and Uta Meta Bauer (eds.) *Under Siege. Four African Cities: Freetown, Johannesburg, Kinshasa, Lagos.* Documenta11_Platform 4. Kassel: Hatje Cantz Publishers, 243–285; Richard Fanthorpe. 2001, Neither Citizen or Subject: "Lumpen" Agency and the Legacy of Native Administration in Sierra Leone. *African Affairs* 100: 363–388; Jeffrey Herbst. 2000, *States and Power in Africa: Comparative Lessons in Authority and Control*. Princeton, N.J.; London: Princeton University Press.

23. Michael Grimm, Charlotte Guénard, and Sandrine Mesplé-Somps. 2002, What Has Happened to the Urban Population in Côte d'Ivoire Since the 1980s? An Analysis of Monetary Poverty and Deprivation over 15 Years of Household Data. *World Development* 30: 1073–1095; Scientific Committee of the African Development Bank–OECD–CILSS. 1995, *West Africa Long-Term Prospective Study*. Paris: OECD; Bamako: Sahel Institute.

24. Human Rights Watch. 2002, *Hidden in Plain Sight: Refugees Living in Nairobi and Kampala*. New York: Human Rights Watch, p. 420.

25. Claude Jacquier. 2005, Can Distressed Areas Become Poles of Urban Growth? OECD International Conference "Sustainable Cities: Linking Competitiveness with Social Cohesion," October 13–14, 2005, Montreal, p. 24.

26. Li Zhang. 2005, Migrant Enclaves and the Impact of Redevelopment Policies in Chinese Cities. In Laurence J.C. Ma and Fulong Wu (eds.) *Restructuring the Chinese City: Changing Society, Economy and Space*. London; New York: Routledge, 243–259; Jiang Jun and Kuang Xiaoming. 2007, The Taxonomy of Contemporary Chinese Cities (We Make Cities). *Architectural Digest* 78: 16–21; Yan Song, Yves Zenou, and Chengri Ding. 2008, Let's Not

Throw Out the Baby with the Bathwater: The Role of Urban Villages in Housing Rural Migrants in China. *Urban Studies* 45: 313–330.

27. Derek Gregory. 2004, *The Colonial Present: Afghanistan, Palestine, Iraq*. Oxford: Blackwell.

28. Homi Bhabha. 1994, *The Location of Culture*. London; New York: Routledge.

29. Stefan Kipfer. 2007, Fanon and Space: Colonization, Urbanization, and Liberation from the Colonial to the Global City. *Environment and Planning D: Society and Space* 25: 701–726.

30. Adriana Allen. 2003, Environmental Planning and Management of the Peri-Urban Interface: Perspectives on an Emerging Field. *Environment and Urbanization* 15: 135–148.

31. Jens Andersson. 2001, Reintegrating the Rural–Urban Connection: Migration Practices and Sociocultural Dispositions of Buhera Workers in Harare. *Africa* 71: 81–111; Harri Englund. 2002, The Village in the City, the City in the Village: Migrants in Lilongwe. *Journal of Southern African Studies* 28: 137–159.

32. The diversity of peri-urban situations is categorized as follows by Axel Dresche and David Iaquinta in a FAO report of 2002 entitled "Urbanization: Linking Development across the Changing Landscape":

Village peri-urban
- non-proximate to the city either geographically or in travel time;
- derives from sojourning, circulation and migration;
- embodies a *Network Induced Institutional Context* (IC) wherein change is effected through diffusion or induction while institutions remain traditional in orientation and stable.

Diffuse peri-urban
- geographically a part of the urban fringe;
- derives from multiple point-source in-migration;
- embodies an *Amalgamated* IC where there is a high demand for negotiating novel institutional forms to address conflicting traditions and worldviews.

Chain peri-urban
- geographically a part of urban fringe;
- derives from chain migration;
- embodies a *Reconstituted* IC wherein links to the donor area remain strong and traditions and institutions are

transplanted with some modification from the donor area and take on a somewhat defensive character.

In-place peri-urban
- geographically close to the city; urban fringe;
- derives from in-place urbanization, natural increase and some migration;
- embodies a *Traditional IC* with long-term stable institutions evidencing strong defensive insulation.

Absorbed peri-urban
- geographically within the city, having been absorbed;
- derives from succession/displacement and traditionalism (ritualism);
- embodies a *Residual IC* wherein the roots of social arrangements lie in the traditions of a previously resident culture group and are now maintained through ritualism.

33. Alan Klima. 2002, *The Funeral Casino: Mediation, Massacre, and Exchange with the Dead in Thailand.* Princeton, N.J.; London: Princeton University Press.
34. Saba Mahmood. 2005, *Politics of Piety: The Islamic Revival and the Feminist Subject.* Princeton, N.J.; London: Princeton University Press.

TWO

1. Sandro Mezzadra. 2007, Living in Transition, Toward a Heterolingual Theory of the Multitude. http://roundtable.kein.org/node/653.
2. Dipesh Chakrabarty. 2000, *Provincializing Europe. Postcolonial Thought and Historical Difference.* Princeton; Oxford: Princeton University Press.
3. Romain Bertrand. 2005, La Politique des "Réunions de l'ombre." Puissances officielles et pouvoirs officieux dans l'Indonésie post-Suharto. Paper presented at the 8ème Congrès de l'Association Française de Science Politiques, Lyon.
4. Richard Robinson and Vedi Hadiz. 2004, *Reorganizing Power in Indonesia: The Politics of Oligarchy in an Age of Markets.* London: Routledge; Ian Douglas Wilson. 2006, Continuity and Change: The Changing Contours of Organized Violence in Post-New Order Indonesia. *Critical Asian Studies* 38: 263–297.
5. Romain Bertrand. 2004, Behave Like Enraged Lions: Civic

Militias, the Army, and the Criminalization of Politics in Indonesia. *Global Crime* 6: 325–344.

6. Donald Brown and Ian Wilson. 2007, Ethnicized Violence in Indonesia: The Betawi Brotherhood Forum in Jakarta. Working Paper 145, Asia Research Centre, Murdoch University.

7. Arjun Appadurai. 2004, The Capacity to Aspire: Culture and the Terms of Recognition. In Viyayendra Rao and Michael Walton (eds.) *Culture and Public Action*. Stanford, Ca.: Stanford University Press, 59–84.

8. Isabelle Stengers. 2008, Experimenting with Refrains: Subjectivity and the Challenge of Escaping Modern Dualism. *Subjectivity* 22: 38–59.

9. Mercy Corps. 2008, Summary of Land Tenure Research Findings in Jakarta. *Urban Bulletin #2*.

10. Richard Sennett. 1990, *The Conscience of the Eye: The Design and Social Life of Cities*. New York: W.W. Norton; Richard Sennett. 1994, *Flesh and Stone: The Body and the City in Western Civilization*. New York: W.W. Norton.

THREE

1. Patrick Le Gales. 2005, Governing Globalizing Cities, Reshaping Urban Policies. OECD International Conference "What Policies for Globalizing Cities: Rethinking the Urban Policy Agenda," March 29–30, 2005, Madrid.

2. Michael Warner. 2002, Publics and Counterpublics. *Public Culture* 14: 49–90.

3. Guillaume Iyenda. 2005, Street Enterprises, Urban Livelihoods and Poverty in Kinshasa. *Environment and Urbanization* 17: 55–67.

4. Filip De Boeck. 2005, The Apocalyptic Interlude: Revealing Death in Kinshasa. *African Studies Review* 48: 11–32.

5. Morag Torrance. 2008, Forging Glocal Governance: Urban Infrastructures as Networked Financial Products. *International Journal of Urban and Regional Research* 32: 1–21.

6. Jochem Monstad, Matthias Naumann, with Verena Meister and Timothy Moss. 2005, *New Geographies of Infrastructure Systems: Spatial Science Perspectives and the Socio-Technical Change of Energy, Water Supply Systems in Germany*. Berlin: Networks Research Association.

7. Jean-Marc Offner. 2000, "Territorial Deregulation": Local Authorities at Risk from Technical Networks. *International Journal of Urban and Regional Research* 24, 1: 171.

8. Karen Bakker, Michelle Koy, Nur Fudah Shotiani, and Ernst-Jan

Martijn. 2006, Disconnected: Poverty, Water Supply and Development in Jakarta, Indonesia. New York: Occasional Paper, Human Development Report 2006, United Nations Development Program.

9. Henri Lefebvre. 1974/1991, *The Production of Space*. Oxford: Blackwell; Bill Hillier and Julienne Hanson. 1984, *The Social Logic of Space*. Cambridge, U.K.: Cambridge University Press; James Vance, Jr. 1990, *The Continuing City: Urban Morphology in Western Civilization*. Baltimore, Md.: Johns Hopkins University Press; N. John Habraken. 1998, *The Structure of the Ordinary: Form and Control in the Built Environment*. Cambridge, Mass.: The MIT Press.

10. Christine Boyer. 1995, *The City of Collective Memory: Its Historical Imagery and Architectural Entertainments*. Cambridge, Mass.: The MIT Press; Dolores Hayden. 1995, *The Power of Place: Urban Landscapes as Public History*. Cambridge, Mass.: The MIT Press; Sharon Zukin. 1995, *The Cultures of Cities*. London: Blackwell; Peter Madsen and Richard Plunz. 2002, *The Urban Lifeworld: Formation, Perception, Representation*. London: Routledge; John Urry. 2002, Mobility and Proximity. *Sociology* 36: 255–274; John Urry. 2004, Small Worlds and the New "Social Physics." *Global Networks* 4: 109–130; David Pinder. 2006, *Visions of the City: Utopianism, Power and Politics in Twentieth Century Urbanism*. London; New York: Routledge.

11. James Holston and Arjun Appadurai. 1996, Cities and Citizenship. *Public Culture* 8: 187–204; John Allen, Doreen Massey, and Michael Pryke (eds.). 1999, *Unsettling Cities*. London: Routledge and The Open University Press; Kenneth Cox. 2001, Territoriality, Politics and the "Urban." *Political Geography* 20: 745–762; Farha Ghannam. 2002, *Remaking the Modern: Space, Relocation and the Politics of Identity in a Global Cairo*. Berkeley, Ca.: University of California Press; Charles Taylor. 2002, Modern Social Imaginaries. *Public Culture* 14: 91–124; Leonie Sandercock. 2003, *Cosmopolis II: Mongrel Cities*. London: Continuum.

12. Phil Hubbard. 1996, Urban Design and City Regeneration: Social Representations of Entrepreneurial Landscapes. *Urban Studies* 33: 1441–1461; Erik Swyngedouw. 1999, Territories of Innovation: Innovation as a Collective Process and the Globalisation of Competition. In Helen Lawton-Smith (ed.) *Technology Transfer and Industrial Change in Europe: The Case of the Electronic Component and the Flow Measuring Industries in the U.K., France and Belgium*. London: Macmillan, 15–33. Bob Jessop. 2000, Globalisation, Entrepreneurial Cities and the Social Economy. In Pierre Hamel,

Henri Lustiger-Thaler, and Margit Mayer (eds.) *Urban Movements in a Globalising World*. London: Routledge; Timothy Bunnell and Neal Coe. 2001, Spaces and Scales of Innovation. *Progress in Human Geography* 25: 569–589; Richard Child Hill and Kuniko Fujita. 2003, The Nested City: Introduction. *Urban Studies* 40: 207–217; Neil Brenner. 2004, *New State Spaces: Urban Governance and the Rescaling of Statehood*. Oxford; New York: Oxford University Press; Ray Hudson. 2004, Conceptualizing Economies and Their Geographies: Spaces, Flows and Circuits. *Progress in Human Geography* 28: 447–471; Groupe Frontière, Christiane Arbaret-Schulz, Antoine Beyer, Jean-Luc Permay, Bernard Reitel, Catherine Selimanovski, Christophe Sohn, and Patricia Zander. 2005, La Frontière, un objet spatial en mutation. *EspacesTemps.net*. Textual. 30.04.2005.http://espacestemps.net/document1317.html; Patsy Healy. 2007, *Urban Complexity and Spatial Strategies: Towards a Relational Planning for Our Times*. London: Routledge.

13. Michael Storper and Michael Mandaville. 2006, Behavior, Preferences, and Cities: Urban Theory and Urban Resurgence. *Urban Studies* 43: 1247–1274.

14. Kian Tajbakhsh. 2001, *The Promise of the City: Space, Identity, and Politics in Contemporary Social Thought*. Berkeley: University of California Press; David Harvey. 2006, *Space of Global Capitalism: Towards a Theory of Uneven Geographical Development*. London: Verso.

15. Edward Soja. 1999, *Postmetropolis: Critical Studies of Cities & Regions*. Oxford: Blackwell; Saskia Sassen. 2000, New Frontiers Facing Urban Sociology at the Millennium. *British Journal of Sociology* 51: 143–160; Lisa Law. 2002, Defying Disappearance: Cosmopolitan Public Spaces in Hong Kong. *Urban Studies* 39: 1625–1645; John Eade and Christopher Mele. 2002, Introduction: Understanding the City. In John Eade and Christopher Mele (eds.) *Understanding the City: Contemporary and Future Perspectives*. Oxford: Blackwell, 1–27; Ash Amin. 2006, The Good City. *Urban Studies* 43: 10,009–10,023; Alev Çinar and Thomas Bender. 2007, Introduction: The City: Experience, Imagination and Place. In Alev Çinar and Thomas Bender (eds.) *Urban Imaginaries: Locating the Modern City*. Minneapolis: University of Minnesota Press, xi–xxvi; Christina Jiménez. 2008, From the Lettered City to the Sellers' City: Vendor Politics and Public Space in Urban Mexico, 1880–1926. In Gyan Prakash and Kevin M. Kruse (eds.) *The Spaces of the Modern City: Imaginaries, Politics and Everyday Life*. Princeton, N.J.: Princeton University Press, 214–246.

16. J. Michael Batty. 2005, *Cities and Complexity: Understanding Cities with*

Cellular Automata, Agent-Based Models, and Fractals. Cambridge, Mass.: The MIT Press.

17. Arturo Escobar. 2001, Culture Sits in Places: Reflections on Globalism and Subaltern Strategies of Localization. *Political Geography* 20: 139–174; Ash Amin and Nigel Thrift. 2002, Cities: *Imagining the Urban*. London: Polity; Anssi Paasi. 2002, Bounded Spaces in the Mobile World: Deconstructing Regional Identity. *Tijdschrift voor Economische en Sociale Geografie* 93: 137–148; Jeffrey Boggs and Normal Rantisi. 2003, The "Relational Turn" in Economic Geography. *Journal of Economic Geography* 3: 109–116; Matthew Gandy. 2005, Cyborg Urbanization: Complexity and Monstrosity in the Contemporary City. *International Journal of Urban and Regional Research* 29: 26–49.

18. Lisa Peattie. 1972, *A View from the Barrio*. Ann Arbor, Mich.: University of Michigan Press; Jane Jacobs. 1996, *Edge of Empire: Postcolonialism and the City*. London: Routledge; Terence McGee. 1999, Urbanization in an Era of Volatile Globalization. In John Brotchie, Peter Newton, Peter Hall, and John Dickey (eds.) *East–West Perspectives on 21st Century Urban Development: Sustainable Eastern and Western Cities in the New Millennium*. Aldershot, U.K.; Brookfield, Vt.: Ashgate, 37–52; Abidin Kusno. 2000, *Behind the Postcolonial: Architecture, Urban Space and Political Cultures*. London; New York: Routledge; Smriti Srinivas. 2001, *Landscapes of Urban Memory: The Sacred and the Civic in India's High-Tech City*. Minneapolis: University of Minnesota Press; Jennifer Robinson. 2002, Global and World Cities: A View from off the Map. *International Journal of Urban and Regional Research* 26: 531–554; Anthony King. 2003, Actually Existing Postcolonialisms: Colonial Urbanism and Architecture after the Postcolonial Turn. In Ryan Bishop, John Phillips, and Wei-Wei Yeo (eds.) *Postcolonial Urbanism: Southeast Asian Cities and Global Processes*. New York; London: Routledge, 167–186; Claudio Lomnitz. 2003, Times of Crisis: Historicity, Sacrifice and the Spectacle of Debacle in Mexico City. *Public Culture* 15: 127–148; Rafael Pizzaro, Liang Wei, and Tridib Bannerjee. 2003, Agencies of Globalization and Third World Urban Form: A Review. *Journal of Planning Literature* 18: 111–130; Filip De Boeck and Marie-Françoise Plissart. 2004, *Kinshasa: Tales of the Invisible City*. Antwerp: Ludion; Michael Peter Smith. 2005, Transnational Urbanism Revisited. *Journal of Ethnic and Migration Studies* 31: 235–244.

19. John Browder and Brian Godfrey. 1997, *Rainforest Cities: Urbanization, Development and Globalization of the Brazilian Amazon*. New York: Columbia University Press; Richard Grant and Jan Nijman.

2002, Globalization and the Corporate Geography of Cities in the Less-Developed World. *Annals of the Association of American Geographers* 92: 320–340; Douglas Webster and Larissa Muller. 2002, The Challenges of Peri-Urban Growth in East Asia: The Case of China's Hangzhou–Ningbo Corridor. In Mila Freire and Belinda Yuen (eds.) *Enhancing Urban Management in East Asia*. Aldershot, U.K.: Ashgate, 23–54; Vivienne Wee and Kanishka Jayasuriya. 2002, New Geographies and Temporalities of Power: Exploring the New Fault-Lines of Southeast Asia. *The Pacific Review* 15: 475–495; Aihwa Ong. 2005, Splintering Cosmopolitanism. In Thomas Blom Hansen and Finn Stepputat (eds.) *Sovereign Bodies*. Princeton, N.J.; London: Princeton University Press, 257–275; Peter Rowe. 2005, *East Asia Modern: Shaping the Contemporary City*. London: Reaktion; Richard Ingersoll. 2006, *Sprawltown: Looking for the City on Its Edges*. New York: Princeton Architectural Press; Timothy Bunnell, Hamzah Muzaini, and James Sidaway. 2006, Global City Frontiers: Singapore's Hinterland and the Contested Socio-Political Geographies of Bintan, Indonesia. *International Journal of Urban and Regional Research* 30: 3–22.

FOUR

1. Kris Olds. 1995, Globalization and the Production of New Urban Spaces: Pacific Rim Megaprojects in the Late 20th Century. *Environment and Planning A* 27: 1713–1743; Michael Pryke and John Allen. 2000, Monetized Time–Space: Derivatives: Money's New "Imaginary." *Economy and Society* 29: 264–284; Bent Flyvbjerg, Nils Bruzelius, and Werner Rothengatter. 2003, *Megaprojects and Risk: An Anatomy of Ambition*. Cambridge, U.K.: Cambridge University Press.

2. As John Lanchester lucidly points out:

> The power of derivatives has a way of proving irresistible to those people who aren't just sure that the market is going up, but are beyond sure, are super-sure, are possessed by absolute knowledge. In that event, it is very tempting indeed to buy an option that increases your level of risk, in the certainty that this will increase your level of reward. In the above example, instead of hedging the position with an option to sell, you could magnify it with options to buy more shares at the same price, which will be worth a lot if you're right—sorry, *when* you're right. When you're right

and the market goes up by half, your £10,000 option will be worth £50,000 (that's the £50,000 by which the shares have gone up). In fact, instead of buying £100,000 of shares and a £10,000 option to buy, why not instead buy £100,000 worth of options? This is called leverage: you have leveraged your £100,000 to buy £1,000,000 worth of exposure to the market. That way when you get your price rise, you have just made £500,000, and all with borrowed money. In fact, since you're not just confident but certain, why not skip the option and instead buy some futures, which are cheaper (because riskier)—let's say half the price. These futures, at £5000 each, oblige you to buy 20 lots of the shares for £100,000 each in a year's time. Hooray! You're rich! Unless the market, instead of doubling, halves, and you are saddled with an obligation to buy £2 million worth of shares which are now worth only £1 million. You've just borrowed £100,000 and through the power of modern financial instruments used it to lose £1 million. Oops.

3. Larry Ford. 1998, Midtowns, Megastructures and World Cities. *The Geographical Review* 88: 528–547; Lilly Kong and Brenda Yeoh. 2003, *The Politics of Landscape in Singapore: Constructions of Nation.* Syracuse, N.Y.: Syracuse University Press; Karen Till. 2005, *The New Berlin: Memory, Politics, Place.* Minneapolis: University of Minnesota Press; Keller Easterling. 2005, *Enduring Innocence: Global Architecture and Its Political Masquerades.* Cambridge, Mass.: The MIT Press; Jane Jacobs. 2006, A Geography of Big Things. *Cultural Geographies* 13: 1–27.

4. David Harvey. 1989, *The Condition of Postmodernity: An Enquiry into the Origins of Cultural Change.* Oxford: Blackwell.

5. Erik Swyngedouw, Frank Moulaert, and Arantxa Rodriguez. 2002, Neoliberal Urbanization in Europe: Large Scale Urban Development Projects and the New Urban Policy. *Antipode* 34: 542–577.

6. Saskia Sassen. 2007, *The Repositioning of Cities and Urban Regions in a Global Economy: Pushing Policy and Governance Options.* Paris: OECD.

7. Ibid.

8. Allen Scott. 1998, *Regions and the World Economy: The Coming Shape of Global Production, Competition, and Political Order.* Oxford: Oxford University Press; Peter Dicken, Phillip Kelly, Kris Olds, and Henry Wai-Chung Yeung. 2001, Chains and Networks, Territories and

Scales: Towards a Relational Framework for Analysing the Global Economy. *Global Networks* 1: 89–112; Gavin MacLeod. 2001, New Regionalism Reconsidered: Globalization and the Remaking of Political Economic Space. *International Journal of Urban and Regional Research* 25: 804–829; K.C. Ho. 2002, Globalization and Southeast Asian Urban Futures. *Asian Journal of Social Science* 30: 1–7; Eric Sheppard. 2002, The Spaces and Times of Globalization: Place, Scale, Networks, and Positionality. *Economic Geography* 78: 307–330; Allen Scott and Michael J. Storper. 2003, Regions, Globalization, Development. *Regional Studies* 37: 579–593; Richard Smith. 2003, World City Topologies. *Progress in Human Geography* 27: 561–582.

9. Anirudh Paul, Prasad Shetty, and Shekhar Krishnan. 2005, The City as Extracurricular Space: Re-instituting Urban Pedagogy in South Asia. *Inter-Asia Cultural Studies* 6: 386–409.

10. Steven Graham and Simon Marvin. 2001, *Splintering Urbanism: Networked Infrastructures, Technological Mobilities, and the Urban Condition.* London; New York: Routledge.

11. Racquel Rolnik. 1999, Territorial Exclusion and Violence: The Case of São Paolo, Brazil. *Woodrow Wilson Center Occasional Papers Series on Comparative Urban Studies* 26.

12. Henri Lefebvre 1996, *Writings on Cities.* New York: Wiley.

13. Saskia Sassen 1996, Analytic Borderlands: Race, Gender and Representation in New York City. In Anthony King (ed.) *Representing the City: Ethnicity, Capital and Culture in the 21st Century Metropolis.* New York: New York University Press, 183–202.

14. Asef Bayat. 1997, Uncivil Society: The Politics of the "Informal People." *Third World Quarterly* 18: 53–72; Solomon Benjamin. 2000, Governance, Economic Settings and Poverty in Bangalore. *Environment and Urbanization* 12: 35–56; Jane Guyer, Denzer LaRay, and Agbaje Adigun. 2002, *Money Struggles and City Life: Devaluation in Ibadan and Other Urban Areas in Southern Nigeria, 1986–96.* Portsmouth, NH: Heinemann; Rem Koolhaas. 2000, Lagos. In Rem Koolhaas, Stefano Boeri, Sanford Kwinter, Nadia Tazi, and Hans-Ulrich Obrist (eds.) *Mutations.* Barcelona: ACTAR; Bordeaux: Arc en Rêve Centre d'Architecture; Karin Bakker. 2003, Archipelagos and Networks: Urbanisation and Water Privatisation in the South. *Geographical Journal* 169: 328–341; Sanjoy Chakravorty. 2003, Urban Development in the Global Periphery: The Consequences of Economic and Ideological Globalization. *Annals of Regional Science* 37: 357–367; Daniel Goldstein. 2004, *The Spectacular City: Violence and Performance in Urban Bolivia.* Durham, N.C.;

London: Duke University Press; Monica Narula and the Raqs Media Collective. 2004, Notes of Practice: Stubborn Structures and Insistent Seepage in a Networked World. In Marina Vishmidt and Melanie Gilligan (eds.) *Immaterial Labour: Work, Research and Art*. London; New York: Black Dog Publishing.

15. Akbar Abbas. 1997, *Hong Kong: Culture and the Politics of Disappearance*. Minneapolis: University of Minnesota Press; Alberto Corsin-Jiménez. 2003, On Space as a Capacity. *Journal of the Royal Anthropological Institute* 9: 137–153; Francisco Ferrándiz. 2004, The Body as Wound: Possession, *Malandros* and Everyday Violence in Venezuela. *Critique of Anthropology* 24: 107–133.

16. Marcelo Lopez de Souza. 2001, Metropolitan Deconcentration, Socio-Political Fragmentation and Extended Suburbanisation: Brazilian Urbanisation in the 1980s and 1990s. *Geoforum* 32: 437–447; Miguel Lacabana and Cecilia Cariola. 2003, Globalization and Metropolitan Expansion: Residential Strategies and Livelihoods in Caracas and Its Peripheries. *Environment and Urbanization* 15: 65–74; Sako Musterd. 2005, Social and Ethnic Segregation in Europe: Levels, Causes, and Effects. *Journal of Urban Affairs* 27: 331–348.

17. David Sattherwaithe. 2007, The Transition to a Predominantly Urban World and Its Underpinnings. *Human Settlements Discussion Paper* 4. London: International Institute of Environment and Development.

FIVE

1. Karel Arnaut. 2004, Performing Displacements and Rephrasing Attachments: Ethnographic Explorations of Mobility in Art, Ritual, Media, and Politics. Doctoral Dissertation, Department of Anthropology, Gent University, Gent, Belgium.

2. Richard Waller. 2006, Rebellious Youth in Colonial Africa. *Journal of African History* 47: 77–92.

3. Sarah Newell. 2006, Estranged Belongings: A Moral Economy of Theft in Abidjan. *Anthropological Theory* 6: 179–203.

4. Gilles Deleuze and Félix Guattari. 1987, *A Thousand Plateaus*. Minnesota, Minn.; London: University of Minnesota Press.

5. Jane Guyer. 2007, Prophecy and the Near Future: Thoughts on Macroeconomic, Evangelical and Punctuated Time. *American Ethnologist* 34: 409–421.

6. Manuel De Landa. 2006, *A New Philosophy of Society: Assemblage Theory and Social Complexity*. London; New York: Continuum.

7. Maria Kaika and Erik Swyngedouw. 2000, Fetishizing the Modern City: The Phantasmagoria of Urban Technological Networks. *International Journal of Urban and Regional Research* 24: 120–138.

8. Michael Dear and Jennifer Wolch. 1987, *Landscapes of Despair: From Deinstitutionalization to Homelessness.* Princeton, N.J.; London: Princeton University Press; Loïc Wacquant. 1997, Three Pernicious Premises in the Study of the American Ghetto. *International Journal of Urban and Regional Research* 21: 341–353; William Julius Wilson. 1987, *The Truly Disadvantaged: The Inner City, the Underclass, and Public Policy.* Chicago: University of Chicago Press.

9. Loïc Wacquant 2002, Scrutinizing the Street: Poverty, Morality, and the Pitfalls of Urban Ethnography. *American Journal of Sociology* 107: 1468–1532.

10. Alan Latham. 2003, Urbanity, Lifestyle and Making Sense of the New Urban Cultural Economy: Notes from Auckland, New Zealand. *Urban Studies* 40:1699–1724; Loretta Lees. 2002, Rematerializing Geography: The "New" Urban Geography. *Progress in Human Geography* 26: 101–112; Michel Maffesoli. 1996, *The Contemplation of the World: Figures of Community Style*, Minneapolis: University of Minnesota Press; Karen Simondsen. 2005, Bodies, Sensations, Space and Time: The Contribution from Henri Lefebvre. *Geografiska Annaler: Series B, Human Geography* 87: 1–14.

11. Alberto Corsin-Jiménez. 2003, On Space as a Capacity. *Journal of the Royal Anthropological Institute* 9: 137–153.

12. Michel de Certeau. 1984, *The Practice of Everyday Life.* Berkeley; Los Angeles: University of California Press.

13. Solomon Benjamin. 2008, Occupancy Urbanism: Radicalizing Politics and Economy Beyond Policy and Programs. *International Journal of Urban and Regional Research* 32: 719–729; Rem Koolhaas and Edgar Clejine. 2007, *Lagos, How It Works.* Heidelberg; New York: Springer Verlag.

14. Erving Goffman. 1971, *Relations in Public: Microstudies of the Public Order.* New York: Basic Books.

15. Elizabeth Wilson. 1991, *The Sphinx in the City: Urban Life, Control of Disorder and Women.* Berkeley; Los Angeles: University of California Press.

16. Ananya Roy. 2003, Paradigms of Propertied Citizenship: Transnational Techniques of Analysis. *Urban Affairs Review* 38: 463–491; Matthew Gandy. 2006, Zones of Indistinction: Biopolitical Contestations in the Urban Arena. *Cultural Geographies* 13: 497–516.

17. Elizabeth Grosz. 2004, *The Nick of Time: Politics, Evolution, and the Untimely.* Durham, N.C.; London: Duke University Press.

18. Henri Lefebvre. 1977, Reflections on the Politics of Space. In Richard Peet (ed.) *Radical Geography: Alternative Viewpoints in Contemporary Social Issues*. London: Methuen, 339–352.

19. Michael Jones. 2005, Towards "Phase Spatiality": Regions, Regional Studies, and the Limits to Thinking Space Relationally. Paper presented at the Regional Studies Association "Regional Growth Agendas" Conference, Aalborg, Denmark, May 28–31, 2005.

20. Teresa Caldeira. 2000, *City of Walls. Crime, Segregation, and Citizenship in São Paulo*. London: Routledge; Lisa Drummond. 2000, Street Scenes: Practices of Public and Private Space in Urban Vietnam. *Urban Studies* 37: 2377–2391; Andrea Dawson. 2004, Squatters, Space, and Belonging in the Underdeveloped City. *Social Text* 22: 17–34; Ananya Roy and Nezar Al Sayyad. 2006, Medieval Modernity: On Citizenship and Urbanism in a Global Era. *Space and Polity* 10: 1–20.

21. Pietro Garau, Elliot Sclar, and Gabriella Carollini. 2005, A Home in the City. London: Earthscan; Ananya Roy. 2005, Urban Informality: Toward an Epistemology of Planning. *Journal of the American Planning Association* 71: 147–158; Lyn Schler. 2003, Ambiguous Spaces: The Struggle over African Identities and Communities in Colonial Douala, 1914–45. *Journal of African History* 44: 51–72.

22. Asef Bayat. 2000, From "Dangerous Classes" to Quiet Rebels: Politics of Urban Subaltern in the Global South. *International Sociology* 15: 533–557; Julia Elychar. 2002, Empowerment Money: The World Bank, Non-Governmental Organizations, and the Value of Culture in Egypt. *Public Culture* 14: 493–513.

23. Guido Martinotti. 1999, A City for Whom? Transients and Public Life in the Second-Generation Metropolis. In Robert Beauregard and Sophie Body-Gendrot (eds.) *The Urban Moment: Cosmopolitan Essays on the Late-20th-Century City*. London: Sage, 155–184.

24. Paul Virilio. 1991, The Overexposed City. In Paul Virilio and Sylvere Lontringer (eds.) *Lost Dimension*. New York: Semiotext(e); Cambridge, Mass.: The MIT Press, 9–27.

25. Nigel Clark. 2000, Botanizing on the Asphalt? The Complex Life of Cosmopolitan Bodies. *Body and Society* 6: 12–33.

26. Vyjayanthi Rao. 2007, Proximate Distances: The Phenomenology of Density in Mumbai. *Built Environment* 33: 227–248.

27. Scott McQuire. 2006, The Politics of Public Space in the Media City. *First Monday* 11. http://www.firstmonday.org/issues/special11_2/mcquire/index.html.

28. Stephen Read. 2005, Questions of Form: Foldings, Topologies and Large Urban Bodies. Paper of the Center for Spatial Syntax, Technical University of Delft. http://www.spacesyntax.tudelft.nl/media/longpapers2/stephenread2.pdf; James Sidaway and Michael Pryke. 2000, The Strange Geographies of "Emerging Markets." *Transactions of the Institute of British Geographers* 25: 187–201.

29. Nicoli Nattrass. 1994, Economic Restructuring in South Africa: The Debate Continues. *Journal of Southern African Studies* 20: 517–531; Ben Fine and Zavareh Rustomjee. 1996, *The Political Economy of South Africa. From Minerals-Energy Complex to Industrialization.* London: Hurst; Adam Habib and Vishnu Padayachee. 2000, Economic Policy and Power Relations in South Africa's Transition to Democracy. *World Development* 28: 245–263.

30. Jonathan Crush and David McDonald. 2000, Transnationalism, African Immigration, and New Migrant Spaces in South Africa: An Introduction. *Canadian Journal of African Studies* 34: 1–19; John Oucho. 1998, Regional Integration and Labour Mobility in Eastern and Southern Africa. In Reginald Appleyard (ed.) *Emigration Dynamics in Developing Countries: Volume 1.* Aldershot: Gower, 264–300; Larry Swatuk and David R. Black (eds.). 1997, *Bridging the Rift: The New South Africa in Africa.* Boulder, Col.: Westview Press; Fred Ahwrieng-Obeng and Patrick McGowan. 1998, Partner or Hegemon? South Africa in Africa. *Journal of Contemporary African Studies* 16: 5–38; 16, 2: 165–195; Robert Davies. 1996, South Africa's Economic Relations with Africa: Current Patterns and Future Perspectives. In Adebayo Adedeji (ed.) *South Africa and Africa: Within or Apart?* Cape Town: Southern Africa Development Research Institute; London: Zed Books; Ijebu-Ode, Nigeria: African Centre for Development and Strategic Studies, 167–192.

31. Johannes Fedderke and Wai-Man Liu. 1999, Modelling the Estimation of Capital Flows and Capital Flight with Application to South African Data from 1960–95. http://www.wits.ac.za/economics/research/capflight2.pdf.

32. Peter Gastrow. 2003, *Penetrating State and Business: Organized Crime in Southern Africa.* Monograph 89, Institute for Security Studies, Pretoria, South Africa.

33. Jo Beall, Owen Crankshaw, and Sue Parnell. 2002, *Uniting a Divided City: Governance and Social Exclusion in Johannesburg.* London; Sterling, Va.: Earthscan.

34. Lindsay Bremner. 2000, Reinventing the Johannesburg Inner City. *Cities* 17: 195–293.

35. Denis Kadima and Gaston Kalombo. 1995, *The Motivation for Emigration and Problems of Integration of the Zairean Community in South Africa*. Johannesburg: University of Witwatersrand; Christian Rogerson. 1997, African Immigrant Entrepreneurs and Johannesburg's Changing Inner City. *Urban Forum* 27: 49–70; AbdouMaliq Simone. 1998, Globalization and the Identity of African Urban Practices. In Judin Hilton and Ivan Vladislavic (eds.) *Blank____ Architecture, Apartheid and After*. Rotterdam: NAi

36. Maxine Reitzes, Zico Tamela, and Paul Thulare. 1997, *Strangers Truer than Fiction: The Social and Economic Impact of Migrants on the Johannesburg City*. Johannesburg: Center for Policy Studies.

37. Owen Crankshaw and Caroline White. 1995, Racial Desegregation and Inner City Decay in Johannesburg. *International Journal of Urban and Regional Research* 19: 622–638; Jo Beall and Owen Crankshaw. 1999, Victims, Villains and Fixers: Urban Services and Johannesburg's Poor. Paper presented to the Conference on African Environments, St. Anthony's College, Oxford, July 22.

38. Based on work conducted by AbouMaliq Simone as part of conjoint Planact/Foundation for Contemporary Research project on unconventional economic networks in the inner city of Johannesburg between 1994 and 1996. Also see Christian Rogerson and J.M. Rogerson. 1996, *Manufacturing Location in the Developing Metropolis: The Case of Inner City Johannesburg*. Washington, D.C.: The World Bank; Urban Market Joint Venture. 1999, *Inner City Street Trading Management Strategy*. Johannesburg: Greater Johannesburg Metropolitan Council.

39. http://www.skyscrapercity.com/showthread.php?t=481722 &page=11.

40. Note from Neil Fraser, November 27, 2007.

41. Pheng Cheah. 2003, *Spectral Nationality: Passages of Liberation from Kant to Postcolonial Literatures of Liberation*. New York: Columbia University Press.

42. See Michel Serres. 1995, *Angels: A Modern Myth*. Paris; New York: Flammarion.

SIX

1. Gayatri Chakravorty Spivak. 2004, Harlem. *Social Text* 22: 117.

2. Ananya Roy. 2008, The 21st Century Metropolis: New Geographies of Theory. *Regional Studies*. http://rsa.informaworld.com/10.1080/00343400701809665.

3. Gayatri Chakravorty Spivak. 2004, Harlem. *Social Text* 22: 113–139.

4. Ananya Roy. 2008, Post-Liberalism: On the Ethico-Politics of Planning. *Planning Theory* 7: 92–102.

5. Kyeong-Ae Kay Choe and Aprodicio Laquian. 2008, *City Cluster Development: Toward an Urban-Led Development Strategy*. Manila: Asian Development Bank; Peter Daniels and John Bryson. 2002, Manufacturing Services and Servicing Manufacturing: Knowledge-Based Cities and Changing Forms of Production. *Urban Studies* 39: 977–991; Jinn-yuh Hsu. 2005, A Site of Transnationalism in the "Ungrounded Empire": Taipei as an Interface City in the Cross-Border Business Networks. *Geoforum* 36: 654–666; Lachang Lu and Yehuda Dennis Wei. 2007, Domesticating Globalisation: New Economic Spaces and Regional Polarisation in Guangdong Province, China. *Tijdschrift voor Economische en Sociale Geografie* 98: 225–244; Bae-Gyoon Park. 2008, Uneven Development, Inter-Scalar Tensions, and the Politics of Decentralization in South Korea. *International Journal of Urban and Regional Research* 32: 40–59; Ngai-Ling Sum. 2002, Globalization, Regionalization and Cross Border Modes of Growth in East Asia: The Reconstruction of "Time–Space Governance." In Markus Perkmann and Ngai-Ling Sum (eds.) *Globalization, Regionalization and Cross Border Regions*. London: Palgrave, 50–76; Geoff Vigar, Stephen Graham, and Patsy Healey. 2005, In Search of the City in Spatial Strategies: Past Legacies, Future Imaginings. *Urban Studies* 42: 1391–1410; Kai Wen Wong and Timothy Bunnell. 2006, "New Economy" Discourse and Spaces in Singapore: A Case Study of One-North. *Environment and Planning A* 38: 69–83; Anthony Venables. 2005, Spatial Disparities in the Developing Countries: Cities, Regions and International Trade. *Journal of Economic Geography* 5: 3–21.

6. Martha Carr and Marilyn Chen. 2002, *Globalization and the Informal Economy: How Global Trade and Investment Impact on the Working Poor*. Geneva: International Labor Office; Jennifer Robinson. 2006, *Ordinary Cities: Between Modernity and Development*. London: Routledge; Jeffrey Sellers. 2002, *Governing from Below: Urban Regions and the Global Economy*. New York: Cambridge University Press.

7. Willem van Schendel and Itty Abraham (eds.). 2005, *Illicit Flows and Criminal Things: States, Borders, and the Other Side of Globalization*. Bloomington, Ind.: Indiana University Press.

8. Gregory Mann. 2003, Immigrants and Arguments in France and West Africa. *Comparative Studies in Society and History* 45: 362–385; Catherine Quiminal. 1997, Familles immigrées entre deux espaces. In Didier Fassier, Alain Morice, and Catherine Quiminal

(eds.) *Les Lois de l'inhospitalité: Les Politiques de l'immigration à l'épreuve des sans-papiers*. Paris: La Découverte, 67–82.

9. Abdoulaye Gueye. 2006, The Colony Strikes Back: African Protest Movements in Postcolonial France. *Comparative Studies of South Asia, Africa, and the Middle East* 26: 225–242; Dominic Thomas. 2007, *Black France: Colonialism, Immigration, and Transnationalism*. Bloomington, Ind.: Indiana University Press.

10. Abdelkader Belbahri. 1987, *Immigration et situation postcoloniale*. Paris: CIEMI/L'Harmattan.

11. Rada Ivekovic. 2006, Le Retour du politique oublié par les banlieues. *Ruptures* 19: 64–88; Didier Nourisson, Yves Perrin, Marie-Françoise Baslez, and Abdelkader Belbahri. 2004, *Le Barbare, létranger: images de l'autre: Actes de colloque organisé par le CEHRI*. Université de Saint-Etienne.

12. Cyprian Avenel and Françoise de Singly. 2004, *Sociologie des quartiers sensibles*. Paris: Armand Colin; Abel El Quandili and Hafid Hamdani. 2005, *Grand (le) frères des banlieues*. Paris: Fayad; Eric Maurin. 2004, *Ghetto (Le) français: Enquête sur la separation social*. Paris: Seuil; Loïc Wacquant. 2006, Les Banlieues populaires à l'heure marginalité avancée. *Les Grands Dossiers des sciences humaines* 4: 30–34.

13. Tiffany Ruby Patterson and Robin Kelley. 2000, Unfinished Migrations: Reflections on the African Diaspora and the Making of the Modern World. *African Studies Review* 43: 11–46; Patrick Manning. 2003, Africa and the African Diaspora: New Directions of Study. *Journal of African History* 44: 487–506; Paul Zeleza. 2005, Rewriting the African Diaspora – Beyond the Black Atlantic. *African Affairs* 104: 35–68.

14. David Scott. 1999, *Refashioning Futures: Criticism after Postcoloniality*. Princeton, N.J.: Princeton University Press.

15. Paul Goodwin. 2006, Notes toward a Black Urbanism. Centre for Urban and Community Research, Goldsmiths College, University of London.

16. C.L.R. James. 1989, *The Black Jacobins: Touissant l'Ouverture and the Santo Domingo Revolution*. New York: Vintage.

17. Michael Eric Dyson. 1997, *Race Rules: Navigating the Color Line*. New York: Vintage; Paul Gilroy. 2000, *Against Race*. Cambridge, Mass.: Harvard University Press; Tommie Shelby. 2005, *We Who Are Dark: The Philosophical Foundations of Black Solidarity*. Cambridge, Mass.: Harvard University Press.

18. Tommie Shelby. 2005, *We Who Are Dark: The Philosophical Foundations of Black Solidarity*. Cambridge, Mass.: Harvard University Press.

19. Ernesto Laclau. 2005, *On Populist Reason*. London; New York: Verso.

When these demands become more heterogeneous in the living experience of a people, it is their unity around a "taken-for-granted" group that is questioned. At points, the logics constructing the "people" as a contingent entity become more autonomous from social immanence, but, for that very reason, more constitutive in their effects. This is the point at which the *name*, as a highly cathected rallying, does not *express* the unit of the ground, but becomes its *ground*.

(pp. 230–231)

20. David Theo Goldberg. 2001, *The Racial State*. New York: Wiley.
21. Mary Patillo. 2003, Negotiating Blackness, for Richer or Poorer. *Ethnography* 4: 61–93.
22. Michael Taussig. 1992, *The Nervous System*. New York: Routledge, 145.
23. John L. Jackson, Jr. 2005, A Little Black Magic. *South Atlantic Quarterly* 104: 393–402.
24. Ibid., p. 399.
25. But as a device, blackness has nothing to hide; it confidently can draw attention to itself because it has no ulterior motives, and therefore passes attention along to other domains and areas of consideration.
26. Celia Lury. 2004, *Brands: The Logos of the Global Economy*. London; New York: Routledge.
27. Robert Gooding-Williams. 2004, Politics, Racial Solidarity, Exodus! *Journal of Speculative Philosophy* 18: 126.
28. Michael Keith. 2005, *After the Cosmopolitan: Multicultural Cities and the Future of Racism*. London: Routledge.
29. Douglas Massey and Nancy Denton. 1993, *American Apartheid: Segregation and the Making of the Underclass*. Cambridge, Mass.: Harvard University Press; Thomas Sugrue. 1996, *The Origins of the Urban Crisis: Race and Inequality in Postwar Detroit*. Princeton, N.J.: Princeton University Press.
30. Matthew Gandy. 2005, Cyborg Urbanization: Complexity and Monstrosity in the Contemporary City. *International Journal of Urban and Regional Research* 29: 26–49.
31. Achille Mbembe. 2004, Necropolitics. *Public Culture* 15: 11–40.
32. Henri Lefebvre. 1991, *The Production of Urban Space*. Oxford: Blackwell.
33. Stefan Kipfer. 2007, Fanon and Space: Colonization, Urbanization, and Liberation from the Colonial to the Global City. *Environment and Planning D: Society and Space* 25: 701–726.

34. Homi Bhabha. 1994, *The Location of Culture*. New York; London: Routledge.

35. Harry Chang. 1985, Towards a Marxist Theory of Racism. *Review of Radical Political Economics* 1, 7: 44, a synthesis of two essays compiled by Paul Liem and Eric Montague.

36. Brian Massumi. 2002, *Parables for Virtue: Movement, Affect, Sensation (Post-Contemporary Interventions)*. Durham, N.C.; London: Duke University Press, p. 85.

37. Derek Hook. 2005, A Critical Psychology of the Postcolonial. *Theory and Psychology* 15: 475–505.

38. John Hartigan. 2005, Culture Against Race: Reworking the Basis for Racial Analysis. *South Atlantic Quarterly* 104: 543–560.

39. Nigel Thrift. 2004, Intensities of Feeling: Towards a Spatial Politics of Affect. *Geografiska Annaler, Series B* 86: 57–78; Nigel Thrift. 2005, But Malice Aforethought: Cities and the Natural History of Hatred. *Transactions of the Institute of British Geographers* 30: 133–150.

40. Denise Ferreira Da Silva. 2005, Bahia Pêlo Negro: Can the Subaltern (Subject of Raciality) Speak. *Ethnicities* 5: 323.

41. Ibid.

42. Robin Kelley. 1999, Black History's Global Vision, 1883–1950. *Journal of American History* 86: 1045–1077.

43. Filip De Boeck and Marie-Françoise Plissart. 2004, *Kinshasa: Tales of the Invisible City*. Antwerp: Ludion.

44. Achille Mbembe. 2004, Necropolitics. *Public Culture* 15: 11–40.

45. David Scott. 2004, *Conscripts of Modernity: The Tragedy of Colonial Enlightenment*. Durham, N.C.; London: Duke University Press.

46. Hortense Spillers. 2003, *Black, White, and in Color: Essays on American Literature and Culture*. Chicago: University of Chicago Press.

47. Achille Mbembe. 2004, Necropolitics. *Public Culture* 15: 31.

48. Achille Mbembe and Janet Roitman. 1995, Figures of the Subject in Times of Crisis. *Public Culture* 7: 323–352.

49. Lynn Schler. 2003, Ambiguous Spaces: The Struggle over African Identities and Urban Communities in Colonial Douala 1914–1945. *Journal of African History* 44: 51–72.

50. Basile Ndjio. 2005, Carrefour de la Joie: Popular Deconstruction of the African Postcolonial Public Sphere. *Africa* 75: 265–294; Basile Njdio. 2006, Intimate Strangers: Neighborhood, Autochthony, and the Politics of Belonging. In Piet Konings and Dick Foeken (eds.) *Crisis and Creativity: Exploring the Wealth of the African Neighborhood*. Leiden: Brill, 66–86.

51. Michael Watts. 2004, Antinomies of Community. *Transactions of the Institute of British Geographers* 29: 195–216.

52. Mike Davis. 2004, The Urbanization of Empire: Megacities and the Laws of Chaos. *Social Text* 22: 9–15.
53. Mahmood Mamdani. 1996, *Citizen and Subject: Contemporary Africa and the Legacy of Colonialism*. Princeton, N.J.: Princeton University Press; AbdouMaliq Simone. 2004, *For the City Yet to Come: Changing Urban Life in Four African Cities*. Durham, N.C.: Duke University Press.
54. Suhail Malik. 2005, Information and Knowledge. *Theory, Culture, and Society* 22: 29–49.

References

Abbas, Akbar. 1997, *Hong Kong: Culture and the Politics of Disappearance.* Minneapolis: University of Minnesota Press.

Ahwrieng-Obeng, Fred and Patrick McGowan. 1998, Partner or Hegemon? South Africa in Africa. *Journal of Contemporary African Studies* 16: 5–38; 16, 2: 165–195.

Allen, Adriana. 2003, Environmental Planning and Management of the Peri-Urban Interface: Perspectives on an Emerging Field. *Environment and Urbanization* 15: 135–148.

Allen, John, Doreen Massey, and Michael Pryke (eds.). 1999, *Unsettling Cities.* London: Routledge and The Open University Press.

Amin, Ash. 2002, Ethnicity and the Multicultural City: Living with Diversity. www.cwis.livjm.ac.uk/cities/Papers/ash_amin.pdf.

Amin, Ash. 2006, The Good City. *Urban Studies* 43: 10,009–10,023.

Amin, Ash and Nigel Thrift. 2002, *Cities: Imagining the Urban.* London: Polity.

Andersson, Jens. 2001, Reintegrating the Rural–Urban Connection: Migration Practices and Sociocultural Dispositions of Buhera Workers in Harare. *Africa* 71: 81–111.

Appadurai, Arjun. 2004, The Capacity to Aspire: Culture and the Terms of Recognition. In Viyayendra Rao and Michael Walton (eds.) *Culture and Public Action.* Stanford, Ca.: Stanford University Press, 59–84.

Arnaut, Karel. 2004, Performing Displacements and Rephrasing Attachments: Ethnographic Explorations of Mobility in Art, Ritual, Media, and Politics. Doctoral Dissertation, Department of Anthropology, Gent University, Gent, Belgium.

Avenel, Cyprian and Françoise de Singly. 2004, *Sociologie des quartiers sensibles.* Paris: Armand Colin.

Azam, Jean-Paul. 2002, Looting and Conflict between Ethno-Regional Groups: Lessons for State Formation in Africa. *Journal of Conflict Resolution* 46: 131–153.

Azam, Jean-Paul. 2002, Statecraft in the Shadow of Civil Conflict. *International Forum on African Perspectives*. African Development Bank and OECD Development Centre, Paris, February 4–5, 2002.

Bakker, Karen. 2003, Archipelagos and Networks: Urbanisation and Water Privatisation in the South. *Geographical Journal* 169: 328–341.

Bakker, Karen, Michelle Koy, Nur Fudah Shotiani, and Ernst-Jan Martijn. 2006, Disconnected: Poverty, Water Supply and Development in Jakarta, Indonesia. New York: Occasional Paper, Human Development Report 2006, United Nations Development Program.

Batty, J. Michael. 2005, *Cities and Complexity: Understanding Cities with Cellular Automata, Agent-Based Models, and Fractals*. Cambridge, Mass.: The MIT Press.

Bayat, Asef. 1997, Uncivil Society: The Politics of the "Informal People." *Third World Quarterly* 18: 53–72.

Bayat, Asef. 2000, From "Dangerous Classes" to Quiet Rebels: Politics of Urban Subaltern in the Global South. *International Sociology* 15: 533–557.

Beall, Jo and Owen Crankshaw. 1999, Victims, Villains and Fixers: Urban Services and Johannesburg's Poor. Paper presented to the Conference on African Environments, St. Anthony's College, Oxford, July 22.

Beall, Jo, Owen Crankshaw, and Sue Parnell. 2002, *Uniting a Divided City: Governance and Social Exclusion in Johannesburg*. London; Sterling, Va.: Earthscan.

Belbahri, Abdelkader. 1987, *Immigration et situation postcoloniale*. Paris: CIEMI/L'Harmattan.

Benjamin, Solomon. 2000, Governance, Economic Settings and Poverty in Bangalore. *Environment and Urbanization* 12: 35–56.

Benjamin, Solomon. 2008, Occupancy Urbanism: Radicalizing Politics and Economy Beyond Policy and Programs. *International Journal of Urban and Regional Research* 32: 719–729.

Berlant, Lauren. 2007, Nearly Utopian, Nearly Normal: Post-Fordist Affect in *La Promesse* and *Rosetta*. *Public Culture* 19: 273–301.

Bertrand, Romain. 2004, Behave Like Enraged Lions: Civic Militias, the Army, and the Criminalization of Politics in Indonesia. *Global Crime* 6: 325–344.

Bertrand, Romain. 2005, La Politique des "Réunions de l'ombre." Puissances officielles et pouvoirs officieux dans l'Indonésie post-Suharto. Paper presented at the 8ème Congrès de l'Association Française de Science Politiques, Lyon.

Bhabha, Homi. 1994, *The Location of Culture*. London; New York: Routledge.

Biaya, Tshikala Kayembe. 2001, Parallel Society in the Democratic Republic of Congo. In Simon Bekker, Martine Dodds, and Meshack Khosa (eds.) *Shifting African Identities*. Pretoria: Human Sciences Research Council, 43–60.

Boggs, Jeffrey and Normal Rantisi. 2003, The "Relational Turn" in Economic Geography. *Journal of Economic Geography* 3: 109–116.

Boyer, Christine. 1995, *The City of Collective Memory: Its Historical Imagery and Architectural Entertainments*. Cambridge, Mass.: The MIT Press.

Bremner, Lindsay. 2000, Reinventing the Johannesburg Inner City. *Cities* 17: 195–293.

Brenner, Neil. 2004, *New State Spaces: Urban Governance and the Rescaling of Statehood*. Oxford; New York: Oxford University Press.

Browder, John and Brian Godfrey. 1997, *Rainforest Cities: Urbanization, Development and Globalization of the Brazilian Amazon*. New York: Columbia University Press.

Brown, Donald and Ian Wilson. 2007, Ethnicized Violence in Indonesia: The Betawi Brotherhood Forum in Jakarta. Working Paper 145, Asia Research Centre, Murdoch University.

Bunnell, Timothy and Neal Coe. 2001, Spaces and Scales of Innovation. *Progress in Human Geography* 25: 569–589.

Bunnell, Timothy, Hamzah Muzaini, and James Sidaway. 2006, Global City Frontiers: Singapore's Hinterland and the Contested Socio-Political Geographies of Bintan, Indonesia. *International Journal of Urban and Regional Research* 30: 3–22.

Caldeira, Teresa. 2000, *City of Walls. Crime, Segregation, and Citizenship in São Paulo*. London: Routledge.

Carr, Martha and Marilyn Chen. 2002, *Globalization and the Informal Economy: How Global Trade and Investment Impact on the Working Poor*. Geneva: International Labor Office.

Chabal, Patrick and Jean-Pascal Daloz. 2006, *Culture Troubles: Politics and the Interpretation of Meaning*. Chicago: University of Chicago Press.

Chakrabarty, Dipesh. 2000, *Provincializing Europe. Postcolonial Thought and Historical Difference*. Princeton; Oxford: Princeton University Press.

Chakravorty, Sanjoy. 2003, Urban Development in the Global Periphery: The Consequences of Economic and Ideological Globalization. *Annals of Regional Science* 37: 357–367.

Chang, Harry. 1985, Towards a Marxist Theory of Racism. *Review of Radical Political Economics* 1, 7:34–45, a synthesis of two essays compiled by Paul Liem and Eric Montague.

359 **References**

Cheah, Pheng. 2003, *Spectral Nationality: Passages of Liberation from Kant to Postcolonial Literatures of Liberation*. New York: Columbia University Press.

Choe, Kyeong-Ae Kay and Aprodicio Laquian. 2008, *City Cluster Development: Toward an Urban-Led Development Strategy*. Manila: Asian Development Bank.

Çinar, Alev and Thomas Bender. 2007, Introduction: The City: Experience, Imagination and Place. In Alev Çinar and Thomas Bender (eds.) *Urban Imaginaries: Locating the Modern City*. Minneapolis: University of Minnesota Press, xi–xxvi.

Clark, Nigel. 2000, Botanizing on the Asphalt? The Complex Life of Cosmopolitan Bodies. *Body and Society* 6: 12–33.

Collier, Paul and Jan Willem Gunning. 1998, Explaining African Performance. WPS/97–2.2, Working Paper Series of the Centre for the Study of African Economies, University of Oxford.

Corsin-Jiménez, Alberto. 2003, On Space as a Capacity. *Journal of the Royal Anthropological Institute* 9: 137–153.

Cox, Kenneth. 2001, Territoriality, Politics and the "Urban." *Political Geography* 20: 745–762.

Crang, Mike and Steve Graham. 2007, Sentient Cities: Ambient Intelligence and the Politics of Urban Space. *Information, Communication and Society* 10: 789–817.

Crankshaw, Owen and Caroline White. 1995, Racial Desegregation and Inner City Decay in Johannesburg. *International Journal of Urban and Regional Research* 19: 622–638.

Crush, Jonathan and David McDonald. 2000, Transnationalism, African Immigration, and New Migrant Spaces in South Africa: An Introduction. *Canadian Journal of African Studies* 34: 1–19.

Daniels, Peter and John Bryson. 2002, Manufacturing Services and Servicing Manufacturing: Knowledge-Based Cities and Changing Forms of Production. *Urban Studies* 39: 977–991.

Da Silva, Denise Ferreira. 2005, Bahia Pêlo Negro: Can the Subaltern (Subject of Raciality) Speak? *Ethnicities* 5: 321–342.

Davies, Robert. 1996, South Africa's Economic Relations with Africa: Current Patterns and Future Perspectives. In Adebayo Adedeji (ed.) *South Africa and Africa: Within or Apart?* Cape Town: Southern Africa Development Research Institute; London: Zed Books; Ijebu-Ode, Nigeria: African Centre for Development and Strategic Studies, 167–192.

Davis, Mike. 2004, The Urbanization of Empire: Megacities and the Laws of Chaos. *Social Text* 22: 9–15.

Davis, Mike. 2006, *Planet of the Slums*. London: Verso.

Dawson, Andrea. 2004, Squatters, Space, and Belonging in the Underdeveloped City. *Social Text* 22: 17–34.

de Certeau, Michel. 1984, *The Practice of Everyday Life*. Berkeley; Los Angeles: University of California Press.

Dear, Michael and Jennifer Wolch. 1987, *Landscapes of Despair: From Deinstitutionalization to Homelessness*. Princeton, N.J.; London: Princeton University Press.

De Boeck, Filip. 2003, Kinshasa: Tales of the "Invisible City" and the Second World. In Okwui Enwezor, Carlos Basualdo, and Uta Meta Bauer (eds.) *Under Siege. Four African Cities: Freetown, Johannesburg, Kinshasa, Lagos. Documenta11_Platform* 4. Kassel: Hatje Cantz Publishers, 243–285.

De Boeck, Filip. 2005, The Apocalyptic Interlude: Revealing Death in Kinshasa. *African Studies Review* 48: 11–32.

De Boeck, Filip and Marie-Françoise Plissart. 2004, *Kinshasa: Tales of the Invisible City*. Antwerp: Ludion.

De Landa, Manuel. 2006, *A New Philosophy of Society: Assemblage Theory and Social Complexity*. London; New York: Continuum.

de Souza, Marcelo Lopez. 2001, Metropolitan Deconcentration, Socio-Political Fragmentation and Extended Suburbanisation: Brazilian Urbanisation in the 1980s and 1990s. *Geoforum* 32: 437–447.

Deleuze, Gilles and Félix Guattari. 1987, *A Thousand Plateaus*. Minnesota, Minn.; London: University of Minnesota Press.

Dicken, Peter, Phillip Kelly, Kris Olds, and Henry Wai-Chung Yeung. 2001, Chains and Networks, Territories and Scales: Towards a Relational Framework for Analysing the Global Economy. *Global Networks* 1: 89–112.

Drummond, Lisa. 2000, Street Scenes: Practices of Public and Private Space in Urban Vietnam. *Urban Studies* 37: 2377–2391.

Dubois, W.E.B. 1995 (edition) *The Philadelphia Negro: A Social Study*. Philadelphia: University of Pennsylvania Press.

Dyson, Michael Eric. 1997, *Race Rules: Navigating the Color Line*. New York: Vintage.

Eade, John and Christopher Mele. 2002, Introduction: Understanding the City. In John Eade and Christopher Mele (eds.) *Understanding the City: Contemporary and Future Perspectives*. Oxford: Blackwell, 1–27.

Easterling, Keller. 2005, *Enduring Innocence: Global Architecture and Its Political Masquerades*. Cambridge, Mass.: The MIT Press.

El Quandili, Abel and Hafid Hamdani. 2005, *Grand (le) frères des banlieues*. Paris: Fayad.

Elychar, Julia. 2002, Empowerment Money: The World Bank, Non-Governmental Organizations, and the Value of Culture in Egypt. *Public Culture* 14: 493–513.

Emizet, Kisangani. 1998, Confronting the Apex of the State: The Growth of the Unofficial Economy in Congo. *African Studies Review* 41, 1: 99–137.

Englund, Harri. 2002, The Village in the City, the City in the Village: Migrants in Lilongwe. *Journal of Southern African Studies* 28: 137–159.

Escobar, Arturo. 2001, Culture Sits in Places: Reflections on Globalism and Subaltern Strategies of Localization. *Political Geography* 20: 139–174.

Fanthorpe, Richard. 2001, Neither Citizen or Subject: "Lumpen" Agency and the Legacy of Native Administration in Sierra Leone. *African Affairs* 100: 363–388.

Fedderke, Johannes and Wai-Man Liu. 1999, Modelling the Estimation of Capital Flows and Capital Flight with Application to South African Data from 1960–95. http://www.wits.ac.za/economics/research/capflight2.pdf.

Ferrándiz, Francisco. 2004, The Body as Wound: Possession, *Malandros* and Everyday Violence in Venezuela. *Critique of Anthropology* 24: 107–133.

Fine, Ben and Zavareh Rustomjee. 1996, *The Political Economy of South Africa. From Minerals-Energy Complex to Industrialization*. London: Hurst.

Flyvbjerg, Bent, Nils Bruzelius, and Werner Rothengatter. 2003, *Megaprojects and Risk: An Anatomy of Ambition*. Cambridge, U.K.: Cambridge University Press.

Ford, Larry. 1998, Midtowns, Megastructures and World Cities. *The Geographical Review* 88: 528–547.

Fox, Sean. 2007, Blue Cities: Encompassing Governance, Urban Integration, and Economic Reform. World Bank Urban Research Symposium 2007. Washington, D.C.: The World Bank.

Gandy, Matthew. 2005, Cyborg Urbanization: Complexity and Monstrosity in the Contemporary City. *International Journal of Urban and Regional Research* 29: 26–49.

Gandy, Matthew. 2006, Zones of Indistinction: Biopolitical Contestations in the Urban Arena. *Cultural Geographies* 13: 497–516.

Garau, Pietro, Elliot Sclar, and Gabriella Carollini. 2005, A Home in the City. London: Earthscan,

Gastrow, Peter. 2003, *Penetrating State and Business: Organized Crime in Southern Africa*. Monograph 89, Institute for Security Studies, Pretoria, South Africa.

Geschiere, Peter. 1997, *The Modernity of Witchcraft: Politics and the Occult in Postcolonial Africa*. Charlottesville, Va.; London: University Press of Virginia.

Ghannam, Farha. 2002, *Remaking the Modern: Space, Relocation and the Politics of Identity in a Global Cairo*. Berkeley, Ca.: University of California Press.

Gilroy, Paul. 2000, *Against Race*. Cambridge, Mass.: Harvard University Press.

Goffman, Erving. 1971, *Relations in Public: Microstudies of the Public Order*. New York: Basic Books.

Goldberg, David Theo. 2001, *The Racial State*. New York: Wiley.

Goldstein, Daniel. 2004, *The Spectacular City: Violence and Performance in Urban Bolivia*. Durham, N.C.; London: Duke University Press.

Gooding-Williams, Robert. 2004, Politics, Racial Solidarity, Exodus! *Journal of Speculative Philosophy* 18: 118–127.

Goodwin, Paul. 2006, Notes toward a Black Urbanism. Centre for Urban and Community Research, Goldsmiths College, University of London.

Graham, Steven and Simon Marvin. 2001, *Splintering Urbanism: Networked Infrastructures, Technological Mobilities, and the Urban Condition*. London; New York: Routledge.

Grant, Richard and Jan Nijman. 2002, Globalization and the Corporate Geography of Cities in the Less-Developed World. *Annals of the Association of American Geographers* 92: 320–340.

Gregory, Derek. 2004, *The Colonial Present: Afghanistan, Palestine, Iraq*. Oxford: Blackwell.

Grimm, Michael, Charlotte Guénard, and Sandrine Mesplé–Somps. 2002, What Has Happened to the Urban Population in Côte d'Ivoire Since the 1980s? An Analysis of Monetary Poverty and Deprivation over 15 Years of Household Data. *World Development* 30: 1073–1095.

Grosz, Elizabeth. 2004, *The Nick of Time: Politics, Evolution, and the Untimely*. Durham, N.C.; London: Duke University Press.

Groupe Frontière, Christiane Arbaret-Schulz, Antoine Beyer, Jean-Luc Permay, Bernard Reitel, Catherine Selimanovski, Christophe Sohn, and Patricia Zander. 2005, La Frontière, un objet spatial en mutation. *EspacesTemps.net*. Textual. 30.04.2005. http://espaces temps.net/document1317.html.

Gueye, Abdoulaye. 2006, The Colony Strikes Back: African Protest Movements in Postcolonial France. *Comparative Studies of South Asia, Africa, and the Middle East* 26: 225–242.

Guyer, Jane. 2007, Prophecy and the Near Future: Thoughts on

Macroeconomic, Evangelical and Punctuated Time. *American Ethnologist* 34: 409–421.

Guyer, Jane, Denzer LaRay, and Agbaje Adigun. 2002, *Money Struggles and City Life: Devaluation in Ibadan and Other Urban Areas in Southern Nigeria, 1986–96*. Portsmouth, N.H.: Heinemann.

Habib, Adam and Vishnu Padayachee. 2000, Economic Policy and Power Relations in South Africa's Transition to Democracy. *World Development* 28: 245–263.

Habraken, N. John. 1998, *The Structure of the Ordinary: Form and Control in the Built Environment*. Cambridge, Mass.: The MIT Press.

Hartigan, John. 2005, Culture Against Race: Reworking the Basis for Racial Analysis. *South Atlantic Quarterly* 104: 543–560.

Harts-Broekhuis, Annelet. 1997, How to Sustain a Living: Urban Households and Poverty in a Sahelian Town of Mopti, Africa. *Africa* 67: 106–131.

Harvey, David. 1989, *The Condition of Postmodernity: An Enquiry into the Origins of Cultural Change*. Oxford: Blackwell.

Harvey, David. 2006, *Space of Global Capitalism: Towards a Theory of Uneven Geographical Development*. London: Verso.

Hayden, Dolores. 1995, *The Power of Place: Urban Landscapes as Public History*. Cambridge, Mass.: The MIT Press.

Healy, Patsy. 2007, *Urban Complexity and Spatial Strategies: Towards a Relational Planning for Our Times*. London: Routledge.

Herbst, Jeffrey. 2000, *States and Power in Africa: Comparative Lessons in Authority and Control*. Princeton, N.J.; London: Princeton University Press.

Hibou, Beatrice. 1999, The Social Capital of the State as an Agent of Deception. In Jean-François Bayart, Beatrice Hibou, and Stephen Ellis (eds.) *The Criminalization of the State in Africa*. London: James Currey; Bloomington, Ind.: Indiana University Press.

Hill, Richard Child and Kuniko Fujita. 2003, The Nested City: Introduction. *Urban Studies* 40: 207–217.

Hillier, Bill and Julienne Hanson. 1984, *The Social Logic of Space*. Cambridge, U.K.: Cambridge University Press.

Ho, K.C. 2002, Globalization and Southeast Asian Urban Futures. *Asian Journal of Social Science* 30: 1–7.

Holston, James and Arjun Appadurai. 1996, Cities and Citizenship. *Public Culture* 8: 187–204.

Hook, Derek. 2005, A Critical Psychology of the Postcolonial. *Theory and Psychology* 15: 475–505.

Hsu Jinn-yuh. 2005, A Site of Transnationalism in the "Ungrounded Empire": Taipei as an Interface City in the Cross-Border Business Networks. *Geoforum* 36: 654–666.

Hubbard, Phil. 1996, Urban Design and City Regeneration: Social Representations of Entrepreneurial Landscapes. *Urban Studies* 33: 1441–1461.

Hudson, Ray. 2004, Conceptualizing Economies and Their Geographies: Spaces, Flows and Circuits. *Progress in Human Geography* 28: 447–471.

Human Rights Watch. 2002, *Hidden in Plain Sight: Refugees Living in Nairobi and Kampala*. New York: Human Rights Watch.

Ingersoll, Richard. 2006, *Sprawltown: Looking for the City on Its Edges*. New York: Princeton Architectural Press.

International Labor Organization. 1998, *Jobs for Africa: A Policy Framework for an Employment-Intensive Growth Strategy*. Geneva: International Labor Organization.

Ivekovic, Rada. 2006, Le Retour du politique oublié par les banlieues. *Ruptures* 19: 64–88.

Iyenda, Guillaume. 2005, Street Enterprises, Urban Livelihoods and Poverty in Kinshasa. *Environment and Urbanization* 17: 55–67.

Jackson, John L., Jr. 2005, A Little Black Magic. *South Atlantic Quarterly* 104: 393–402.

Jacobs, Jane. 1996, *Edge of Empire: Postcolonialism and the City*. London: Routledge.

Jacobs, Jane. 2006, A Geography of Big Things. *Cultural Geographies* 13: 1–27.

Jacquier, Claude. 2005, Can Distressed Areas Become Poles of Urban Growth? OECD International Conference "Sustainable Cities: Linking Competitiveness with Social Cohesion," October 13–14, 2005, Montreal.

James, C.L.R. 1989, *The Black Jacobins: Touissant l'Ouverture and the Santo Domingo Revolution*. New York: Vintage.

Jessop, Bob. 2000, Globalisation, Entrepreneurial Cities and the Social Economy. In Pierre Hamel, Henri Lustiger-Thaler, and Margit Mayer (eds.) *Urban Movements in a Globalising World*. London: Routledge.

Jiménez, Christina. 2008, From the Lettered City to the Sellers' City: Vendor Politics and Public Space in Urban Mexico, 1880–1926. In Gyan Prakash and Kevin M. Kruse (eds.) *The Spaces of the Modern City: Imaginaries, Politics and Everyday Life*. Princeton, N.J.: Princeton University Press, 214–246.

Jones, Michael. 2005, Towards "Phase Spatiality": Regions, Regional Studies, and the Limits to Thinking Space Relationally. Paper presented at the Regional Studies Association "Regional Growth Agendas" Conference, Aalborg, Denmark, May 28–31, 2005.

Jun, Jiang and Kuang Xiaoming. 2007, The Taxonomy of Contemporary Chinese Cities (We Make Cities). *Architectural Digest* 78: 16–21.

Kadima, Denis and Gaston Kalombo. 1995, *The Motivation for Emigration and Problems of Integration of the Zairean Community in South Africa*. Johannesburg: University of Witwatersrand.

Kaika, Maria and Erik Swyngedouw. 2000, Fetishizing the Modern City: The Phantasmagoria of Urban Technological Networks. *International Journal of Urban and Regional Research* 24: 120–138.

Kanji, Nazneen. 1995, Gender, Poverty, and Economic Adjustment in Harare, Zimbabwe. *Environment and Urbanization* 7: 37–55.

Keith, Michael. 2005, *After the Cosmopolitan: Multicultural Cities and the Future of Racism*. London: Routledge.

Kelley, Robin. 1999, Black History's Global Vision, 1883–1950. *Journal of American History* 86: 1045–1077.

King, Anthony. 2003, Actually Existing Postcolonialisms: Colonial Urbanism and Architecture after the Postcolonial Turn. In Ryan Bishop, John Phillips, and Wei-Wei Yeo (eds.) *Postcolonial Urbanism: Southeast Asian Cities and Global Processes*. New York; London: Routledge, 167–186.

King, Kenneth. 1996, *Jua Kali Kenya: Change and Development in an Informal Economy 1970–95*. Nairobi: East African Educational Publishers.

Kipfer, Stefan. 2007, Fanon and Space: Colonization, Urbanization, and Liberation from the Colonial to the Global City. *Environment and Planning D: Society and Space* 25: 701–726.

Klima, Alan. 2002, *The Funeral Casino: Mediation, Massacre, and Exchange with the Dead in Thailand*. Princeton, N.J.; London: Princeton University Press.

Kong, Lilly and Brenda Yeoh. 2003, *The Politics of Landscape in Singapore: Constructions of Nation*. Syracuse, N.Y.: Syracuse University Press.

Koolhaas, Rem. 2000, Lagos. In Rem Koolhaas, Stefano Boeri, Sanford Kwinter, Nadia Tazi, and Hans-Ulrich Obrist (eds.) *Mutations*. Barcelona: ACTAR; Bordeaux: Arc en Rêve Centre d'Architecture.

Koolhaas, Rem and Edgar Clejine. 2007, *Lagos, How It Works*. Heidelberg; New York: Springer Verlag.

Kusno, Abidin. 2000, *Behind the Postcolonial: Architecture, Urban Space and Political Cultures*. London; New York: Routledge.

Lacabana, Miguel and Cecilia Cariola. 2003, Globalization and Metropolitan Expansion: Residential Strategies and Livelihoods in Caracas and Its Peripheries. *Environment and Urbanization* 15: 65–74.

Laclau, Ernesto. 2005, *On Populist Reason*. London; New York: Verso.

Lanchester, John. 2008, Cityphobia. *London Review of Books*, October 23, 2008.

Latham, Alan. 2003, Urbanity, Lifestyle and Making Sense of the New Urban Cultural Economy: Notes from Auckland, New Zealand. *Urban Studies* 40: 1699–1724.

Law, Lisa. 2002, Defying Disappearance: Cosmopolitan Public Spaces in Hong Kong. *Urban Studies* 39: 1625–1645.

Lees, Loretta. 2002, Rematerializing Geography: The "New" Urban Geography. *Progress in Human Geography* 26: 101–112.

Lefebvre, Henri. 1974/1991, *The Production of Space*. Oxford: Blackwell.

Lefebvre, Henri. 1977, Reflections on the Politics of Space. In Richard Peet (ed.) *Radical Geography: Alternative Viewpoints in Contemporary Social Issues*. London: Methuen, 339–352.

Lefebvre, Henri. 1996, *Writings on Cities*. New York: Wiley.

Le Gales, Patrick. 2005, Governing Globalizing Cities, Reshaping Urban Policies. OECD International Conference "What Policies for Globalizing Cities: Rethinking the Urban Policy Agenda," March 29–30, 2005, Madrid.

Lomnitz, Claudio. 2003, Times of Crisis: Historicity, Sacrifice and the Spectacle of Debacle in Mexico City. *Public Culture* 15: 127–148.

Lu, Lachang and Yehuda Dennis Wei. 2007, Domesticating Globalisation: New Economic Spaces and Regional Polarisation in Guangdong Province, China. *Tijdschrift voor Economische en Sociale Geografie* 98: 225–244.

Lugalla, Joe. 1995, *Crisis, Urbanization and Urban Poverty in Tanzania: A Study of Urban Poverty and Survival Politics*. Lanham, Md.; London: University Presses of America.

Lury, Celia. 2004, *Brands: The Logos of the Global Economy*. London; New York: Routledge.

McGee, Terence. 1999, Urbanization in an Era of Volatile Globalization. In John Brotchie, Peter Newton, Peter Hall, and John Dickey (eds.) *East–West Perspectives on 21st Century Urban Development: Sustainable Eastern and Western Cities in the New Millennium*. Aldershot, U.K.: Brookfield, Vt.: Ashgate, 37–52.

MacLeod, Gavin. 2001, New Regionalism Reconsidered: Globalization and the Remaking of Political Economic Space. *International Journal of Urban and Regional Research* 25: 804–829.

McQuire, Scott. 2006, The Politics of Public Space in the Media City. *First Monday* 11. http://www.firstmonday.org/issues/special11_2/mcquire/index.html.

Madsen, Peter and Richard Plunz. 2002, *The Urban Lifeworld: Formation, Perception, Representation*. London: Routledge.

Maffesoli, Michel. 1996, *The Contemplation of the World: Figures of Community Style*, Minneapolis, Minn.: University of Minnesota Press.

Mahmood, Saba. 2005, *Politics of Piety: The Islamic Revival and the Feminist Subject*. Princeton, N.J.; London: Princeton University Press.

Malik, Suhail. 2005, Information and Knowledge. *Theory, Culture, and Society* 22: 22–49.

Mamdani, Mahmood. 1996, *Citizen and Subject: Contemporary Africa and the Legacy of Colonialism*. Princeton, N.J.: Princeton University Press.

Mann, Gregory. 2003, Immigrants and Arguments in France and West Africa. *Comparative Studies in Society and History* 45: 362–385.

Manning, Patrick. 2003, Africa and the African Diaspora: New Directions of Study. *Journal of African History* 44: 487–506.

Martinotti, Guido. 1999, A City for Whom? Transients and Public Life in the Second-Generation Metropolis. In Robert Beauregard and Sophie Body-Gendrot (eds.) *The Urban Moment: Cosmopolitan Essays on the Late-20th-Century City*. London: Sage, 155–184.

Massey, Douglas and Nancy Denton. 1993, *American Apartheid: Segregation and the Making of the Underclass*. Cambridge, Mass.: Harvard University Press.

Massumi, Brian. 2002, *Parables for Virtue: Movement, Affect, Sensation (Post-Contemporary Interventions)*. Durham, N.C.; London: Duke University Press.

Maurin, Eric. 2004, *Ghetto (Le) français: Enquête sur la separation social*. Paris: Seuil.

Mbembe, Achille. 2004, Necropolitics. *Public Culture* 15: 11–40.

Mbembe, Achille and Janet Roitman. 1995, Figures of the Subject in Times of Crisis. *Public Culture* 7: 323–352.

Mercy Corps. 2008, Summary of Land Tenure Research Findings in Jakarta. *Urban Bulletin* #2.

Mezzadra, Sandro. 2007, Living in Transition, Toward a Heterolingual Theory of the Multitude. http://roundtable.kein.org/node/653.

Monstad, Jochem, Matthias Naumann, with Verena Meister and Timothy Moss. 2005, *New Geographies of Infrastructure Systems: Spatial Science Perspectives and the Socio-Technical Change of Energy, Water Supply Systems in Germany*. Berlin: Networks Research Association.

Musterd, Sako. 2005, Social and Ethnic Segregation in Europe: Levels, Causes, and Effects. *Journal of Urban Affairs* 27: 331–348.

Narula, Monica and the Raqs Media Collective. 2004, Notes of Practice: Stubborn Structures and Insistent Seepage in a Networked World. In Marina Vishmidt and Melanie Gilligan (eds.) *Immaterial Labour: Work, Research and Art*. London; New York: Black Dog Publishing.

Nattrass, Nicoli. 1994, Economic Restructuring in South Africa: The Debate Continues. *Journal of Southern African Studies* 20: 517–531.

Ndjio, Basile. 2005, Carrefour de la Joie: Popular Deconstruction of the African Postcolonial Public Sphere. *Africa* 75: 265–294.

Ndjio, Basile. 2006, Intimate Strangers: Neighborhood, Autochthony, and the Politics of Belonging. In Piet Konings and Dick Foeken (eds.) *Crisis and Creativity: Exploring the Wealth of the African Neighborhood.* Leiden: Brill, 66–86.

Newell, Sarah. 2006, Estranged Belongings: A Moral Economy of Theft in Abidjan. *Anthropological Theory* 6: 179–203.

Nourisson, Didier, Yves Perrin, Marie-Françoise Baslez, and Abdelkader Belbahri. 2004, *Le Barbare, l'étranger: images de l'autre: Actes de colloque organisé par le CEHRI.* Université de Saint-Etienne.

Offner, Jean-Marc. 2000, "Territorial Deregulation": Local Authorities at Risk from Technical Networks. *International Journal of Urban and Regional Research* 24, 1: 165–182.

Olds, Kris. 1995, Globalization and the Production of New Urban Spaces: Pacific Rim Megaprojects in the Late 20th Century. *Environment and Planning A* 27: 1713–1743.

Ong, Aihwa. 2005, Splintering Cosmopolitanism. In Thomas Blom Hansen and Finn Stepputat (eds.) *Sovereign Bodies.* Princeton, N.J.; London: Princeton University Press, 257–275.

Osborne, Thomas and Nikolas Rose. 1999, Governing Cities: Notes on the Spatialisation of Virtue. *Environment and Planning D: Society and Space* 17: 737–760.

Oucho, John. 1998, Regional Integration and Labour Mobility in Eastern and Southern Africa. In Reginald Appleyard (ed.) *Emigration Dynamics in Developing Countries: Volume 1.* Aldershot: Gower, 264–300.

Paasi, Anssi. 2002, Bounded Spaces in the Mobile World: Deconstructing Regional Identity. *Tijdschrift voor Economische en Sociale Geografie* 93: 137–148.

Park, Bae-Gyoon. 2008, Uneven Development, Inter-Scalar Tensions, and the Politics of Decentralization in South Korea. *International Journal of Urban and Regional Research* 32: 40–59.

Patillo, Mary. 2003, Negotiating Blackness, for Richer or Poorer. *Ethnography* 4: 61–93.

Patterson, Tiffany Ruby and Robin Kelley. 2000, Unfinished Migrations: Reflections on the African Diaspora and the Making of the Modern World. *African Studies Review* 43: 11–46.

Paul, Anirudh, Prasad Shetty, and Shekhar Krishnan. 2005, The City as Extracurricular Space: Re-instituting Urban Pedagogy in South Asia. *Inter-Asia Cultural Studies* 6: 386–409.

Peattie, Lisa. 1972, *A View from the Barrio.* Ann Arbor, Mich.: University of Michigan Press.

Pinder, David. 2006, *Visions of the City: Utopianism, Power and Politics in Twentieth Century Urbanism*. London; New York: Routledge.

Pizzaro, Rafael, Liang Wei, and Tridib Bannerjee. 2003, Agencies of Globalization and Third World Urban Form: A Review. *Journal of Planning Literature* 18: 111–130.

Pryke, Michael and John Allen. 2000, Monetized Time–Space: Derivatives: Money's New "Imaginary." *Economy and Society* 29: 264–284.

Quiminal, Catherine. 1997, Familles immigrées entre deux espaces. In Didier Fassier, Alain Morice, and Catherine Quiminal (eds.) *Les Lois de l'inhospitalité: Les Politiques de l'immigration à l'épreuve des sans-papiers*. Paris: La Découverte, 67–82.

Rahem, Karim. 2005, "Maladie, anomie et monothéisme à Khartoum: Le Cas de Mayo Farm. Dossier Khartoum: Lettre de l'oucc no. 6–7. Centre d'Etudes et de Documentation Economiques, Juridiques et Sociales.

Rao, Vyjayanthi. 2007, Proximate Distances: The Phenomenology of Density in Mumbai. *Built Environment* 33: 227–248.

Read, Stephen. 2005, Questions of Form: Foldings, Topologies and Large Urban Bodies. Paper of the Center for Spatial Syntax, Technical University of Delft. http://www.spacesyntax.tudelft.nl/media/longpapers2/stephenread2.pdf.

Reitzes, Maxine, Zico Tamela, and Paul Thulare. 1997, *Strangers Truer than Fiction: The Social and Economic Impact of Migrants on the Johannesburg City*. Johannesburg: Center for Policy Studies.

Robertson, Claire. 1997, *Trouble Showed the Way: Women, Men and Trade in the Nairobi Area 1890–1990*. Bloomington, Ind.; Indianapolis: Indiana University Press.

Robinson, Jennifer. 2002, Global and World Cities: A View from off the Map. *International Journal of Urban and Regional Research* 26: 531–554.

Robinson, Jennifer. 2006, *Ordinary Cities: Between Modernity and Development*. London: Routledge.

Robinson, Richard and Vedi Hadiz. 2004, *Reorganizing Power in Indonesia: The Politics of Oligarchy in an Age of Markets*. London: Routledge.

Rogers, Richard. 1990, *Return Migration, Migrant's Savings and Sending Countries: Economic Development Lessons from Europe*. Washington, D.C.: Commission for the Study of International Migration and Cooperative Economic Development. No. 30, May.

Rogerson, Christian. 1997, African Immigrant Entrepreneurs and Johannesburg's Changing Inner City. *Urban Forum* 27: 49–70.

Rogerson, Christian and J.M. Rogerson. 1996, *Manufacturing Location in the Developing Metropolis: The Case of Inner City Johannesburg*. Washington, D.C.: The World Bank.

Roitman, Janet. 1998, The Garrison-Entrepôt. *Cahiers d'études africaines* 150–152: 297–329.

Rolnik, Racquel. 1999, Territorial Exclusion and Violence: The Case of São Paolo, Brazil. *Woodrow Wilson Center Occasional Papers Series on Comparative Urban Studies* 26.

Rowe, Peter. 2005, *East Asia Modern: Shaping the Contemporary City*. London: Reaktion.

Roy, Ananya. 2003, Paradigms of Propertied Citizenship: Trans-national Techniques of Analysis. *Urban Affairs Review* 38: 463–491.

Roy, Ananya. 2005, Urban Informality: Toward an Epistemology of Planning. *Journal of the American Planning Association* 71: 147–158.

Roy, Ananya. 2008, The 21st Century Metropolis: New Geographies of Theory. *Regional Studies.* http://rsa.informaworld.com/10.1080/00343400701809665.

Roy, Ananya. 2008, Post-Liberalism: On the Ethico-Politics of Planning. *Planning Theory* 7: 92–102.

Roy, Ananya and Nezar Al Sayyad. 2006, Medieval Modernity: On Citizenship and Urbanism in a Global Era. *Space and Polity* 10: 1–20.

Sandercock, Leonie. 2003, *Cosmopolis II: Mongrel Cities*. London: Continuum.

Sassen, Saskia. 1996, Analytic Borderlands: Race, Gender and Representation in New York City. In Anthony King (ed.) *Re-presenting the City: Ethnicity, Capital and Culture in the 21st Century Metropolis*. New York: New York University Press, 183–202.

Sassen, Saskia. 2000, New Frontiers Facing Urban Sociology at the Millennium. *British Journal of Sociology* 51: 143–160.

Sassen, Saskia. 2007, *The Repositioning of Cities and Urban Regions in a Global Economy: Pushing Policy and Governance Options*. Paris: OECD.

Sattherwaithe, David. 2007, The Transition to a Predominantly Urban World and Its Underpinnings. *Human Settlements Discussion Paper* 4. London: International Institute of Environment and Development.

Schler, Lyn. 2003, Ambiguous Spaces: The Struggle over African Identities and Communities in Colonial Douala, 1914–45. *Journal of African History* 44: 51–72.

Scientific Committee of the African Development Bank–OECD–CILSS. 1995, *West Africa Long-Term Prospective Study*. Paris: OECD; Bamako: Sahel Institute.

Scott, Allen. 1998, *Regions and the World Economy: The Coming Shape of Global Production, Competition, and Political Order*. Oxford: Oxford University Press.

Scott, Allen and Michael J. Storper. 2003, Regions, Globalization, Development. *Regional Studies* 37: 579–593.

Scott, David. 1999, *Refashioning Futures: Criticism after Postcoloniality*. Princeton, N.J.: Princeton University Press.

Scott, David. 2004, *Conscripts of Modernity: The Tragedy of Colonial Enlightenment*. Durham, N.C.; London: Duke University Press.

Sellers, Jeffrey. 2002, *Governing from Below: Urban Regions and the Global Economy*. New York: Cambridge University Press.

Sennett, Richard. 1990, *The Conscience of the Eye: The Design and Social Life of Cities*. New York: W.W. Norton.

Sennett, Richard. 1994, *Flesh and Stone: The Body and the City in Western Civilization*. New York: W.W. Norton.

Serres, Michel. 1995, *Angels: A Modern Myth*. Paris; New York: Flammarion.

Sethuraman, S.V. 1997, *Africa's Informal Economy*. Geneva: International Labor Office.

Shelby, Tommie. 2005, *We Who Are Dark: The Philosophical Foundations of Black Solidarity*. Cambridge, Mass.: Harvard University Press.

Sheppard, Eric. 2002, The Spaces and Times of Globalization: Place, Scale, Networks, and Positionality. *Economic Geography* 78: 307–330.

Sidaway, James and Michael Pryke. 2000, The Strange Geographies of "Emerging Markets." *Transactions of the Institute of British Geographers* 25: 187–201.

Simondsen, Karen. 2005, Bodies, Sensations, Space and Time: The Contribution from Henri Lefebvre. *Geografiska Annaler: Series B, Human Geography* 87: 1–14.

Simone, AbdouMaliq. 1998, Globalization and the Identity of African Urban Practices. In Judin Hilton and Ivan Vladislavic (eds.) *Blank _____ Architecture, Apartheid and After*. Rotterdam: NAi.

Simone, AbdouMaliq. 2004, *For the City Yet to Come: Changing Urban Life in Four African Cities*. Durham, N.C.: Duke University Press.

Smith, Michael Peter. 2005, Transnational Urbanism Revisited. *Journal of Ethnic and Migration Studies* 31: 235–244.

Smith, Richard. 2003, World City Topologies. *Progress in Human Geography* 27: 561–582.

Soja, Edward. 1999, *Postmetropolis: Critical Studies of Cities & Regions*. Oxford: Blackwell.

Song, Yang, Yves Zenou, and Chengri Ding. 2008, Let's Not Throw Out the Baby with the Bathwater: The Role of Urban Villages in Housing Rural Migrants in China. *Urban Studies* 45: 313–330.

Spillers, Hortense. 2003, *Black, White, and in Color: Essays on American Literature and Culture*. Chicago: University of Chicago Press.

Spivak, Gayatri Chakravorty. 2004, Harlem. *Social Text* 22: 113–139.

Srinivas, Smiriti. 2001, *Landscapes of Urban Memory: The Sacred and the*

Civic in *India's High-Tech City*. Minneapolis: University of Minnesota Press.

Stengers, Isabelle. 2008, Experimenting with Refrains: Subjectivity and the Challenge of Escaping Modern Dualism. *Subjectivity* 22: 38–59.

Storper, Michael and Michael Mandaville. 2006, Behavior, Preferences, and Cities: Urban Theory and Urban Resurgence. *Urban Studies* 43: 1247–1274.

Sugrue, Thomas. 1996, *The Origins of the Urban Crisis: Race and Inequality in Postwar Detroit*. Princeton, N.J.: Princeton University Press.

Sum, Ngai-Ling. 2002, Globalization, Regionalization and Cross Border Modes of Growth in East Asia: The Reconstruction of "Time–Space Governance." In Markus Perkmann and Ngai-Ling Sum (eds.) *Globalization, Regionalization and Cross Border Regions*. London: Palgrave, 50–76.

Swatuk, Larry and David R. Black (eds.). 1997, *Bridging the Rift : The New South Africa in Africa*. Boulder, Col.: Westview Press.

Swyngedouw, Erik. 1999, Territories of Innovation: Innovation as a Collective Process and the Globalisation of Competition. In Helen Lawton-Smith (ed.) *Technology Transfer and Industrial Change in Europe: The Case of the Electronic Component and the Flow Measuring Industries in the U.K., France and Belgium*. London: Macmillan, 15–33.

Swyngedouw, Erik, Frank Moulaert, and Arantxa Rodriguez. 2002, Neoliberal Urbanization in Europe: Large Scale Urban Development Projects and the New Urban Policy. *Antipode* 34: 542–577.

Tajbakhsh, Kian. 2001, *The Promise of the City: Space, Identity, and Politics in Contemporary Social Thought*. Berkeley: University of California Press.

Taussig, Michael. 1992, *The Nervous System*. New York: Routledge, 145.

Taylor, Charles. 2002, Modern Social Imaginaries. *Public Culture* 14: 91–124.

Thomas, Dominic. 2007, *Black France: Colonialism, Immigration, and Transnationalism*. Bloomington, Ind.: Indiana University Press.

Thrift, Nigel. 2004, Intensities of Feeling: Towards a Spatial Politics of Affect. *Geografiska Annaler, Series B* 86: 57–78.

Thrift, Nigel. 2005, But Malice Aforethought: Cities and the Natural History of Hatred. *Transactions of the Institute of British Geographers* 30: 133–150.

Till, Karen. 2005, *The New Berlin: Memory, Politics, Place*. Minneapolis, Minn.: University of Minnesota Press.

Torrance, Morag. 2008, Forging Glocal Governance: Urban Infrastructures as Networked Financial Products. *International Journal of Urban and Regional Research* 32: 1–21.

Urban Market Joint Venture. 1999, *Inner City Street Trading Management Strategy*. Johannesburg: Greater Johannesburg Metropolitan Council.

Urry, John. 2002, Mobility and Proximity. *Sociology* 36: 255–274.

Urry, John. 2004, Small Worlds and the New "Social Physics." *Global Networks* 4: 109–130.

Van Arkadie, Brian. 1995, The State and Economic Change in Africa. In Ha-Joon Chang and Robert Rowthorn (eds.) *The Role of the State in Economic Change in Africa*. Oxford: Clarendon Press.

van Schendel, Willem and Itty Abraham (eds.). 2005, *Illicit Flows and Criminal Things: States, Borders, and the Other Side of Globalization*. Bloomington, Ind.: Indiana University Press.

Vance, James Jr. 1990, *The Continuing City: Urban Morphology in Western Civilization*. Baltimore, Md.: Johns Hopkins University Press.

Venables, Anthony. 2005, Spatial Disparities in the Developing Countries: Cities, Regions and International Trade. *Journal of Economic Geography* 5: 3–21.

Vigar, Geoff, Stephen Graham, and Patsy Healey. 2005, In Search of the City in Spatial Strategies: Past Legacies, Future Imaginings. *Urban Studies* 42: 1391–1410.

Virilio, Paul. 1991, The Overexposed City. In Paul Virilio and Sylvere Lontringer (eds.) *Lost Dimension*. New York: Semiotext(e); Cambridge, Mass.: The MIT Press, 9–27.

Virilio, Paul. 1995. *The Art of the Motor*. Minneapolis, Minn.: University of Minnesota Press.

Wacquant, Loïc. 1997, Three Pernicious Premises in the Study of the American Ghetto. *International Journal of Urban and Regional Research* 21: 341–353.

Wacquant, Loïc. 2002, Scrutinizing the Street: Poverty, Morality, and the Pitfalls of Urban Ethnography. *American Journal of Sociology* 107: 1468–1532.

Wacquant, Loïc. 2006, Les Banlieues populaires à l'heure marginalité avancée. *Les Grands Dossiers des sciences humaines* 4: 30–34.

Waller, Richard. 2006, Rebellious Youth in Colonial Africa. *Journal of African History* 47: 77–92.

Warner, Michael. 2002, Publics and Counterpublics. *Public Culture* 14: 49–90.

Watts, Michael. 2004, Antinomies of Community. *Transactions of the Institute of British Geographers* 29: 195–216.

Webster, Douglas and Larissa Muller. 2002, The Challenges of Peri-Urban Growth in East Asia: The Case of China's Hangzhou–Ningbo

Corridor. In Mila Freire and Belinda Yuen (eds.) *Enhancing Urban Management in East Asia*. Aldershot, U.K.: Ashgate, 23–54.

Wee, Vivienne and Kanishka Jayasuriya. 2002, New Geographies and Temporalities of Power: Exploring the New Fault-Lines of Southeast Asia. *The Pacific Review* 15: 475–495.

Wilson, Elizabeth. 1991, *The Sphinx in the City: Urban Life, Control of Disorder and Women*. Berkeley; Los Angeles: University of California Press.

Wilson, Ian Douglas. 2006, Continuity and Change: The Changing Contours of Organized Violence in Post-New Order Indonesia. *Critical Asian Studies* 38: 263–297.

Wilson, William Julius. 1987, *The Truly Disadvantaged: The Inner City, the Underclass, and Public Policy*. Chicago: University of Chicago Press.

Wong, Kai Wen and Timothy Bunnell. 2006, "New Economy" Discourse and Spaces in Singapore: A Case Study of One-North. *Environment and Planning A* 38: 69–83.

Zeleza, Paul. 2005, Rewriting the African Diaspora—Beyond the Black Atlantic. *African Affairs* 104: 35–68.

Zhang, Li. 2005, Migrant Enclaves and the Impact of Redevelopment Policies in Chinese Cities. In Laurence J.C. Ma and Fulong Wu (eds.) *Restructuring the Chinese City: Changing Society, Economy and Space*. London; New York: Routledge, 243–259.

Zukin, Sharon. 1995, *The Cultures of Cities*. London: Blackwell.

Index

intersections 137, 143; patrols 5; recharging 192, 197, 201, 214, 216–20; rights 333; shadow worlds 302; street 225

seed money 204

segregation 6, 47, 50, 178–79, 239, 278, 288, 290–91

selectivity 223

self-organization 294–98, 307

selfhood 58

semiotics 288

Semper 66

Senegal 201, 243, 273

Senegalese 244

Sennett, Richard 113

Sereysothea, Ros 323

servants 28

services 6, 17, 21, 23, 25–26; anticipation 63, 69, 71, 80, 83–84, 86, 88, 90, 94, 106, 112; blackness 288, 295; circulations 166, 169, 174–75, 177–85, 187, 189; cityness 30, 33, 37, 49; connections 264–65, 268, 274, 276; finance 164; inner cities 239, 241, 245–46, 252–54, 257, 260; intersections 127, 130, 137–38, 145–46, 148–54, 156–57, 160, 202, 281; markets 316–18; popular culture 312; recharging 195, 197–98, 201, 205, 208–11, 213; rights 333; street 229, 233, 235, 237

settlement patterns 287

sewerage 182

sex workers 4, 28, 34–35, 37, 90, 204, 222, 301–302, 311

shadow worlds 188, 299–306

Shanghai 280

shanty towns 33

shareholders 163–64

Shelby, Tommie 282

shelter 17, 41, 53, 98, 124, 188, 275, 311

Shenzhen 10, 43–44

Shi'a 206

Shilluk people 28, 30, 32

shipping 63, 105, 107, 109, 181, 188, 281

shopping 31, 54, 63, 86, 154; black urbanism 274, 277, 308; circulations 170, 181, 187; intersections 195, 197, 209, 240–41, 243–44, 255, 257

short futures 169–72

SIM cards 30

skills 192, 197, 207, 219, 222, 240, 311, 317–18

slang 307

slavery 278–79, 282, 291, 297, 300

slummification 246, 257

slums 17, 19, 23, 26, 28, 30, 38, 47, 182, 300

smart buildings 12

smuggling 318

social engineering 43

social movements 33, 91

social relations 6–7, 19, 22–23, 27, 39; anticipation 67, 74, 81–84, 88, 93, 98, 109, 113; black urbanism 299; blackness 288–89; circulations 162; cityness 53–55, 57; connections 276; inner cities 240, 245, 248, 259; intersections 130, 145–46, 154; popular culture 326; recharging 194, 197–98, 203, 205, 209, 219; shadow worlds 301, 304; street 221–22, 229